RUNAWAY

RuNAWAY
diary of a street kid

———

EVELYN LAU

COACH

HOUSE

Coach House Press
50 Prince Arthur Avenue, Suite 107,
Toronto, Canada M5R 1B5

First Edition
3 5 7 9 8 6 4 2

PRINTED IN CANADA

*All the events described in this book are true. However, with the
exception of Denny Boyd, and the parents and sister of the
writer, names and descriptions of people and some places have
been changed to protect the identity and privacy of individuals,
and in these cases any resemblance to identifiable persons is
entirely coincidental.*

Canadian Cataloguing in Publication Data
Lau, Evelyn, 1971–
Runaway : diary of a street kid

ISBN 0-88910-491-3

1. Lau, Evelyn, 1971–   – Biography – Youth. 2. Prostitution, Juvenile — British
Columbia — Vancouver. 3. Runaway teenagers — British Columbia —
Vancouver — Biography. 4. Authors, Canadian (English) – 20th century –
Biography.*   I. Title.

HQ799.C22V36 1995   362.7'4'092   C95-931956-5

For my psychiatrist, who took care of me,
and
for Fred Kerner, who believed in this book

contents

prologue

I decided to become a writer when I was six years old. It wasn't a passing whim; it was an obsession. By that age, I had already become an avid reader—reading was like living in a fantasy world; it had become my form of escape. I thought that by writing I could give that same feeling to other people, that they could open one of my books and disappear for a while. Even then, it was important to me not to stay rooted in reality.

I was born in Vancouver to Chinese immigrants. I was a shy and introspective child, exceedingly sensitive to the tensions and emotions around me. My parents were strict, overprotective and suspicious of the unknown society around them. By kindergarten, I was already expected to excel in class, as the first step in my pre-planned career as a doctor or lawyer. I wasn't allowed to spend much time with the neighborhood children; consequently, I always had my nose in a book.

My father spent a lot of time with me during those early years. We were very close; he was calm and gentle and gave me the nurturing I needed. My mother was a small, thin woman; she had a great deal of nervous energy and was always racing around the house, cooking and cleaning and getting upset without apparent reason. Sometimes my parents would start fighting late at night, which terrified me—I assumed my mother would end up hurting my father or making him leave the house.

It was a bit later in elementary school that I began feeling pressured from all sides. My parents expected me to be the top student in school, and even a few of the teachers expressed disappointment when I didn't achieve the highest mark. My mother would be enraged. Every afternoon, she would call me out to the living room, where she would be sitting on the couch, rapping a ruler impatiently against her palm

9

and forcing me to recite the answers to textbook questions. She would become hysterical with frustration if I didn't come up with the right answers. I dreaded these sessions and started becoming frightened of people, especially my parents. I escaped by writing cheerful entries in my journal and assuming the personalities of different characters in novels.

Outwardly, I was not rebellious. I never displayed anger, since that invited punishment. Instead, I became painfully sensitive to everything around me—I just didn't seem to be able to protect myself from hurt.

Once in Grade 5, I received 89 percent on an exam. I couldn't go home with this imperfect mark and frantically told a friend that I was going to commit suicide. The teacher overheard and arranged a session for me with a school psychiatrist, but I wouldn't say anything to the woman. She asked to see my parents—my mother went but afterwards, on the way home, she made me promise not to tell anyone about the incident for fear it would bring shame upon the family.

My father became unemployed when I was ten years old. This was one of the most traumatic events in my childhood because it caused an abrupt separation between us. He withdrew into himself, working till the early hours of the morning in the basement, going to job interviews, straining to keep food on the table by securing brief contracts that kept him busy for a few weeks before he would have to pound the pavement again. I could never get close to him after that, partially because he now thought I was too old and my mother should be taking responsibility for me. Which she did, with a frenzy. I seldom saw my father after that—we'd say hello to each other when he came home from work, but that was all. Tension was building in the household, with the lack of money and the need to maintain a house and a car, the trappings of security. My mother taunted my father for not supporting the family properly, since that was his traditional role. She felt powerless over his employment, but she wasn't powerless over me, and that was where she poured all her energy. She was going to make sure that I would somehow redeem them.

The final year of elementary school, adolescence hit my classmates hard; along with it, clothes became the standard for judging people. It wouldn't have been difficult for my parents to buy me a pair of jeans and a sweatshirt. Instead, I arrived at school each day in ridiculous attire dug out of my mother's trunk, bright green bell-bottoms and the like. From the moment I stepped into the schoolyard, I was ridiculed mercilessly till I left in the afternoon. I used to pray every night for hours that I would die in my sleep, so I wouldn't have to face the same thing the next day. My parents wouldn't listen to my pleas, and that one year lasted a lifetime.

As a child I had become quite skilled in dissociation, but during that year I mastered it. I fantasized about living alone in a submarine deep in an ocean far away from people; I fantasized so hard that it would surprise me that the fantasies didn't come true. I seldom remained in my body but floated farther and farther away from it. I hardly ever opened my mouth in class, paralyzed by fear, so my marks dropped sharply and my mother's anxiety increased. She kept me in my bedroom, studying between one school day and the next, and it was in there that my writing developed in the form of short stories, poetry and even two book-length manuscripts.

Entering high school was a bit easier, in a sense. I made a few friends; I became involved in the peace movement; my name was on the honor roll every year; I began publishing in literary magazines and winning writing competitions. My parents did not approve of my writing or of my involvement in the peace movement. They forbade me to write unless I brought home straight A's from school, and right up until I left home at fourteen I was not allowed out of my house except to attend school and take piano lessons—not on weekends, not after school. I went submissively to my bedroom and stayed there, descending into months of depression alleviated only by the fact that I would continue to write secretly under a math textbook. My mother would sneak into the room very quietly to check if I were doing my homework; I would hold my textbook tilted upwards with one hand and write with the other, slamming the book down when I heard her footsteps. As a result, I was in constant panic, a kind of fight-or-flight reaction to all that went on.

At the same time, I had developed bulimia, which my parents didn't understand; I had also begun developing severe stress symptoms which I have to treat medically to this day. I would lapse into incredible depressions, just going down and down and not being able to come back up. It was like living under a cloud. I frequently thought about killing myself but could never handle the thought of disappointing and embarrassing my parents by actually doing it.

The volume of mail I received posed another problem, and it was yet another fight about the mail that precipitated my running away. It consisted mostly of rejection slips, correspondence with editors who responded kindly to the 'age thirteen' scrawled at the bottom of the page, a few acceptances and checks. By that time I was terrified of my mother, her outbursts of screaming and abuse, her constantly telling me that I wasn't worthy and wasn't good enough. I became what could be considered a model daughter—I never went out, helped with the housework, had no boyfriend and few friends, brought home good grades, never experimented with alcohol or drugs. I would win writing awards, but my parents would become angry rather than proud, rebuking me for not doing my homework instead. I never felt like I was loved, or that I could ever satisfy them or anyone else in the world.

And that was what it was all about. Feeling that no matter what I did, I could never justify being alive and being their daughter. Sometimes, when my parents were away from the house, I would start screaming and not be able to stop. It was worse than anything else I could imagine, stuck for hours and hours inside my bedroom. My mother wouldn't leave me alone and my father was just not there. I reached the point where I was willing to give up everything that had been familiar to me, including my writing, to run away. It was unplanned; I just did it one day. Somehow I knew that if I didn't, I would kill myself or go crazy.

This journal covers the two years of my life after I ran away from home. It is, in one sense, no different from all the destroyed diaries preceding it—it is a story of survival. Although it may sound hard to believe, all the events that took place during these two years were easier on me emotionally than living at home, which is why I have never gone back there to live.

PART I

march 22 to june 28 1986

March 22

It is morning, and I'm at the office of a youth newspaper. I ran away from home yesterday, calling the people at the newspaper from the school library to beg them to take me in for a while. I emptied my locker of the journals I had stashed there, hauling them down the corridor and dumping them into a garbage bin, listening to them tumble to the bottom. They certainly couldn't come with me—my schoolbag was already stuffed with poems and stories, a book of writers' markets, a change of clothing and ten dollars.

Huddled in the living room, away from the window, I look out at the mountains, managing to convince myself that I never existed before this day, that my parents would not be expecting their teenage daughter to come home after school. I crouch on the floor and concentrate hard on my fantasy: It never happened, I was not born until today.

The people at the newspaper are trying to bolster each other up, keep us all from collapsing. Tommy has taken me under his wing and seems to understand my need not to be left alone. He pretends to be enjoying the situation, tossing comforting smiles in my direction every few minutes.

Don is warm and funny; he tells stories there on the couch, his arms flailing. Standing over the stove in the kitchen in his grey sweater, he looks like the father of the house—watching him, I feel protected. But both Don and his girlfriend, Crystal, are over nineteen, so they could be charged with harboring a runaway. And they are doing this for someone they never met before. I glance at Crystal and see the creases across her forehead, how she's waiting for the police to knock on her door.

Evening

Today we decided I should get out of Vancouver and go up to the coast. The people at the newspaper have a friend named Joe who lives in a cabin there. The police had started contacting several people connected with the newspaper, and after we left they came to the door of this house.

Tommy and I took the ferry to Joe's cabin. I was terrified about making the trip; it seemed safer to stay in the house, out of the light.

Tommy is here with me now, bent over the kitchen table and reading poetry aloud. He feels obliged to stay, although he's done too much already, including cutting college classes when it's approaching exam time.

Joe's an old hippie with hair down to his waist, a fringed shawl wrapped around his shoulders. The cabin has a wood stove but no hot water, heat or refrigeration. There is a huge, sprawling garden outside, haunted by ghostly tents where his friends sleep in the summertime. Incredible, living in a cabin, complete with organic food, trees as far as the eye can see, a creek, chickens. At night, though, it freezes here.

Joe reassured me with the old ideology: 'Help people who need it; accept help when you need it.' He told me I'm safe here, for as long as I want to stay. He did point out that he couldn't support me for another four years, naturally, but I could be moved from one safe place to the next. For how long? I still nurture vague notions of making it to the States; eventually I suppose I'd have to leave this province anyway.

Tommy and Joe are convinced that I can negotiate with my parents, but they don't fully understand. Why would I have had to hurt them so much by running away, if we'd been able to talk? I wonder if I will ever see my school friends, the street I lived on, again. Will I ever feel safe venturing outside again?

This morning I became depressed thinking about how I couldn't continue a writing career. I could still submit to magazines and contests, putting the cost of stamps aside, but with the lack of address I'd never know if any of the material got accepted. After a while, what if I lost my determination and remained content with the odd letter or journal entry?

March 24

I'm beginning to relax at last, though I feel guilty about this content-ment, wondering what my parents must be going through. Tommy is amused by what my parents would think of this cabin and its inhabi-tants: 'Subversive, unclean—with drugs, hippie food and long hair!' Beyond their most impossible nightmares.

These people are confident about an anarchist revolution. When I became worried that I would hinder the newspaper's political activi-ties by arousing the authorities' suspicion, they all said no, this expe-rience would only prepare them for the revolution. Then they'd know how to act if they were caught.

'Stick it out till the anarchist revolution is over, and then you'll be free,' one of them said. They're serious, and it's beautiful.

Evening

Silent disapproval on Tommy's face as he watches me smoking pot for the first time, sharing a joint with Joe. It's so cold here. Oh fuck, lis-ten to this: America and Libya have done it and launched guns, mis-siles and shit at each other today.

Tommy's going to mail my letters to school friends and writer friends, from another municipality. Yesterday he and I handwashed a bathtubful of clothes; today we raked up the garden. He's wonderful. Joe's right: HIPPIE TRIP IS STILL VALID!

March 25

Yesterday Tommy remarked that my best option would be to seek a compromise with my parents and then go home. I knew that I was being unreasonable by refusing to talk to them, but I also knew that they would respond with rage and even tighter rules if I did. I can't go back, yet no one will believe me; everyone had been secretly hoping my attitude would change after a week or so.

I started feeling cornered, especially by Tommy. Joe came home and hugged me, saying I looked teary and depressed.

After Tommy went to bed (he left early this morning for Vancouver;

missed his bus last night), I started drinking. Finally the tears came, thinking of my school friend Patricia and the scrapes she'd saved me from, her maturity, the stability I drew from being around her. I never even got to say goodbye.

And my writing, gone. The journals I'd had to throw in a garbage bin because they wouldn't fit into my schoolbag. The future I'd thrown away in the same gesture—how easily it had disappeared.

Then Don and Crystal, how I'd almost forced myself on them, and now Joe ...

I cried for hours, the first time since leaving home. Joe came into the kitchen, held me, rocked me like a baby, guided me to bed. He was silent except for when he murmured hypnotically that everything would be all better, it would. He repeated this over and over until I stopped shaking, then he kissed me goodnight and left, and I fell asleep exhausted under twisted covers.

March 26

I feel like I've been raped. Feelings of self-hatred, disgust and hatred of men, unfamiliar, are racing through me.

Last night I had a couple of drinks on an empty stomach—they made me sick, dizzy. The cabin was empty. I sat on the edge of Joe's bed and we talked. Eventually I asked to sleep on the floor of his room, since he builds a fire there every night and my room is unbearably cold. He dragged a mattress and blankets inside, then hugged me and asked if I wanted to sleep with him instead.

It sounded like a good idea. I was feeling very alone and needed a warm bed with someone beside me. (How naive, perhaps, to believe that a girl could crawl into a man's bed for the night and expect to be left alone. But how could I have understood this?) Joe stripped and I shrugged off my jacket, tired and nauseated, and buried myself in the pillow. But then he pulled my pants off and started exploring me with his dirt-stained fingers. It hurt, and with panic I rose out of my stupor and told him to stop, but he wouldn't. Then he came onto my hand and the sheets.

This morning Joe admitted that he knew I hadn't wanted to go so far. He explained that he hadn't been with a woman for eight months, and I turned him on. He thought I'd come on to him! He told me he'd be thrown in jail if I ever told anybody, and that most of his friends would refuse to see him again if they found out about what happened.

Did I let him do what he did so maybe he'd let me stay here longer? But now I want to leave.

March 27

I don't know how to deal with what's happening between Joe and me. We slept together last night, then the same thing happened again this morning. It hurts. I wonder, what's so great about sex? It's my fault; I can't bear the thought of sleeping alone.

Now Joe's in his room, asleep, after working in the garden. This morning's sexual incident is going to be the last. So far I've tried not to hurt him by insisting that he stop, but I'm not exactly in love with pain.

March 28

What is my future? I've escaped—but to where? It's funny, but I still want to make something of myself. Maybe what I'd like to do is escape from myself; don a mask into which I could melt.

Funny too how Joe takes it for granted that emotional involvement comes after sexual contact, not before. He admits with surprise in his voice that he's getting to like me. (O magnanimous gesture!)

All I have to sell is my personality and, as someone once said, my ass. But it'll never come down to that. All I'm willing to give is myself as a person, not a body.

Night

Tommy arrived in the afternoon. He said everything was basically okay; the letters had been dropped off, and he'd called my parents. My father went to their house to retrieve my letter. He told Tommy that his former manager was going to pay for an ad in the main section of the Vancouver Sun, asking me to come home. My father had been called to work but hadn't wanted to go.

An unexpected rage welled up inside me. He was wasting his time and energy for nothing! I flung myself onto Joe's bed, cranked up some music full volume, and stared blankly at the wall while the noise fucked the space between my ears. Tommy came and sat beside me, but left because I ignored him, lost in my sulking.

Later Tommy came back into the room quietly and switched off the music. I sobbed that he had to keep it on. Then he told me: Crystal was on the phone; the police had discovered that she and Don had harbored me.

It turned out that they had given the letters to Crystal's older sister to mail. The six o'clock news had carried a spot on my disappearance, showing clips of the letters I'd sent, and hinting that I'd been kidnapped. Crystal's sister freaked out and went to the police.

I didn't think this could happen except in nightmares. Crystal told Tommy to tell me that it wasn't my fault, that she and Don would have helped anyway, even if they'd known this was going to happen.

What's happened since then is a blur. Just now I hear the story has been on the late news—my parents have played it out to be like I was snatched away. Tommy is facing kidnapping charges. His lawyer was on the phone with him a while ago, Joe is busy scrambling around the cabin hiding his dope ... I'm as good as dead. They'll all get arrested.

I've gotten everybody into shit. It's hard to be lucid. Tommy's mom is freaked out about this and is going to tell the cops where we are if they ask her. I should kill myself. Joe wants me to leave. The cops could come any minute—the news was broadcast province-wide. People on the coast have noticed me.

I don't know what to do, or how to live with this.

Tommy plunks a note on the table in front of me: 'She who trips on what is behind her lacks foresight.' I haven't just tripped, I've collapsed and dragged. God knows how many others with me.

I called Patricia. She said that the cops have been to some of our other friends' houses, and that it's pretty well all over the school by now.

I called Crystal and screamed that I was sorry, she and Don had to believe I was sorry!

What I'm supposed to do is return to Vancouver with Tommy tomorrow, to Emergency Services downtown. I hate you, Joe. But that's the only way to clear this mess up. They'll probably dump me into a group home.

I'm torn but still selfish. I can't go back, face my parents and then (at my choice, I'm assured) either go back home or into the care of the government. Fuck Joe. He wants me out, just like that.

I can't go home, but it would be fruitless to stay here, waiting to be picked up by the police. I can't even run away from here because there's nowhere to go without getting caught.

So it's a choice between Emergency Services, committing suicide, and trying to persuade someone else to take me in. That last is most appealing, but it really shows how selfish I am.

It's 2 a.m. Tommy's probably still awake, staring at the ceiling. Hours ago we were sitting around the table talking. I said I didn't want to return to Vancouver, but wanted to find another place to hide. Joe spat out that if I really did care about Tommy, like I claimed, then I wouldn't be so fucking pigheaded about going back to Vancouver!

'Oh my God, look, I'm sorry. I shouldn't have said that,' he blurted immediately afterwards, as Tommy's eyes darkened.

We ran around spilling things, bumping into things, dialing wrong numbers. Dismaying, that it's just over me. It'd be cool if it was for some worthwhile cause, but it's just over me.

There's guilt and fear, but no decisions. The best way out is suicide. But there's so much I can't bear to leave, haven't even experienced yet.

And I'm terrified of the blackness.

March 29

This morning I swallowed thirty aspirin from the bathroom cabinet, with great difficulty, while Tommy hovered nervously outside the door wondering if he should break it down or if he was just being paranoid. Bob Dylan was singing 'It's All Over Now, Baby Blue' as I went into my room to lie down. I woke up an hour later; the pills had not done their job.

It turned out that moving to another safe house wasn't even an option. Everyone we called said no. Joe turned over in his bed and mumbled that he didn't approve of my decision to try hiding from the cops and social services, that I was being 'silly.'

The plans had already been arranged: Joe would drive Tommy and me down to the 4:30 p.m. ferry to Vancouver, and we would head straight for Emergency Services. I was really depressed. I wondered if I could still slip out the door when they weren't looking and hitchhike somewhere, or melt away from Tommy along the bus route in Vancouver.

Then the phone rang. It was a reporter from the Province armed with whiny persistent questions. A male 'anonymous caller' had phoned the newspaper and provided them with Joe's number and address. Sputtering furiously into the mouthpiece, I hung up.

Tommy and I clambered into Joe's truck and the three of us barrelled down the dirt roads towards the ferry. Along the way, Tommy slipped me twenty dollars, and Joe began singing 'Om Mani Padhme Hum' out the open window, his voice rising and flowing into the wind. Tommy and I joined in timidly, trying to relax. Joe could hardly contain his excitement at the possibility that a reporter might interview him, giving him the chance to expound his anarchist ideals.

The police were waiting for us when we got to the ferry terminal. Joe hugged me; Tommy and I were guided into a cop car. It would have been funny under other circumstances—everybody who was waiting for the ferry had their faces squished against the glass, staring at us.

At the police station we were shut inside a white room with a desk, under glaring fluorescent lights. The pills were starting to wreak havoc in my stomach. I finally had to tell Tommy about the overdose; he in turn told the policemen. One of them stared at me with bulging eyes and asked sarcastically, 'If you took thirty aspirin, why aren't you passed out on the floor?' He didn't believe me!

Tommy was ordered to pay a traffic fine and then released.

Alone, I was guided into the cell block, leaving my shoes, jacket and bags in a locker. I touched my hair and skin, frightened by their sudden strange texture—as though I had been slathered with grease.

Two policemen, one with a scrubbed ruddy face, the other with protuberant eyes, slipped a key into the lock on the door of one of the cells. The cell contained two bunks covered with green mattresses, a metal toilet and a sink. They slid the bewildering construction of bars shut, twisting the key in the lock.

I sat on the closest bunk, realizing that the cell was windowless and virtually airless. A woman gave me a pat-down, her fleshy hands exploring my pockets, socks and bra, then paced back and forth outside the bars, jiggling with fat, watching me. She could have suffocated me between her breasts. She brought out an ancient-looking bag of Jelly Bears—'An Easter treat for my daughter'—allowing me three of the synthetic creatures. Afterwards, when the nausea won and I had to race for the sink, the vomit was a candy-colored substance clogging the drain.

The fluorescent lights leaked into me. Somehow, on the walls and the frames of the bunks, other people had managed to scratch their message: 'FUCK PIGS.' I sat there, too stunned to move. The toilet didn't work; the taps didn't work. The lights and the recycled air kept rushing at me; the emptiness in my ears separated into a universe of clanging dots. The lights were hard and oily, inhuman. For one breath of clean air, for a sympathetic blue sky, I would have thrown the world away.

I tried to stand up and in the process banged my head thunderously against the metal frame of the bunk. Holding my breath, waiting for the accusations—another suicide attempt? How much do you have left when somebody takes away their last shred of trust in you?

Windowless. Trapped in an experiment, cornered. Look, Mommy and Daddy, they've locked up your little girl. White walls, white ceiling, white buzzing in my ears. The scratches on the walls and bunks were futile: hairpin art.

The ringing wouldn't stop; the little white pills wouldn't stay down. After a while I fell asleep, through the naked brightness, the bile-colored mattress, the blood- and vomit-stained floor ...

A vision of Hell.

April 22

The police put me on the ferry to Vancouver with a social worker, Michael. It's evening and I'm now in an emergency group home in Vancouver, a temporary shelter for teens. I'm sharing a bedroom with a fourteen-year-old, Rachel—we've been having long conversations while lying in the dark, before falling asleep; she wonders about God and whether there's anything after death. She's on probation and will be living here until her court appearance and until her social worker finds a place for her in a permanent home. Rachel had been living with friends for some time before being taken into care.

'But they finked on me. They told a bunch of lies and threatened to kick my boyfriend's head in.' One of her 'friends' had led her into an alley and stabbed her in the hand. There was a deep knife slash on her palm where infection was starting to set in, making it turn black.

Rachel's mother had, in the meantime, taken off to California and left her daughter to fend for herself.

The other morning I woke up to find Rachel perched on the edge of her bed, changing the dressing on her wound. 'Morning.'

'Hi.'

'How's your hand doing?'

'Good,' she said at last, as if surprised that anyone would care enough to remember.

* * *

The *Vancouver Sun* splashed me on their front page, under their New Look headline. They wrung my voice from the long-distance line, pulling it apart like taffy, so many electrical impulses flashing into a reporter's cubicle in the newsroom. Denny Boyd's [real name] words—'I've never met a kid who could write like that'—the only kind words they allow. They snatched the words from my mouth and hung them up to drip-dry in their darkroom, black print flailing from a line. They stole my words and bled them limp, beat them with truncheons until they lay on the cell floor, locked up, in their own puddle of Jelly Bear-colored vomit. Lies. Headlines ('Young Woman Hunted') sprinkled with color; articles typeset and flushed both sides. A reporter picked through my words like an old Chinese amah would pick through the hair of her child, searching for lice, pinching them away.

The ink of the newspaper comes off on our hands, painting the housemother's fingernails black.

* * *

I called up a close friend, Patricia, down in the basement with the sticky root beer stain on the floor, the lukewarm soft drink in the bottle on the desk flecked with cigarette ashes. I call her to say hi, to say

I'm okay and are you? When I ask for her she replies, smoothly, 'She's not home right now.'

'Pat, I can recognize your voice.' What was going on?

'I know,' she sighs tonelessly, then tells me her parents have been screaming at her incessantly since the police called them to ask if I was there. Her parents don't want her to see or talk to me again.

Patricia's voice remained lifeless, polite. I kept my own voice bright, saying at the end that I hoped I hadn't gotten her into too much trouble, but she didn't give me the reassurance I needed.

'Yeah, I hope not,' was all she said.

Week-old root beer swims black in its open bottle. I run up the green-carpeted stairs, up through the dimness, up into the social services group home, away from the years of school and family and friends.

April 3

They've assigned May Wong to be my social worker because she speaks Cantonese. Watching George Orwell's *1984* on TV, I turn to Rachel and tell her how much I want Michael to be my worker. He was the man who came to fetch me from the coast back to Vancouver, taking my hand under the descending night when I stepped out of the police car.

Maybe he belongs just in Emergency Services, to give bright beams of himself to everyone entering with their broken lives. That kind of caring shouldn't be hogged. Michael was a tiny man, meeting me at the ferry, almost buried inside his coat—he had light green eyes, tired, in a pleasing face. Through the aspirin-haze of nausea and distortions, he took me to the hospital, leaning against the white walls at 2 a.m., waiting for a nurse to arrive and take a blood test to check for poisoning from the pills. She extracted tubes of blood from my arm, a spill like a wet flower plastered afterwards on the floor at my feet.

Michael's silver-rimmed driving glasses sparkled in the rushing darkness, in the tan interior of the government car. He wore jeans tucked inside leather ankle boots. I'd felt I'd found a friend in him— but, so much for friends. Watch, I shall go and crawl across the floor to Patricia's parents whom I have never met, fling myself at their feet, hug their ankles. What have they to fear from this wreck? This is the bitch who tried to 'subvert' your daughter, who brought the blue-clad boys to your pillar-of-society door.

While all the other social workers and counsellors try to make me talk, thus enabling them to betray me, Michael merely sits quietly and finally reaches out to warm me. Fuck the doctors' medical charts, their analyses, their poison creeping insidious through my veins. Their analyses may even lead to the psychiatric ward at the hospital. HAVEN'T MY PARENTS OSTRACIZED ME ENOUGH? Michael makes me feel secure and clean—I haven't felt clean for so long. It's like he reassures me that I'm real and everything is all right; I'm not lost or homeless at all.

You know, he'll just be another face drifting through the crowd in the end, another of the people I attach myself to in times of crisis. There is no security to return to anymore. And Michael too backs off from me, falls away with the rest of the dominoes, a pawn moved away from me on the chess board.

April 4

I didn't know the daffodils were out, my little sister Karen. They must be overflowing the garden now, in clumps, pleasing blossoms of yellow. You treat me like an invalid, bringing me the flower with its stem wrapped in tissue, and I have to take it shamefully from you. I feel my parents have succeeded again in revealing me as cruel and wrong in running away.

I lay the daffodil on the table. It has a long, healthy green stem, billowing open into delicate primrose-yellow sheets. It looks good on the table, like it belongs there; if I inch away, I can pretend it isn't mine.

The family session. Here we are, around the kitchen table, in the kitchen that the housemother desperately cleaned for the occasion. My father shakes her hand—she is diminutive even beside him, oversized glasses perched over her forehead.

Michael's eyes never leave Karen's face, which is traumatic; I want to smack the pale little hand scuttling up my knee like a spider. Fuck you, bitch, you're part of the conspiracy too: 'Look, your little sister loves you so; how could you be so cold?' I can and I will ... No, I'm hot, hot with the hilarity of this situation. I want to stand up and overturn the table with its cream-colored cloth onto these people's laps; I want to see Michael's beautiful green eyes widen in astonishment, his mouth fall a little open under that neatly trimmed beard ... to laugh in my parents' faces ... but I won't; I hold it in, biting the inside of my mouth to control the hysteria, the desperate barks of laughter.

Another social worker from Emergency Services is a shadow to my right; Michael is an anchor at my left, his fingers entwining nervously in his lap—his only sign of tension. A relief, to know I'm not the only one under stress. There is a sugar jar on this table, an ashtray with curled butts and loops of ash ... I want to upset this table; what a release it would be.

Love you, Mommy and Daddy, your little girl wants to hear you laugh, can't you understand that? Sugar and cream and spice and everything nice, on your stiff hands, in your laps ...

So, the daffodils are out.

April 5

It is always morning in the Quiet Room.

I remember feeling superior in the waiting room, dismissing the psychiatric patients as crazies I'd never have to join. There was the scrawny Chinese woman with the greasy hair, the mumbling Caucasian woman with the wiglike hair she brushed from her face with nervous hands. Loonies. I was going to get out; I belonged to the outside world.

Then they hand me hospital clothing, dull blue, and the walls begin to spin. The door to the corridor is locked; the bathroom door cannot be locked. Someone keeps pushing my heart against my ribs. Wigwoman informs me that all they live for in the ward are the meals—waiting for breakfast, lunch and dinner. Bewildered children that we have become, children turned guinea pigs crouching in hospital corridors. The Chinese woman runs to me in her fluffy yellow slippers that remind me involuntarily of Big Bird (just another way of degrading the patients here), holding me, her sharp face begging, 'Don't hurt her. Please don't hurt her.' The man on duty drags me to the floor, so used to doing it that he no longer needs a reason. I feel the tiles; the fear is so engulfing it comes close to exhilaration. I make a run for the wash-room—they betrayed me, you know, the whole lot of them: the psy-chiatrists and the social workers and the counsellors. Trusting them, brushing aside my lawyer's warnings to make room for the good in people. (My friends found me a feminist lawyer, who cautioned, 'Don't let them make you see a psychiatrist. He'll make you go into a psychiatric ward; then they'll never let go of you.') A nurse forces her way through the bathroom door, then another; white-clad nurses spill into the bathroom, murmuring, hands searching my pockets for sharp objects. I'm kicking, screaming, crying, wrenched from former freedom.

I'd rather be living on the streets, standing in puddles of glistening black and neon—at least I'd be free.

Trying to saunter casually out the door—next, I'm grabbed with steely fingers and carried into the Quiet Room, dropped like a sack of potatoes onto the mattress. High cement walls, a mattress mounted on a cement block, the hum of air conditioning. It is windowless and fluorescent, with the eye of a TV camera watching steadily from above the door, and the inevitable metal sink and toilet in the corner. My company consists of a 1984 *Reader's Digest* I remember having read before. In one of the other rooms a man roars without pause, banging his head against the wall; policemen parade into the waiting room, forcing in other screaming, biting people. The hospital is reduced to a blur seen through a slit in the door—they took away my glasses, the nurse claiming I might try to swallow them. How appetizing.

Quiet Room #4 rings from my screams. More blood tests, red liq-uid burbling up needles from a hole in the arm. More physicals, hands scuttling over my breasts, prodding my stomach. Blue shampoo in a plastic cup to match the hospital pajamas. My defiance is reduced to refusing to wear the woolly housecoat and the shapeless socks.

Betrayed. I was allowed only one phone call, after wheedling the uncertain nurse, using Crystal's birthday as an excuse. A sign on my door reads: NO VISITORS, NO PHONE CALLS, NO PRESS. One nurse admits that Tommy has been calling, tirelessly. I beg Crystal to help me; how can they do this to a fourteen-year-old? Before we hang up, her friend Frannie calls: 'We love you ...' Will that help, in here? Just the night before, things were normal; going shopping with the group home mother, then waking up and exchanging makeup. A normal life, like any teenager should be allowed to lead. This morning we prepared to meet with my parents to persuade them that I should be left in social services' care. Instead, my social worker brought me to a counsellor's office, where three psychiatrists had already decided to commit me. My parents showed up here at the hospital later, but I couldn't face them.

* * *

Here now in PAU (Psychiatric Assessment Unit). A step up, after putting on a mask of calm. The people in this ward look dead; it must be worse than death. The TV is on all the time—it's what they live for, plus the meals. Bells to ring and switches to flick for a nurse to come running. A deaf, dumb and blind woman performs the Thorazine shuffle endlessly, methodically, from early morning till bedtime. Shuffling is a group activity here, helped along by the funny slippers. Soon it turns into whining. I try to hold in my tears but can't, the misplaced trust is too hurtful … the feeling of foreverness, confined in a mental ward. Even Tommy had promised that returning to Vancouver wouldn't mean giving up my rights—thinking of that, I feel betrayed by him too.

So many walls: separating, confining, closing in. When they allow me to step outside for a few minutes, the plants growing by the door are brambly: holly. Is that all they want the patients to see in PAU? So close to the outside world! Yet I remain in my hospital clothes, the plastic band around my wrist as unbreakable as a pair of handcuffs.

There is just one thought that holds the spinning fragments of my head together—Michael. None of this would have happened if he'd had any say in the matter! I remember the night at the ferry, released from the RCMP cell, the back of the police car. I want to see him again; he wouldn't have hurt me this way. Would he?

April 6

Pissing into a styrofoam cup for a urine sample: dark red, it's that time of the month again. They have pads here, long and impossibly narrow, held up the old way, with belts. It's the second day of my period, and under these circumstances I have to sit tight—they don't allow underwear—afraid a sudden angry streak of scarlet will explode onto the light fabric of the hospital trousers.

Oh Michael. Where are you? That beautiful face with its bleary eyes, sunken and reddened. My doctor hurls her recriminations at me: he has kids, probably a wife, you're bothering him—you're bothering everyone! They're doing everything to me he said they shouldn't do: trapping, cornering, guilt-tripping.

There are yellow curtains around my bed. Shaken awake to my box of cheery yellow. Here the patients talk incessantly about food, complaining loudly if there is not enough on their trays, snatching bits from their neighbor's meals. Medication is pumped into these people until they shuffle listlessly through the days, sightless, tuned inwards to the dances in their heads. Even now, I want to be the Prince who awakens these Sleeping Beauties from their drugged apathy. Let them scream! Let them fight! Together we could shatter the glass and tumble into the streets underneath the blue sky; what is beyond this world inside a paperweight.

I wish I could be optimistic enough to believe I could get out of this place. They've cut off all communication. Last night I waited tensely on my bed for the nurses to leave, hoping I could race to the telephone to put through that one precious call to my lawyer. But before they left, they gave a whispered rundown of each patient to the man left in charge, eventually reaching me: 'Girl ... no visitors, no telephone calls ...' Hemmed in on each side.

The woman on the opposite bed is old, with frizzy grey hair, and she snores, choking up a tortured cough throughout the night. The Chinese woman is convinced she'll be free on Monday, but she still screams in her sleep. Her husband comes to visit several times a day, bringing their two children—I held the smallest, three months old, a girl who's all muscle. Her mother wants to go home. Most of us want to go home. Why do I have to abide by these rules if I don't have anything wrong with me mentally? HOW COULD I, OR ANYONE, BELIEVE FROM NOW ON THAT I AM SANE? Sanity is too elusive, undefinable. It doesn't help that my case doesn't lie with social services anymore, but with the psychiatrists here.

* * *

Just finished talking to another psychiatrist, who tells me that May and the others brought me here because of my suicide attempt with the aspirin. Once three doctors decide that a person should be hospitalized—well, heaven and earth may be moved, but what they decide is final, for up to two weeks. My lawyer can't even help me. I just have to prove that I've calmed down enough and am in control enough to be released, and that I'm capable of making sensible decisions. You have no idea the rage I feel at having to wear this mask of obedience.

I must be quiet. Must think peaceful thoughts: rolling green hills, flowing blue streams. Come on, Ev, you can do it. For God's sake, of course you're sane.

April 7

Wedged between the bars of my cage, a blue pajama'd figure blown by the wind. It's gorgeous outside. As I stand in the doorway of the Psychiatric Assessment Unit, the breeze on my skin is a perfume as dry as baby powder and as soft. The air whirls around me, through the thin material of my clothing, fretting my hair. Light, feathery, playful. I stand in shadow, sun a touch away, but it's the touch that's forbidden, the touch that (the nurses warn gravely) will alert brawny-armed men to hoist me away. Now I wouldn't want that, would I? Not the Quiet Room again.

What a sharp contrast the cement walls of the hospital make against the spring sky, cutting into its heart, bleeding it blue. Holly grows within the confines of the railings, rusting. Barefoot, I could dance down the cement walk to freedom, arms held aloft, face free.

Things will work out, even if the psychiatrists tell me I can't see my lawyer because of my age. However, she must still be working on my case ...

After talking to the psychiatrists, I realize that I'd been too confused on Friday. I hadn't known that because my parents' contract with social services ended on Friday, social services wouldn't have any more jurisdiction over me. In other words, I'd become my parents' belonging once more, a toy to be bent or broken.

This realization ripped through me a few hours ago. I felt like the biggest idiot in the world, having fucked it all up like that. Maybe if I'd sat down with my parents on Friday, they might have signed an agreement allowing me to be taken into care by social services for a longer period of time. As it is now, my only choices are to stay in PAU (eventually to be moved to the adolescent ward) or to go home.

* * *

So Father Dearest arrives unheralded, believing I am crazy but that I will heal with rest, food and hard work in school. It fills me with an ironic sadness. Strange being in these impossible situations—it's making me feel like the wronged heroine in every TV drama.

I'm in better spirits because a school teacher called and I was allowed to call back. She made me feel good about what had happened, appeared delighted that I'd 'gone crazy.' The vice-principal had entered her office the day before, and she'd told him that I'd been committed to the psych ward at the hospital. She empathizes with me, knowing I'd been the good little Chinese girl all my life, jumping through every hoop my parents had set up, and now I'd finally broken away. She admits in her bubbly voice that she admires me. It helps like anything to know that there are people backing me up.

If this experience has taught me anything, it's not to do anything later in life that would result in hospitalization or imprisonment. It's just not worth it.

April 8

Once more the world, a paperweight, has been upended; I'm forced to balance on the concave sky, snow tumbling from the ground. A plastic world with snowflakes the color of coconut, grayed from being on the shelves too long.

At noon my parents arrived at the hospital; even with my apprehension I didn't expect what happened. The head doctor in his tailored suit and polished shoes (I should have known; you can't trust anyone in a tailored suit and polished shoes) drew me into another room and told me that social services had decided to withdraw from my case, that they felt I belonged at home. His face, though tanned and not unpleasant, had a startling stony quality, as though it were carved, and his lips wriggled like snakes above his chin.

I was taken into the meeting room, a room surrounded by mirrors, and the doctor stated that I wasn't crazy, social services didn't want anything more to do with me, and he was going to release me into my parents' care again.

I climbed into my street clothes; my runners were still muddy from the walk I took with Joe through the woods. I told the nurse I wasn't going home and that's it; why were they putting my parents through this: I would almost rather stay in the psych ward scumhole than live at home and didn't understand why I was being kicked out like this when the doctors had been waiting for an available bed for me in the adolescent unit.

My family and I walked to the nearest coffee shop, inside the medical building. My mother had packed clothes for me, food. This gesture touched me, bled me somewhere inside.

I jumped up from the table as soon as we were seated. 'I have to go to the washroom.' I walked briskly past the blank coffee-shop faces into the medical building lobby, then ran! Not much hope, not a cent in my pocket, but that was the way it would have to be. I ran along Broadway Street, dashing past the open-mouthed, wide-eyed passersby—what fragile hope that I would not be stopped. Slowing down, gasping with pain, I weaved my way through alleys and side streets: I hadn't realized I was this out of shape. My runners weighed my feet down like cement, my heart shrieked, the yellow man danced enticingly on the walk signal.

A man said hello to me. He wasn't bad looking, had a slight accent; perhaps he could smell my desperation. He followed me into an alley, then suddenly kissed me, squeezing my right breast so hard that when I looked down there was blood on my T-shirt. He dragged me towards the underground parking lot of an apartment building. Oh God. There's no one in sight, but this is impossible, it's broad daylight! And honor roll students are never raped. Dying now, alone? I kept screaming, my runners scraping against cement as he pushed me into a corner behind a garbage bin. My eyes searched wildly for any face in any window, but each was blank, gray, glass and metal frame. Fear jerked in electric jolts through my body, suffusing my mind. This can't be real. Someone screamed and screamed ... With a sigh the man released me; I ran again.

Finally I made it to the youth newspaper, several miles away. Adrenalin had flooded into my legs, and I had no trouble identifying the house, which rocked with loud music. Pounding on the door, I found it unlocked. Tommy was there—and safety.

We left the house (probably the first place the cops would look), and followed the cement path of the Skytrain to the nearest park. The water gleamed, ripples painted a deep gray. I was free; no more hospital clothes! The grass was so green I was afraid to step on it. Ducks bobbed like decoys in the distance, on the water's surface. A man attached bait from a Dairyland milk bag onto a pole, flung it into the lake, glanced back at Tommy and me on the park bench, uninterested.

We went to the downtown eastside to a street worker's office. Presently my lawyer arrived. She had deep-set eyes and a ready smile, and was dressed in respectable dark clothing. Will she help me, or throw me out like social services did?

Now I'm sitting in her chair, in her office—the sky is darkening to a bruised color above the skylight. Central America and Amnesty International posters plaster the walls: the Amnesty poster depicts a single chair in a cell with bars over the window, a chain draped across the chair. Bamboo snakes across the crumpled black and white poster, something green, something alive. Ivy spiders up the walls, its leaves spreading like palms opened in appeal.

I wasn't abandoned in the psych ward. My lawyer had prepared to go to court today with the head doctor to seek permission to see me, her client. The hospital apparently didn't have the right to refuse me a lawyer and they became frightened—hence the sudden release this morning. Previously they had planned to keep me locked in the Psychiatric Assessment Unit for a few more days until there was room available in the adolescent ward.

Tommy has gone off to arrange a place for me to stay tonight. I need a shower, and another shirt—I can't look down at the bloodstain ...

Crystal and Tommy have typed up extensive transcripts of their involvement in my situation. My lawyer has been working late on my case for the past few nights, putting in countless calls to the hospital. I'm starting to shake, can't stop. Social services would take me in if I ran away another fifteen times or so—oh sure, sounds like great fun.

April 16

Last night I talked to Michael on the phone. He was merely a voice through a plastic receiver hooked into the wall, a bad connection that whined and whistled—but he was Michael.

He said he'd felt like shit when he heard I had been committed to the hospital; only the day before he'd told his supervisor that to dump me in the psych ward would be the worst thing they could do to me then. He had wanted to visit me in the hospital, but the staff wouldn't allow it, and if he'd gotten too involved against the wishes of his supervisor and May, he would have jeopardized his job. 'And then I'd end up resenting you for it. I'm glad I didn't do what I'd wanted to.'

My father was right in that last stab he delivered in his letter: 'You will be suffering for the rest of your life for your actions.' But not in the way he thought. I will suffer the most for my inability to pay back the people who have helped me over the past few weeks.

April 26

I'm staying at my friend Lana's house. I've been alone here all day, the rain drowning the world outside. I feel I shall never be happy again. A rage so red it explodes in my head; all day it's been the same, and the depression ... maybe I need to go back to the psych ward. What a thing to consider. I need escape from people—God, I must be one of the unhappiest kids around.

Yesterday, across the dining room table, Lana's dad pinned his eyes to my T-shirt. He began yelling, ordering me to take it off, anger tightening his face. 'I'd given you more credit than to wear profanity in my house!' I was speechless, and the insulting T-shirt did come off (it was printed with slogans: 'Fuck Expo 86,' 'Fuck Being Poor,' 'Fuck the BC Government,' etc.), forgetting about rebellion and knowing only the threat of humiliated tears.

No one can give me the security I threw away. I want to be safe, but there's no such thing as safety; I want love and not tolerance, not pity.

May 9

Things are not okay; when will they ever be okay again? Life is a torture, imposed by some freak accident. This planet developing in the universe, coloring itself blue and green, was an accident. It shouldn't have happened. At any rate, it shouldn't have populated itself.

I've been drinking with Crystal's friend Frannie and some other people. I'm becoming too adept at swallowing booze, its liquid flowing golden down my throat. I don't know how to be happy otherwise.

In the downtown eastside, I am approached by a man wearing an Expo button. He draws me into a pub. Too deadened to feel apprehension, I follow him and the need for another drink.

He thinks I'm a whore, this man with the villain's smile and eyes that beckon, coerce. He's an Expo volunteer and in his drunkenness thinks my name is Veronica. Suddenly he says he wants to marry me, needs a girl; I put my feet up, feeling sorry for him. I wonder what happened in his life to lead him here, the hows and whys. Gesturing at his wallet, he resorts to lying and says he's got five hundred dollars for sex.

I head home, leaving him with his eyes darting behind his glasses, unable to write down my name. Leave him alone in the pub, waiting for some blurry vision of a girl named Veronica to come back and redeem him.

Home, or what passes for home this month—another new friend has taken me in—I slouch on the green-tiled kitchen floor. There's more beer in the fridge. I smash a bottle against the wooden leg of the table and it breaks into hundreds of brown pieces and translucent shards, flying around the kitchen, glass showering before my eyes in rainbow colors. Someone comes in as I aim the larger pieces at the wall. I slump as glass crunches and tinkles, and she sweeps it up, all up, and I lie on the floor thinking: I've done it this time. REALLY DONE IT THIS TIME.

May 11

I wandered around the downtown eastside yesterday after midnight, along the streets where women sold their bodies and men's cars slid to a stop, indistinguishable from the blackness, their lights flashing. I walked in the sandwich of night, darting between the girls' inviting smiles and the cars slowing, slowing.

A cold night; the sidewalk was powdered white. I tried to call Michael, the one person I could talk to, but: 'Oh, Michael has a client, he can't speak to you right now.' I can envision him in a chair in Emergency Services, hands between his knees, green eyes concerned.

The community is trying to evict the tenants of the house across the street. They play loud music at all hours. 'White hippies, no politics, just do a lot of booze and drugs,' my friends claim, standing in their nightgowns at 11 p.m. while music pounds into their living room from the speakers the hippies moved onto the roof.

At two in the morning, I stumble from the house and knock on the white hippies' door. My life is enough of a shambles; they could do anything to me and I wouldn't care.

Faces stare out through the half-opened door, suspicious. I squeeze inside and slump in their hallway, eyeing an enormous knife on the crates packed in front of me.

'Who are you, man? What're you doing here?'

The house reeks of marijuana. There are a few people strumming guitars in the room behind me, but the guy who's talking to me immediately shuts their door. Wide-eyed, unsmiling, these people who call themselves gypsies question me, worried I'm out to bust them. Their dog wanders over, though, and immediately tries to make friends.

A guy named Dave hands me a beer; he's nineteen but looks older, brown hair falling around his shoulders. He asks if I'm strung out and I slump there and say, 'No, but do you have any dope?' He doesn't trust me quite yet, face grave with suspicion, and blurts, 'No, man, no dope.' The other people continue wandering in and out, but he takes responsibility for me—somehow fatherly.

They think politics is a waste of time; Dave says I've got to live, live. 'Who gives a shit about Sexpo?' They may be right: there's nothing I can do. If I don't like ten thousand dollars' worth of fireworks going off every night while people are starving, why don't I just ignore them?

His friend peers down at me from the top of the stairway. 'So now you're on your own and you've got a skull on your T-shirt and you're hanging around with all us guys—and you think you're all grown up, eh!' They laugh at me. 'Come upstairs if you want, but you'll have to

give us head first,' Dave's friend warns, then they all smile and admit
they're just kidding and I'm shaking my head and we start laughing
together.

Their attic is lit by a teetering lamp that sometime during the night
crashes onto the floor and leaves us in pitch blackness. The stairway is
dark and narrow, and upstairs music is going full blast, guitars are scattered around together with clothes, ashtrays, beer bottles. Blankets are
strung across the ceiling and the mattresses on the floor are buried
beneath miscellaneous articles. It's wild! They're into spirituality and
dropping LSD to see God. Dave's friend starts panicking because 'if the
cops come here right now looking for you I'd shit,' but nonetheless
they'd invite me to join their band, except I'm 'too young.' Through
the music, Dave's friend deftly divides a puddle of cocaine into several
lines, the razor flicking silver, sharp. Innocuous snow on glass. Beer is
passed around, a layer of foam coating the murky liquid.

I'm really happy, like it here. Dave and his friends are full of smiles,
and I know they've accepted me. Dave thinks me unusual because I'm
appreciating this: 'You're not like this chick who came once and
grabbed all the hash and started rolling joints for herself and drinking
our beer and smoking our cigarettes without even asking.'

We become so stoned we can't talk. One guy sits on a mattress withdrawing into himself and looking miserable, empty. I sprawl on the
floor, unable to move, wanting to sleep and puke at the same time.
Nausea rises sour into my mouth and my head won't stop spinning,
and I've got to get back to my friends' home but my lips can't form
the word 'Goodbye.' The music becomes intolerable, and there are too
many lumps of hash still waiting on the table. Our heads are back,
eyes lidded and mouths speechless. I start hallucinating that the people around me are in my head and my head becomes so stuffed with
their bodies that it almost explodes. How can you have several people
living inside your head? There isn't enough room.

My lips mobilize themselves enough to tell them I'm leaving—it's
nearly 5 a.m. Dave guides me to the door, and I look at him realizing
how much I love the sensitive person he's revealed himself to be. The
high school dropout and drug dealer who wants to break out of the
life he's leading. I sense someone warm, mature, caring inside him.

We touch each other lightly and he tells me to take care, take it easy,
and then I'm out on the porch, staggering into the unfriendly morning.

'Not every day that someone knocks on the door at two in the morning and sits down in the hallway. Nope, not every day, man. Strange.'

May 25

The street lamp splatters light like egg yolk onto the road; it oozes through the window blinds into the trash can. Rain showers from these lamps, in orange slivers of water. It is black and cold and pouring out there.

I'm in Emergency Services with Michael opposite me, in the family conference room. The flower prints on the walls and the orange-cushioned chairs trigger memories of another night, long ago. Michael hooks one leg over the arm of his chair, looking different from the last time we'd seen each other—or maybe just different from my fabrications. The shirt he's wearing is too tight, revealing small lumps of fat, and his face is very pale. Michael looks faintly ridiculous, but do you know something? It doesn't matter. He smiles rarely and doesn't reach over to touch me.

I wonder how much of him I've used up. It's Friday night. I stood in the rain outside, seeking out the dry corners around Emergency Services. Finally I pressed the intercom, giving my name, and they said they were closed.

'I've got to come in.'

'How old are you, Evelyn?'

'Fourteen.'

Silence, then Michael hurries to the door.

He spends most of his eight-hour shift with me, and as usual I screw up, sitting there with my wet shoes plastered to my feet, looking outside. It's an effort to talk through the fog of depression—words come out tiny, after long spaces. Michael waits for a sentence to work its way out. Watching him, I wish for a smile to color his eyes blue, but when it comes it is so fleeting it crumbles like sawdust.

I ramble on while people are turned away from the door. Some women are brought in for child neglect; others, after being raped. I sit there wishing for Michael's closeness, his warmth, and most of all his smile, which would return the caring to his face. It doesn't take long for someone to stop caring: I should have known this. It doesn't take very long at all.

A curtain has fallen over his eyes.

Sometime during the graveyard shift a man is turned away from the door. He was supposed to be in his hostel by 2:30 a.m., but it's 3:00 and he wants shelter in the empty, lit offices of E.S. He is sent back into the furious rain. 'You only have to walk the streets for a few hours before we open in the morning,' a social worker tells him.

That enrages me. What kind of condition might that man have been in? What if he was knifed, or beaten up, during those 'few hours?'

'I'll go in his place. Please, Michael, just let him come in and I'll leave, okay?'

A worker thrusts his head into the doorway and catches what I said. He laughs, tries to exchange winks with Michael, who doesn't smile or make fun of me but sits there silently. Suddenly my words sound tinselly in the air, fake concern, and I realize how tired I am.

Michael scribbles something on a notepad. Why is he carrying one? Is he, too, trying to play the role of shrink? I want to keep my social services file bland.

I sit there contorting my hands in my lap, searching his eyes and finding them clouded, obscure.

It's a coffin in this room. He listens patiently, but he shouldn't have to be listening, what I'm saying isn't even important, just thoughts tripping over my tongue. He persuades me to go into care temporarily, just for the weekend, and after a long time mulling it over I agree to do it. He says, 'I'm glad,' but there's no gladness in his eyes. His face is paste-colored and his eyes are weary, but not in an endearing way— not when I'm the one who's made them like that.

I've used him, just like I've used everyone. He flinches and moves away, unclean, eyes bloodshot.

I'm motioned into another office; it is light outside now. At dawn the sky was awash with blue, but now it is gray and the open window is cleansed with rain. It's too cold here, but that helps keep me awake.

As rain blows in from the office window, I talk to my father on the phone, explaining that he's supposed to come down to sign the forty-eight-hour weekend care agreement. He sounds tired, older than when I heard him last. (Okay, is that my fault too?) He asks to talk to

Michael, and I listen in on the extension, hearing him tell Michael that I'm just fourteen, that I'm being exploited, that nobody takes in a fourteen-year-old girl without expecting something back.

Michael murmurs, 'Yeah, yeah,' over and over, tired of hearing the spiel yet again, his eyes red-rimmed. Before he gets another worker to drive me to the emergency group home and goes home himself, we say goodbye and I look at him and think I love him.

June 2

I'm living at New Beginnings, a girls' group home. I lie here nights and watch the traffic outside. All I can see of the cars are rectangular shapes of light passing across the ceiling that slants over my bed. The fan blows stale air into my face; my few possessions are stacked onto a shelf. The rumbling of the trucks and buses drowns out the Top 40 music trickling from the adjacent bedroom:

'I just wanna use your love tonight/ I don't wanna lose your love tonight ...'

Lying here under a tangle of sheets. The sound of the fan screams in my ears, lifting the hair off my face. Won't it stop? I have to squint onto this page as the room is lighted with one bare bulb, hung from a scratched, splotched ceiling. The mountains are black outside the half-open window.

One night, I called Michael at home, when I was wandering around drunk in the downtown eastside, after AWOLing from the emergency group home. I didn't do anything except cry, and it made him angry, till he finally ordered me to start making sense instead of wasting his time.

So I dragged myself to Co-Op Radio, cradling another beer, sitting and crying until somebody kicked me out. I tried, really I did, to stay either drunk or hungover all the time, but it was hard; no one would let me. They stole the beer hidden under my bed, mopped up the carpet and the golden shards of glass.

Someone saw me drinking and buying drugs in the downtown eastside and called my father, who in turn called Emergency Services. They sent a social worker to the youth newspaper. I went back to my friends' home the next morning and got bawled out by everyone despite the worst hangover I'd ever had; then when I was talking to the school counsellor on the phone I couldn't stop crying and she got somebody to trace the call and send the police over.

So they arrived, clanking down the stairs to the basement where I was drinking and sobbing. The constable threatened to break my arm even as he let down the wall for a split second to touch me and say, 'Look, I care.' Maybe I should have accepted that caring, but it sounded rehearsed, so I chose not to believe and suddenly the silver circles knocked my wrists together and they brought me into the blackness that was actually afternoon sunlight, strapping me to a stretcher.

I had to laugh when I opened my eyes and found myself in Quiet Room #1 at the hospital. Before I was rolled in and dumped onto the mattress, one of the ambulance men demanded my address.

'Any address. Sure, her parents' will do. Just so long as I get paid for the ride.'

This room was different from Quiet Room #4 only in that the toilet and sink were in the right corner rather than the left (again there was no water), and I was stripped of blankets, cold. I was wearing the blue pajamas again, with one of the buttons missing on the shirt.

A doctor thrust his fingers into various parts of my body, thinking I was drunk or unconscious, until the pain induced a screamed 'Fuck off!' whereupon he laughed and sauntered out the door. I buried my hot face in the pillow until nurses came to stick a needle into me, while two other people held me down unnecessarily. The needle shuddered and drew, and I almost wished they were drugging me so that I could finally escape.

Kristin, an Emergency Services worker, came to retrieve me, but all I saw of her for half an hour were pink heels as I hid my face in my hands and sobbed. I had been sitting on the floor of the waiting room, back in my own clothes, when a young psych patient in blue pajamas knelt beside me and moved her hands lovingly over me. She was so beautiful. Are they going to destroy her in there?

* * *

Kristin brought me to New Beginnings, and now I'm in this chipped blue room that I share with a twelve-year-old girl who looks about sixteen with her makeup. She went AWOL a while ago, like I did from the emergency group home, because after a while it doesn't matter, you stop caring about whom you might hurt and in fact you just want to hurt more people because that's the only power you've got left.

She took off after leaving her clothes and possessions on the floor, took off with a smile in my direction. I'm left with memories of her as a shadow on the edge of my bed in the middle of the night, confiding about her life of sex and drugs and booze, the traffic lights illuminating bits of her face. So she's on the street now, this twelve-year-old girl, but I'm too tired to cry over her.

June 7

Two a.m., at the bus depot. Crystal standing on the front porch of the youth newspaper house, a curtain of hair covering her white shoulders, arms folded across her chest and watching me grimly. The lines of her face are gray under the harsh light of the bulb. I've AWOL'd from New Beginnings, this time with nowhere to go. I couldn't stand being a case number in social services' computer anymore. Couldn't stand the helpless love songs going all night, the other girls busying themselves with their makeup early in the morning.

Unshaven men are my company tonight, picking out items from the garbage can in front of me. Somehow, in all of this, I've mingled with the stench of sweat and quiet desperation.

In the meantime, two strangers pull up in their car and ask if I need a ride and do I give head, and the night is wracked with the blaring of horns. 'It's good, baby, come on, suck my cock,' and the driver's eyes are glazed. I look at him and his friend with the long blond hair, peering through the fence, standing with my bags.

One man pulls down his pants in front of me, working intensely with the zipper. The wind blows dust into my eyes, without end.

It's graduation night for three of the high schools in the district, and everyone is either drunk or high. The girls laugh at Death, hair wild in their faces in the limousines, while the guys in their tuxedos feel like men.

I'm sure the men in this depot don't feel so grown-up. They shuffle their Salvation Army sneakers, and the traffic remains impersonal.

I wonder if the people in their cars ever think about how secure they are, with their toilets and running water and a place to wash their faces each morning, to do their hair and makeup and set forth looking like everyone else.

A man spits and coughs behind me on the bench, billowing clouds of smoke into my face that thrust little knives of pain into my head. Maybe I should have clambered over that fence and fucked that rather beautiful blond boy, but the street lamps are lonely moons hanging over the alley. There isn't anybody I could call at this hour, no one who hasn't already exhausted themselves pulling me out of situations. A potato chip bag blows forlornly across the cement.

Now I'm in a restaurant; at least it's warm. Poor May; I don't suppose her hours of work on my case mean much now. Another worker, Frank, has been assigned to my case as well.

The staff in this place just kicked out a derelict in his tattered, stained clothing, who apparently seeks out this restaurant each night to slump into a chair and try to sleep. I beg them to let him stay, offering to buy him food, but they refuse and then gossip in the kitchen. Is my anger going to give the man warmth?

A bug-eyed man in a T-shirt wanders unsteadily around the depot, and the guys who wanted head fling back 'Bitch!' into the wind when I don't move. You know, sometimes I begin to wonder about things, especially when less than three months ago I was an honor roll student and labelled a square.

I want to sleep. Would things have turned out differently if Tommy were here, instead of staying in Ontario for seven months? Then I realize his patience and common sense wouldn't make things better. His puppy-dog eyes filled with friendship would still have been incomparable to Michael's, even if they'd been washed pale with the sight of too many dirt-splattered bums kicked back into the night.

The restaurant closes and I migrate to a twenty-four-hour coffee shop, where I meet the derelict again, drinking coffee and shaking. Beside me at the counter, he asks tentatively, 'Can I touch your leg?' and places his fingers there in a curiously obligatory manner, as if he had to because I was female. I shake my head tiredly. He takes his fingers back in silence, and doesn't try again.

June 14

I'm now living with four guys I met through a friend who saw me on the bus. Last night we dropped some T'ai Chi acid—nobody told me it was laced with PCP (angel dust)—supplied by their friend Ken. They were already tripping out by the time I got home to slip the blotter onto my tongue; we decided to head towards the liquor store and then stop at a park on the way back to watch the sunset.

When we left the house, Ken could barely walk. He was doubled over on the sidewalk, staring with glazed eyes at his sandalled feet. I should have been warned by the condition he was in, but I thought I was immune to any heavy trips—after all, my first introduction to LSD several weeks ago had been tame.

We wandered through the park to Commercial Drive. I was experiencing a gradual feeling of excitement, a heightened awareness of the scenery around us. The lake shone with the hardness of glass, and the hills rolled ever so slightly. It was like stepping into a child's book where cardboard figures would spring out of the pages as they were opened. A comfortable sensation spread through me as I gazed at the horizon awash in soft colors.

The acid really hit on Commercial Drive. We were standing at an intersection, and the cars started rippling down the road, gaining weight, undulating. A Labatt's beer carton beckoned to us from the darkening sky, and my school friends sprouted up from the street corners. I had been transported to this amazing reality where objects moved not in a blur but concretely; it was impossible to believe that the rest of the world wasn't seeing the same thing. We passed by store windows where designs on plates whirled and spun; sofas in furniture stores glowed pink and cream; the sidewalk began to roll. Buildings tilted towards us, and the air shimmered in icicles of color. The acid washed over me in sweltering waves, urging me to the brink of nausea, then retreating just in time. It was difficult keeping my balance on the violently heaving pavement. And the passersby were hilarious— their bodies warped, obese one instant and anorexic the next. I was laughing hysterically even while noticing that Ken's eyes had dilated into white, glittering circles. He said he was seeing blood on the mouths of girls walking by.

We stumbled and swayed down Commercial Drive, the lights in the stores blinking madly, that Labatt's carton glowing enticingly in the sky, people in the pool halls moving jerkily as robots. The traffic appeared to be studded with liquidly rotating police lights, stirring within me a sense of danger. I was having a wild time, amazed by the powers of what had been soaked into a tiny rectangle of paper placed on my tongue. Walking the streets, I realized delightedly, would never be the same again. I had discovered the ultimate weapon against boredom. I could have tripped out on the air alone, which was bursting with shimmering rainbows and curved fingers of color. It was like being in the most bizarre circus; my only regret was that I couldn't linger anywhere, because the guys were pulling me forward.

There were so many things to see, all moving and changing. I didn't even complain about the waves of acid when they hit, leaving me sweating and gasping, and the disturbing realization that I could barely keep my balance. As the trip progressed, each block became a different world, even the air changed as it grew darker or lighter, filled with mirages. The pollution from the traffic hung in a swirling fog above us; the traffic lights turned green when they were actually red; people on the sidewalk were there one moment and vanished the next. Buses snaked down the street, flaming with light; teenagers sipping their Cokes on the street corners became victims of my not-so-silent ridicule. In restaurants and pubs, the lights started flickering, and the patrons wore wicked grins glued to their faces, toasting each other with goblets brimming with blood.

The world had become a madhouse.

I waited outside while the others went in to the liquor store. I was becoming worried now but didn't tell anyone—the waves of acid were crashing down too hard on me; the sidewalk continued to rise and bend. I wasn't sure if I was in control anymore; the different worlds rushed at me with increasing speed, trapping me in prism after prism. The buildings bulged outwards, threatening to explode at the seams; the sky was a raging sea, boiling and bubbling.

When the guys returned from the liquor store, I had begun to lose control. We turned around to head back to the park, and they thrust a bottle into my hands. It grew small, then large; flat, then bulbous. The grass was infested with lizards, snapping at my feet, and baby monsters with spiked tails took swipes at me from the branches overhead. It was a far cry from the gentle beginning of the trip.

I wove in and out of blackness, moments without noise or vision, then returned to stare with horrible fascination at the lizards and to take an obligatory sip from the bottle undulating between my palms. I had forgotten who the people sauntering in front of me were. At one point I emerged from a phase of blackness to find myself staring down into my bottle and sobbing quietly, 'I'm sorry, Michael.' I repeated it a few times, then started apologizing to everyone who had tried to help me. I stood in the middle of the sidewalk and did this steadily until one of the guys shouted at me to hurry, and then I snapped out of it enough to stumble a few steps forward.

Suddenly I entered another space, a world of complete darkness except for showers of light that swirled in scarves about me. I was trapped inside this cloak of night and magic, falling between the folds. The guys disappeared; the sidewalk disappeared; I floated through the sparks as if in a dream ... When I awoke I was dead. In reality we had reached the park, but I had died under the Skytrain. The Skytrain was bearing down upon me, yet there was no pain, just the onrush of wind, the gravelly swooshing of the train. It wasn't bad at first. But then my eyes opened and when they looked down at me they saw that my shirt was soaking with blood, my blood! The lake shimmered distantly and I tried to find my way towards it because it was pink and blue and I wanted to drown in the colors.

One of the guys told me later that when they'd finally succeeded in half-dragging, half-carrying me home, I was wandering around in circles talking to myself. A biker had chased them for blocks because he thought they were trying to rape me.

Stupidly enough, my first thought when I woke up the next morning was that no matter what had happened last night, I would take LSD again. After all, I hadn't gone crazy, had I? And there couldn't be another trip worse than last night's. I was sure I'd be able to handle it better next time, aware now of what could happen.

June 18

Today was a new lesson in humiliation. I went to the Food Bank for the first time: St. Jude's Church on Renfrew Street. I can remember a time, back home, when my parents would drive past such depots and

I'd look at the lineups, eyes angry with tears. There was a time when I'd been above this, high enough to hope to change it all.

I walk across the lawn to the church. Some men are sprawled on the curb, wearing lumber jackets and long, greasy hair. They sit there, spoiling the lawn with their dirt. Three girls with carefully made-up eyes weave through the straggling lineup, uncomfortable expressions on their faces.

The air reeks of alcohol. At one of the entrances to the church, men sit silently under the stairs, the whites of their eyes glinting as they glance up without interest. One stumbles, staggers against me; a woman laughs and grabs his arm. There are women here with dyed blond hair; women in flaring green polyester pants; women clinging to thin babies with eyes like shallow pools.

Oh Michael, this wasn't supposed to happen! If there's any glamor in poverty, it's been lost on me. I've fallen far from 2 a.m. in the hospital, your slim jean-clad legs in their leather boots leaning against the wall.

I go in, fill out a registration form using a fake address, show the man identification.

'You're only fourteen?' he asks.

'Yes,' I say, and the question 'Why?' hangs unspoken in the air. Cigarette smoke clouds the air of the church. Volunteers with sagging faces, their hair in rollers, move wearily within this haze, amongst crumpled bags of groceries stacked in a sea around them. Tired people, sometimes eyeing us with contempt.

Clutching my punched orange ticket, I wait with the growing crowd. The lawn is littered with people now. A group of native Indians with sweaty hair wrap their arms around each other, washing the air with the smell of booze.

They line us up like a herd of cattle, straight out onto the sidewalk. We are in groups, we are alone, under the clouds and patches of blue sky. There is a kind of solidarity in this, strange.

I'm inside. A woman hands me a grocery bag. We walk past the tables, in file, as the volunteers drop packages into our bags. I say 'Thank you' hollowly each time and am ignored; occasionally a woman will smile encouragingly at me, but more often I receive hard looks from stone faces.

Coming out into the empty daylight, the guys join me. The food is in the fridge now, milk and carrots and old bags of licorice allsorts ... I can't touch any of it, leave it for my friends.

Yesterday I caught a glimpse of my eyes in the mirror and withdrew, then looked again. They were the eyes of a drug user, unusually shiny. We smoke hash in this house almost twenty-four hours a day.

I'd never turned down any drug after being offered that first joint by Joe, but last night when I was on the couch trying to sleep, Dave came by with hash. He passed the pipe over; when I shook my head he ridiculed me until I succumbed.

The weedy, sharp taste of hashish lingers in my mouth. My lids are heavy and there is a scratchiness in my throat. Okay, I'd been wrong, I admit it, I shouldn't have started using drugs in the beginning.

PART II

june 22 to september 14 1986

June 22

Kim, a writer some friends connected me with, has sent me the money to take a bus to Ottawa. From there, he and his girlfriend are going to arrange to move me to a suburb near Boston, where they live. My suitcases are stacked in the living room. I won't forget these guys, though; they've become a kind of family.

One of them blows smoke into the air and says in his hoarse voice, 'I don't know you mega-well, but still you've become a part of our lives and we're never going to forget you. We'll always be wondering where you are and if you're okay.' I look at him, think how loving they all are in their drugged way. The next morning I wake up to Led Zeppelin sawing at the air, and I hear his words hanging in the early morning, and I can't help crying.

I don't know what I'll do, four thousand miles away from anyone who cares about me, but maybe things will be different there. Maybe I'll finally be able to escape all that's bothering me, without using drugs. But I don't want to say goodbye to these guys, almost wish somebody would chain me to a bed or something.

June 30

Traveling across the country was like walking into a social studies map. Towns that had previously been names memorized for exams became populated, alive. In Alberta and Saskatchewan, the Rockies sank into the earth and the land became flat. Here there would be no security for Crystal, who used to stand at the window and stare at the mountains, arms hugging her body. The trees flowed by the highway, and I remembered what it was like to spend the days in the psych ward fantasizing about escape.

I wanted Michael, buried in his brown coat. I wouldn't have minded being insane in a sane world as long as he was there, as long as he didn't abandon me.

Through the flatness, lakes appeared, stirred into thick milkshakes by the wind. Trees clawed at the cliffs and the sky fell until I could have reached up with thumb and forefinger to pinch a cloud into my pocket.

Kim and Ruth arrived at the Ottawa depot. He was tall, with long arms (the left one sunburned from driving out to 'rescue' me), a bristling beard and thinning waves of brown hair. Ruth was short with blond hair that flowed endlessly down her back.

A woman hurtles into the dim interior of the bus bound for New York. She is muscular, with thick frizzy hair, wearing a gray uniform and a gun at her hip. 'All right people, this is U.S. Customs. Everyone off the bus. Take all your luggage and line up outside!' Her arms go up in command as the neon lights flash STOP at the border.

For one moment terror grips me and my knees go limp, but by the time we're in the Customs office I have to stop myself from laughing. This is no big deal. I'm caught between two places, equally fucked; I've left my future behind in the bottom of that aspirin bottle in Joe's cabinet.

The fake American high school ID passes both officials: 'How was your weekend in Canada visiting friends? So you live in New York— why, I was down there last weekend, shopping.'

In New York, Kim hugs me hard and I feel the leanness of his body; in the waiting car Ruth leaps up, banging on the roof with her fists and screaming with triumph. 'We've won!' they shout excitedly—but against what? I pretend to smile, but my lips are grim. We may have won against the authorities, but nothing has changed.

Men walk around in the American heat, scratching aimlessly at their crotches.

July 2

My birthday. I remember childhood birthdays when I'd wake up with excitement, embarrassingly early, and it would always be sunny. I'd leap up, throwing back the covers. There would be a cake, and smiles for a day. No anger for one day. I remember the aftermath, though, when I was about five—Mom sweeping the gleaming kitchen floor, turning around to scream at me about something. Wishing sadly that it could always be my birthday so no one would yell at me.

I also remember the fireplace in my parents' living room, me sprawled on the carpet at Daddy's feet, subservient. Parents used to be God, didn't they?

Told Kim last night that today I'd legally be fifteen. 'Want us to bake a cake?' he laughed. 'Or we'll take you out to dinner, only I don't know if there's anywhere around here you'd like to eat at.'

I shook my head. 'No, look, I'd rather just not think about it, okay? I'd rather we ignored it.' The healing hasn't started. There are just those previous birthdays to dwell on, reminding me of what had once been home. It's inappropriate to have a birthday here, so far away from family and friends.

Kim is at the word processor now, punk music all much the same roaring from the record player. Slogans shrieked in angry voices. At night I try to lull myself asleep with meditation music recorded inside the Taj Mahal, trying to float on the sounds, but turn and turn hotly on the dog's couch. Dream of Michael, talking with him, then wake up and think I've got to be near him. What day is it? Wednesday? I'll find out when he works next and then go down to Emergency Services. Waking up and focusing on the fuzzy wallpaper, I realize I can't walk to Emergency Services after all; it's four thousand miles away.

July 6

Uninspired. Walking the streets of America, jean jacket slung over one shoulder, alien to the grandmothers on their square porches overlooking neatly trimmed lawns. The air is thick and crouches on my shoulders as I walk past these houses, each one the same as the next, under plastic-looking trees.

Few people in the world have the luxury to follow their impulses, tied down as they are by families, jobs and other responsibilities. But

I'm not bound by anything. It's too important for me to move from one place to the next, savoring this freedom.

Watching two gerbils in their respective cages, I wonder how they handle spending years in a cage little more than a foot long and a foot high, their entire lives behind thin steel barriers, with nothing but a wheel spinning crazily. Yet if I released them they would die. Is this what I've done? My parents' house was a prison; I pried open the bars and leapt out into the world. A naked, raw world, without protection. Didn't I ever think that the bars of a cage might do more than confine?

Still, I believe dying out here 'free' is better than perishing mad and alone inside a bedroom. My head and eyes ache from the heaviness of the air; I can't stand this heat. It looks like another bad night ahead.

July 7

Once upon a time, there was a man named Michael. He was a social worker for a twenty-four-hour branch of social services called Emergency Services. And then there was a kid who had given up her home and identity who came to depend upon him and wrote about him until her nonexistent audience emitted a collective yawn.

It doesn't matter, though. It is pure fantasy for her to think that one day the audience will breathe and her scribblings will be transformed into print on the pages of a book. There were all the diaries she wrote since she was six years old, but she ran away and destroyed those volumes of ink and paper. She tries to compensate now, recording her discoveries and disillusionments, the gradual learning process and the falling apart, but she has no motivation except that writing means life, and it gives her the feeling that she still belongs inside herself.

I love Kim and Ruth, but I can't deal with some of the things going on here—the heat, my allergies, no friends or identity in this tiny suburb. I sit in this house and obediently go outside as little as possible, to avoid being caught. There is nothing glamorous about being an illegal immigrant; glamor fades quickly in the drudgery of a day-to-day existence.

* * *

Drunk again. Not so drunk that I can't write, but drunk enough to be at a loss creatively, though my hand makes motions on the paper. The room smells like mint, the kind my mother used to pull from her garden. I had nightmares about being chased by my parents last night; they wouldn't give up no matter how hard I ran or how loudly I screamed at them.

Falling, falling; I wish there was someone here.

July 8

In the mall today, I stopped one of the security men. He was young with sandy hair and pale, mirrorlike eyes, wearing a starched white shirt and a gun at his hip. He had been standing at one of the stores for fifteen minutes, talking to the girl behind the counter. I approached him and asked where the nearest police station was.

His eyes reflected me instantly. 'What happened?'

What happened? It started happening three and a half months ago. Distance has done nothing except prove that borders and miles can't contain me either, nor this rage banging against the bars of my body, demanding release. It was a mistake, conquering distance, allowing me not just an illusion but a near-reality of infallibility, power, defiance. Was it May who had asked why power was so important to me? I'd shaken my head then and pursued another topic, because she'd been wrong—I'd only wanted freedom.

What happened? I've screwed around with my mind, body and relationships with others; somewhere along the way I went too far. That's all. For a while I thought there was no place left to fall, but that's not true; when you get to this point, you find out that there isn't any bottom so you just keep falling. I have a life to fill, without rules, borders, or conscience. So this is what happens when you tear yourself from your restraints.

Today is the court date set to determine my guardianship, and do you know that a mocking, sallow-skinned May Wong is in Family Court waiting to apprehend me? What has the judge decided? The choice is between a rock and a hard place: parents or government. But

I'd be grateful to be a ward of the court; no surprises then—no more alleys and men squeezing my breasts and dragging me behind garbage bins. NO MORE ALLEYS.

'What happened?' The security man watched me with concern in his pale eyes.

'Nothing's happened,' I said quickly. The muscles of his face relaxed and he pointed me to the nearest exit: left, right, then under a bridge and right again. I decided against going and sat down in the mall instead, reading my diary entries.

Kim looked at me shrewdly across the kitchen table tonight and asked, 'You're not going to turn yourself in, are you?' It was hard meeting his eyes, but I did, laughing and shaking my head.

'Oh God, no, of course not.'

July 9

A part of me yearns for those summer afternoons with my girlfriend, Lana, our schoolbags flung into the ditch, our bodies sprawled among the weeds by the sidewalk. Summer days of leaping from the stone fence in my parents' front yard, playing with her dogs. It occurs to me that if everyone acted like I'm acting now, nothing would ever get done. Yet sometimes I question the purpose of construction when it will all be destroyed anyway—maybe not through nuclear war, but through any multitude of self-destructive schemes humankind will cook up along the way. Nothing is forever (except death).

Graveyards are simple places. Once I was young with peach-fuzz cheeks and attended summer school near a graveyard. After the lessons I would walk back to the car hand in hand with my mother, swatting away the mosquitoes that darted out of the bushes. Once I loved her. Surely once I loved her.

I loved both my parents. My early childhood memories are like photographs: in the back seat of a car, drinking lemonade in the heat with relief, standing in front of a striped tent in the Interior; posing with a cone of blue cotton candy at the fair. Pictures snapped and positioned in an album. But I've learned that things, like photographs, are dispensable and too bulky for travel. In the end, I'll have led a totally anonymous life. Everything is temporary, perhaps even these thoughts on this paper in the withering heat—not even thoughts, just finger movements. Is this fair?

It's the same here in this suburb as it was back in Vancouver, only I have nothing to do, no one to be with. Not very reassuring. Perhaps I came out here to find something, but it didn't materialize, and I am sick of myself.

July 10

Thinking about Crystal, her coldness, started the tears. Once she'd told me to be strong and had held me with so much warmth. Flying into the kitchen with her hair spilling over her long black coat, wearing bright political buttons, dropping her groceries and hugging me fiercely: 'Boy, am I glad to see you!' What happened?

I miss Tommy, his patience, the delight and warmth in his eyes. Tommy who wanted to be locked up with me in that cell up the coast, so I wouldn't be alone. But the cops aren't here when I need them, and when I didn't need them, they stalked around the ferry terminal. It's like that. You might think you've won because you've gotten away with drugs and booze and crossing borders, but those are superficial victories, the ones that whirl around when you least expect it and slap you in the face.

No more men in orange vans coming for me at 2 a.m., placing their hands on my shoulders and stopping me from shattering. No more workers willing to rescue me from myself.

Michael. I'm sorry that I built something out of you that never existed. Somebody had to come along at the beginning, and it happened to be you. I didn't even know you as a person, only as a figure inside a government agency. Kristin made everything clear when she said that she cared about me, and it was in the same stilted, rehearsed voice you used when you said that I mattered. Perhaps you said it with your eyes closed and your teeth clenched. How many clients have you used that line on, anyway? The system captured me through your tired eyes and your smile, but that's the last time.

NEVER AGAIN.

July 11

Kim raises his eyes and looks directly at me across the kitchen table. 'You're free to go back any time you want, you know. You could go back now.'

Ruth is silent, stirring her ice cream absentmindedly. I dig into my own dish of ice cream with sudden interest. A film has settled over Kim's eyes, making them inscrutable.

'Well, I'm sure I'll want to go back in a few years. But not now. I want to stay as far away from the system as possible.'

They laugh, and the moment (the opportunity) passes.

We were in Harvard Square tonight. Stars swung mockingly in the cup of sky over the university grounds, the colored lights. Glasses clinked together, a crowd gathered before a live band, and perfume hung headily in the purple air. Guys with shoulder-length hair, wearing ripped jeans with peace symbols drawn on the knees, strode down the brick pavement; they were accompanied by girls trailing beads and the scent of sandalwood. Older men with wire-rimmed glasses and bushy beards walked more slowly past me, with older women who had long hair and were wrapped in shawls dripping with fringes. The air was thick with the night, the music, the excitement. It was alive around me, its fingers drawing me in, but I remained an observer.

The night was spattered with stars and throngs of laughing people. Wine swirled in glasses beneath glittering propositioning eyes. It had the potential for a cheap romance novel and certainly for drugs, but I didn't have any money.

Maybe eventually I'll make a living selling drugs, then write a best seller about the whole thing and become rich and famous and live happily ever after.

I miss Vancouver, the men with glazed eyes slipping me grams of hash at bus stops. I miss the potential safety of Emergency Services, and perhaps a social worker named Michael, who was sort of a beacon in the night.

July 16

Last night at the nearest square I called the police station, feigning an

American accent, and explained how I'd run across this girl sitting in the square who'd told me she was a runaway from Canada. I gave them a description of 'her' clothing, then hung up and sat down in the center of the empty square. In a few minutes a cop car maneuvered to a stop in front of me and a young policeman emerged. He was tanned and wore an ironic smile.

'I want to talk to you.' He put his hand on my shoulder, comforting. I felt strangely floating and empty. He tried to look into my face and spent several minutes asking me questions, but I was tired and silent. As the worker at Emergency Services had said, I was only playing charades.

The cop was exceptionally nice until I told him to fuck off, then he grabbed my wrists and handcuffed me, with something curiously sad as well as angry in his eyes. At the station we sat together for a few hours, with a sergeant, and talked. The policeman kept smiling at me reassuringly, and the sergeant adopted a paternal attitude, but the lies were difficult to craft: How had I gotten to Boston? Where had I been staying? How long had I been here? My answers were gaping with lapses of time, but they ignored this. Mostly we just discussed life. The cop eventually had to leave, but the sergeant stayed, bringing me coffee and donuts.

He called Emergency Services in Vancouver, but for tonight at least I needed a place here. The sergeant tried several social services without luck, mostly because out-of-towners aren't looked after. Our eyes met above the desk and he shook his head. Then he managed to reach a woman named Janet from a social service called Bridge Over Troubled Waters, which dealt with runaways, drug and alcohol abuse, etc. He emphasized to her that I wasn't eager to stay in a group home and was hoping for either an Independent Living or volunteer foster home.

While we waited for Janet, the sergeant left the office and came back with a T-shirt printed with the emblem of the Boston Police. He held the shirt out with a tentative smile, which looked a little ridiculous on his fleshy face.

'I don't want you to forget us. So here's a souvenir of the cop station you visited in Boston.'

I didn't know whether to laugh or cry. I took the shirt and thanked the sergeant.

Janet was young, outspoken and involved in the peace movement. We drove to an Independent Living house, in a suburb outside of Boston. The house had the capacity to hold twelve kids; there were ten living there. They were asleep, so I took a shower and climbed immediately into bed, grateful for the clean sheets. It didn't bother me much that now my possessions consisted of my writing, the clothes on my back and two hits of LSD I'd stolen from Kim. I sat on the pink cover of the bed and shook my hair dry, squinting through the absolute darkness. The lights were still on in the neighbor's house; I could see them through the mosquito netting over my window. A baby behind the door separating my bedroom from the next one let out a wail. Thinking about Kim and Ruth, I was afraid—it brought back the feelings of running away, the hurt and the guilt. It was hard falling asleep.

The next morning the housemother shook me awake at 7:30, still groggy eyed. There was a clamor for the washroom, then I met the kids staying there. Two of the girls had babies—one a boy and the other a girl, both not yet a year old, with kinky hair and saliva dribbling down their bare chests. The housemother was old and unfriendly, but she managed to maintain discipline over her household.

At 8:30 I called Kim to tell him I was all right; it was horrible, having to lie. His voice was calm, though, and he wanted to call Emergency Services to persuade them to let me stay in the States for a while.

A kid who was 'rehabilitating' under the Bridge Over Troubled Waters program and held the job of placing runaways arrived at the Independent Living house. We took the bus and the subway to downtown Boston; she told me she'd been on the streets for three years, labeling herself a drug addict and alcoholic.

At Bridge I met Allan, Janet's partner in working with runaways. I was told to stay in the waiting room with three guys, one of them buried behind a mass of brown curls. He reminded me of Tommy, though there was none of the puppy-like gentleness in his eyes; he was covered in ripped-up black clothing and decorated with chains. The four of us dived into a conversation about drugs and what it was like on the streets. The curly-haired boy, who turned out to be fifteen though he looked older, peered at me from under his curls. He had a startlingly soft voice.

The three guys had been on the streets ranging from a week and a half to a few months. We discussed what kind of drugs were most available here and in Vancouver. Underneath, I felt unbearably sad, wanting to help them, especially the boy with Tommy's face under the hair. But instead I laughed along with their sexist jokes; laughed and felt safe, so far removed from Emergency Services.

Frank called from Vancouver. I walked into Janet's office and picked up the phone. Though the tone of his voice was obscured by distance, the message wasn't. I concentrated on looking out the window onto Boston Common. A trolley-car ambled by and, squeezing my hands into fists, I wished not for the first time that the thirty aspirin had done a better job.

Frank stated flatly that first of all the plane ticket back to Vancouver would cost $613, and he was sure as hell not going to fork over the money if I was going to run away again. They were going to obtain most of the airfare from my parents.

'There are plenty other kids who can use my help, so I'm not going to waste my time beating my head against the wall if you keep refusing it.'

He told me that the court date had been postponed until August 5 because they had to have a body there—'and hopefully a warm one.' I asked again for a foster home, but he refused. He gave me an hour to decide whether or not to return to Vancouver; long-term services aren't available in the States for a kid who belongs in Canada. I suppose I'll have to go back ... lovingly, I finger the acid against my breast.

July 27

I've been spending the nights at a foster home and days at Bridge, where I've had long talks with Janet and Allan. Both have worked persistently with me, and now I think I might be able to return to Vancouver without screwing up. Janet and Allan have replaced some of the foundation I've been missing. They don't just lecture; they've actually made stuff happen for me—they believe I deserve help and that I have to start convincing social services in Vancouver that it isn't possible for me to return to my parents.

July 28

This morning I dropped the acid at the foster home before going to Bridge. It's frightening how much drugs can unravel—the blocks Allan and Janet had helped me build in the past few days, with some hint at healing, have toppled down. All this through a square of soaked paper. Ironic, how greedily I licked my fingers after taking the blotter.

I got to Bridge okay. The foster father drove me to the subway station, where I took a train to Boston Common. Along the way I ran into a girl who'd been in the waiting room yesterday. We were both heading towards Bridge, but first we walked around downtown and the 'Combat Zone,' the red-light district on the fringe of Chinatown where some drunk had chucked beer bottle pieces at me yesterday. It was populated by prostitutes and drug dealers. The doorways reeked; misshapen women stood waiting for the men whose eyes gleamed with purpose. Construction workers smoked in the billowing dust and watched the girls passing by; the hot, polluted air mingled with the dirt, and bits of garbage swirled around our feet.

The acid began to hit when the girl and I were in the waiting room. I could feel it: the lump in my throat, the heaviness in my chest. Soon the candies in the Lifesavers puzzle pinned to the wall opposite me began wriggling like fat, colorful caterpillars. I told the girl I was tripping and she was right there with me.

Janet came in and motioned me into her office. She asked how I was doing and I said fine, then without warning started crying. I ran for the bathroom, but after a few minutes she dragged me outside and we walked across the street to Boston Common. We sat at the foot of a stone monument where I started giggling uncontrollably; I had to lean against Janet to make it back to Bridge. Everything was too bright, too colorful, wavering in front of my eyes. She left me in one of the offices at my request and I pressed against the window overlooking the Common. The glass bulged out and I thought it would fragment under my weight, spilling in shards onto the sidewalk. Janet came back while I was staring at a framed picture of flowers in baskets inside a greenhouse. Their petals and fronds waved, began dancing; with effort I tore my eyes away.

We went to her office, where I huddled in a chair and became hysterical. My head buried in my arms, I could see policemen in blue suits encircling me, sometimes waving and laughing, sometimes rushing in with sticks. I screamed that no one was going to make me go back to Vancouver! No one was going to make me deal with the ring of asshole social workers, and above all with my parents. Allan came in and urged me to the dental clinic, where it was quiet, but the sight of the institutional walls brought on another fit of screaming.

Back in the office with the waving flowers, with Janet, I babbled something about wanting to hurt May—'she's so small'—and then wanting to kill myself. The acid would dull the second thoughts, the remorse. My eyes purposefully sought the veins in my wrists. Through the drug those wrists looked strong; it would be no different than carving through a piece of meat.

But Janet wouldn't leave. In the meantime, the floor had been cleared and it was very quiet—until two ambulance men in olive uniforms appeared in the doorway. That did it. Behind them were more uniformed men, some of them cops. I flipped out. They cornered me near the window, in front of the heater, and there was a lot of kicking and shouting and scratching. It took a couple of them to get me onto a stretcher; they handcuffed me and tied me firmly down. One of the policemen was apparently 'rough beyond his line of duty,' as Janet told me later; an ambulance attendant apologized for him. Later there were countless bruises over my arms and thighs, and blood dripping from my right elbow.

Ambulance lights twirled orange. My head was blank; sometimes I forgot Janet was with me, and often I thought I was in a bedroom, not in an ambulance, and had just woken up out of a strange nightmare.

They took me to the emergency section of the hospital. Now it's evening and I've been here all day; Janet stayed with me till dinnertime. Hey, how many people have spoken to a psychiatrist while tripping out on LSD and were able to conceal it? It's pretty hard. I kept getting lost inside the mazes of my words and often forgot the questions he asked.

At the end of the session the shrink just looked at me. 'You're tremendous. I wish we could have met under different circumstances.' He stood up and left me there, gaping.

Despite my pleas and protests, I have to spend at least one night in the hospital. I haven't even gone to the bathroom all day because a nurse has to watch—you really wonder. It's impossibly boring, pacing back and forth in here. They're trying to get Frank to fly down to Boston to take me back, because they don't trust me to go alone.

I'm tired. Just one picture keeps floating to my mind: a child's multicolored blocks tumbling to the ground. I'll probably never see Allan again, and the last thing I did was tell him to fuck off along with everyone else.

July 20

I've been on the plane for several hours now; the nurse woke me at 6 a.m., but I had to wait half an hour for the cops, and the night had been interrupted by nurses changing shifts and doctors wandering in with flashlights. I'm trapped in the back seat here, sick of being watched and escorted, beside an old woman with a loud voice who keeps trying to start a conversation.

A nurse, a policeman and a security guard brought me to the airport. They milled about me at all times, one in front and one behind and one standing some distance off. I longed to split a cleaver into the fat, balding head of the hospital security guard who was driving, fantasizing about the blood and brains spewing everywhere.

We've passed Chicago, where several flight attendants made sure I didn't disappear. The rage will probably melt into fear by the time we reach Vancouver, but that's not necessarily going to hinder anything. As Ruth advised, if the workers asked too many questions I could simply back into a corner and curl up in a fetal position.

They can't make me feel guilty, anyway. It's annoying being on this plane, where overweight women in flowered polyester pants sneak glimpses of this page as I write. I'm furious at people who say, 'We want to help,' then give me a hasty hug and push me away.

Sick! I'm sick of not being allowed to go to the washroom alone. I don't need acid; I don't need any crutches.

July 21

It's been four months since I left home. A long time. The voices of the social workers whirl in my head: 'Evelyn, don't you think it's time to go home?' I can't go back, though; that's the only thing that's clear, so I hang on to it.

I was in the washroom when the announcement switched on that we were reaching the Richmond airport, and would all passengers please fasten their seat belts? For a moment sheer panic ran through me, then I went over to one of the escape doors and leaned against the porthole. The sky was blue, and anorexic clouds paddled in the thin atmosphere. Below lay a jigsaw puzzle of earth colors. My fear of the psych ward will always be in the shadows of my mind—the four walls, the TV camera, the needles, the metal toilet. It never goes away. I keep remembering that there are places where everywhere you turn there are sterile walls and no escape except through death.

A stewardess wearing an inhibiting skirt and high heels walked me off the plane and through Customs. I looked around wildly for an escape; getting away from her wouldn't be a problem, but the airport was huge and swarming with people and security guards.

The worker who was to retrieve me hadn't arrived yet, so I was put in a waiting room inside Customs. I paced back and forth as one official watched me with hateful, heavily made-up eyes. Restlessly I sat down and began talking to the other person in the room—he was in his late thirties, a small character huddled in his jacket, his legs shaking uncontrollably. Later I was glad of his presence, because his circumstances made me angry again rather than afraid. He lived in the Philippines but had used fake ID to get into Vancouver, where he'd been caught.

Another Customs official came in and told the man he'd be placed in an RCMP cell for twenty-nine hours before being deported back to the Philippines. The thin face across from me darkened with terror. Something sparked, then began raging like a furnace inside me— flashes of the RCMP cell on the coast, the puke in the sink, the fluorescent lights. My mind spun furiously and I told the official that he had no idea what being locked up was like. There must be alternatives. What about a hostel for the man? What about …?

'Shut up!'

After a while the stewardess found the Emergency Services worker, who as it turned out had been waiting for hours, but the instructions had gotten messed up and she'd been told to wait in the wrong section.

I said goodbye to the little man shaking in the waiting room and he thanked me—it was warming, though I hadn't been able to do anything for him.

The social worker drove me to Seymour House, an emergency group home! I could have leapt up from the seat of the car and banged on the roof just as Ruth had done after crossing the border, shrieking with triumph. How stupid of them, how easily I'll be able to leave.

Evening

Upstairs watching a video, I became drowsy from the darkness and the plane ride and might have gone to bed, then met with Frank the next morning. Maybe stayed inside the system. But something rebelled. Promising I'd be back by midnight, I went downstairs and said goodbye, edging to the door; the child care worker stopped me, asking what time I wanted to be woken up in the morning.

The morning. Why were other peoples' lives normal? Why did they know what it would be like when they opened their eyes in the morning? Why don't they keep running away like me? I shrugged and said I'd probably be up before Frank called, then walked out onto the porch and closed the heavy white door. The clean, invigorating night air imparted some strength, some idea of being okay again.

First I called Kim and Ruth, waking them up (I forgot about the time difference) and chortling. They were less than overjoyed by the phone call, but they humored me anyway.

Then I headed for a journalist friend's apartment in the West End. She'd said before I left for Boston that she didn't ever want to see me on the streets, that her apartment was small but I could stay there for a while. Just to prove my independence, I would have spent the night on the streets, but I really needed to wash up.

She was speechless at finding me on her doorstep. I parked myself on a sofa printed with Oriental flowers and told her briefly what was going on. Her anxiety about my being on the streets vaporized now that I was actually in her apartment. She blinked at me with black eyes and moved her bright red lips thoughtfully; her two sisters were spending the week at her place, and she didn't have any room.

I shrugged and said I wasn't tired anyway. Besides, her perfect little apartment unnerved me; I felt as if I were in a dollhouse where I couldn't touch anything without fear of breaking it. She suggested that I go back to my parents. Then her sisters returned and there was an uncomfortable silence until I stood up with the obligatory, 'Well, it's kind of late—I think I should get going.'

My friend stood in the doorway and smiled tolerantly. What next? I walked quickly downtown, berating myself for fantasizing that Michael would drive past in his government car and somehow make me feel safe. I got on a bus and headed to the home of a political activist's mother.

It was an old house buried behind tons of trees. Two a.m., and I was hungry, tired and dirty, stumbling through the grass to the steps, clawed at from every direction by eager spiderwebs. A woman with white hair eased the door open, squinting suspiciously before realizing who I must be. The house was a mess, and her cat promptly bit my hand when I tried to pet it. After she had stuffed me and generally been maternal, I went to sleep on the couch, tired of thinking all the time.

After breakfast this morning I called Kim; my mouth must have hung open for fifteen minutes afterwards in dismay. He told me that Ruth had flown out to the West Coast and would be in Vancouver by the evening. Talk about being trapped! Fleetingly I remembered Allan on the foster home's doorstep, advising me to tell people what I wanted. Here Ruth was coming out to 'rescue' me and smuggle me back into the States, when I'd run away from her and Kim in the first place! Too much. I gaped and nodded dumbly, agreeing to meet Ruth in the downtown eastside later that evening. Guess I'll just have to let things unfold from here.

July 25

Am I crazy to be screwing with my life and still be calm? There is a weird stillness in me that shouldn't be here.

Many days ago (it seems), I trudged out towards the downtown eastside. Ruth was there, partially concealed by her long hair, perched self-consciously among the bums on the street. Affection rose in me and I called to her, running across the street. She got up slowly, eyes darting around, then approached me without any sign of recognition on her face. I would have hugged her, but she remained aloof until we reached the rented car, where she promptly became hysterical, terrified that the police had spotted us.

We drove along the Trans-Canada Highway till midnight; my parents would have been impressed with the way I navigated. Ruth was becoming increasingly paranoid. She complained about feeling lonely without Kim, about the possibility of being arrested, about my forthright manner with the authorities, about being depressed. I wasn't in much of a position to offer strength. At one rest stop she demanded that I toss out my belongings, including the clothes I was wearing and my journals, but I was able to conceal the latter. She thrust me into the bathroom with a selection of her clothing, and feeling silly I climbed into a short blue skirt and shoes that were several sizes too small. Allan's advice that I should tell people what I want kept coming to mind, but the idea of telling Ruth I didn't want to go through with the plan was too intimidating. I excused myself by rationalizing that I had played no part in this latest development.

Later Ruth worked herself into such a state that she drove all the way back to the rest stop where we'd dumped my belongings, convinced that the guy in the van beside us had been spying and had taken the bag to the police. Well, what to do but humor my 'rescuer?' Sure enough, the clothes were gone, but most likely because the garbage had been emptied.

We found a motel for the night. Ruth promptly crashed and I rearranged our bags on the floor, following her orders so that we'd both have baggage that would look as if we'd gone to visit friends for a few days in Canada.

We continued east next morning, eating fast food along the way, Ruth driving while I struggled with a medley of maps. It began raining towards evening—flashes of lightning skittered across the sky and rain drummed on the windows. Up till then the sky had been blue and the clouds little more than scarves of mist winding around the thickly forested mountains. We stopped and found a cheap motel, with rooms above a bar. Everywhere we stopped, Ruth telephoned Kim. Later my tortured dreams were filled with guilt, images of Kim furious about the stolen acid. ('After all we've done for you …')

Drunk men and women hobbled shrieking into the rain from the bar; Ruth asked me crossly to close the windows. The room was overheated, with mustard-colored curtains and dubious towels. I pulled my ID out of the shoes (it had been concealed there to look worn) and examined it. Ruth had fashioned the identification that morning. Sitting on the edge of the bed, I searched the face on the laminated high school ID. The birth certificate was similar to the one she used the first time. (Ruth had had to do the photo ID twice—the first time she laminated the card without letting me sign it first).

Around noon we arrived in Calgary. The car didn't have to be returned till four, so we walked around downtown for a while. Ruth communicated her restlessness—she was constantly snapping at me to keep my voice down. She was lost, terrified of arrest. I knew, though, that if anyone was going to be arrested, it would be me.

In the evening we bought bus tickets to Winnipeg. I gulped down Dramamine during the ride and drifted in and out of sleep, but I felt okay. Except for the hallucinations that have been preceding every nap for the past few weeks. It doesn't matter if I'm crazy. With the LSD trips, my intense thoughts and feelings, my bouts in the hospital, my secluded childhood—how could it be otherwise?

In Winnipeg we bought tickets to Minnesota. From there Ruth's plans were vague. The green miles fled before my eyes and I stared for hours out the window as we approached the border, head aching from the concentration. By that time I was determined to get caught at the border. The bus was nearly empty, so when we approached Customs, there was no need to line up outside.

An official climbed in, a thin, graying man past middle age. At first he appeared mild mannered, but on closer inspection I could see stern lines etched in his face. He breezed past the other passengers; I pretended to be nervous, clenching my hands together. I filled out the declaration report under his eyes, starting to scribble an E on the signature line before carefully writing 'Susan Young.' After that unintentional slipup I glanced up to find him watching me and asking for ID. I proffered the photo card, certain he'd notice the poorly cut cardboard, but nothing seemed amiss to him, though he turned it over in his hands, giving it back with some reluctance.

'So your name is Susan Young, eh?' he asked tauntingly. Without a word he grabbed my tote bag and sifted restlessly through the contents, opening the cosmetic bag containing money and the bus ticket, lifting up the raincoat concealing the other clothes, feeling around the inner lining of the baggage. Oops, no drugs. He bestowed one last suspicious glare upon me, then spun on his heels and returned to the Customs office. The driver leapt back into his seat and gunned the motor.

I sat there sweating, mechanically filing the ID back into the bag. The night bled through the window. After midnight, we arrived in Fargo, North Dakota; the depot was full and Ruth made a beeline for the pay phone, turning her back on me.

Outside the depot were a few sleazy porn theaters and several drunk, wild-eyed men lurching past. With a fast backwards glance, sure that the other travelers were eyeing me, I slipped out into the night. About two blocks away there was an alley. I wedged myself between a garbage bin and the side of a building, attempting to hide between a chair on one side of me and a box of rotting grapes on the other. Crouching there, the grapes squashing beneath my feet, the reek of garbage surrounding me, I waited for a few minutes before ducking through the streets and into the doorway of a gray building. Shadows; I breathed shallowly, cheek against the cool stone wall. It was silent and dusky in the streets. After about fifteen minutes I darted across the lawn—remembering my childhood fantasy of living under the concealing branches of an evergreen tree—and towards the back of another building. There was a parking lot with two police cars. My eyes rose and were rewarded with a neon sign announcing the police station. Thinking only enough to tear off the tag on my baggage, I walked in.

Through the grim white corridor swamped with fluorescent lights, the duty officer approached me. I asked if there were any places in Fargo where I could take a shower, spend the night—something like a hostel. He regarded me suspiciously, then took me into a room where he filed a report. I answered his questions as naturally as possible, making everything up on the spot. He checked out the volunteer foster homes, but they turned me down because of the lack of concrete information.

'The only place that'll take you for the night will be youth detention.'

Another cop led me to his police car; I was tired and dirty and simply wanted to be safe. Cringing as the cop drove past the Greyhound depot, I peeked through the back window. Ruth was standing outside the station, holding her bag. As we drove on, she flickered like a candle flame in the distance.

We arrived at detention—a flat, solid brick building. The snickering cop assured me it would be just like a motel, except I'd be locked in. A swarm of flies attacked us in the hall before we entered another door, where a woman seated me in the admittance room and asked me a list of questions, mostly medical things. In another room they were having a debate about whether detention could legally hold me, but this question was cleared up when one policeman conveniently announced that I could be lying and they should keep me until my parents could be tracked down.

Good luck, I thought grimly. Then I was subjected to a pat-down against the wall, a strip in the shower. I had to give up my tote bag with the journals inside and the two sets of fake ID (one set left over from the Boston trip) claiming I was Kathy Wong and Susan Young, no matter how I clutched it away from them. Then I was placed in a cell labeled L. It's like the Quiet Room, except that the walls are white and there is a generous window, a plastic stool and slab (intended as a desk) and a steel plate (intended as a mirror) above the metal sink. The window is desperately scarred; the door is a blasphemous orange, clashing with the bile-green mattress.

I was lying on the plastic green mattress in the darkness when a counsellor's voice cut into the room from an intercom in the cement wall. I sat up apprehensively. 'Are you from Canada, Kathy?'

Watching my huddled shadow on the wall, I asked, 'Why?'

'Are you? You've been lying to us and to the police, Kathy, haven't you—and that's very serious.'

They'd obviously searched my bag. There was silence, then, 'Susan Young. You're not Kathy, are you, Susan?'

Afterwards there were many more questions, cornering. The room was black except for the light from a street lamp washing through the double-plated window; silent except for the separate voices intertwining at 2 a.m. in a cell in North Dakota.

July 26

At night the counsellors walk around detention, holding flashlights.

Periodically an orange globe pokes through the slit in the door and into my eyes; then the sound of footsteps fading and darkness again.

Yesterday morning I was woken up at 6:45 and towed out for breakfast. There was a sixteen-year-old girl there, scratching herself incessantly. She'd been there for several weeks, but they were going to release her on Monday into a group home. At least she's company. We spend a total of five hours a day locked in our cells ('jail is not meant to be pleasant,' a counsellor explains): an hour after breakfast, before lunch, in the afternoon, before dinner and after dinner. We trudge back into our rooms accompanied by books, with bored, sleepy eyes, to wait out the hour. I read, stretch or stare out the unbreakable window. The view consists of a parking lot, with a cop car and sheriff van, and the tree-lined street. Sometimes an elderly man will bike past, or a cop will walk by with his brown-paper-bag lunch.

Late in the morning the probation officer, accompanied by another woman, arrives and takes me to a separate room, firing questions. I curl up in the armchair and answer them truthfully, resigned. The woman smiles at me, but the probation officer is muscular and her face rigid. At the end of the interrogation she says briskly, 'You'd better have told me the truth,' and leaves with her notes, adding that my detention hearing will be on Monday or Tuesday.

More hours in the cell. No pens are allowed when we're locked up. A counsellor visits from Red River Runaway, the runaway service in Fargo. It's a Christian organization, and he ended up talking about God. In my vulnerability tears came to my eyes—had he talked longer, I would have believed. He had gone through the drugs and rebellion of the sixties and now his quick smile was hidden behind a bushy beard. He had deep dimples at the corners of his mouth and seemed human.

Then one of the counsellors said I was going to court today! I leapt up and followed her through the exit door in my stockinged feet, but was disappointed to discover that we weren't going to enter the outside world. We simply walked down a short, carpeted hallway and I was introduced to an attorney—an elderly man with greased-back, thinning gray hair who drew me into another room, closed the door and handed over a document for me to sign. A few steps away there was a small courtroom, built right into the detention center. We sat down together with the probation officer and one of the counsellors, and then the judge entered. The court procedure was short. I said all of two words, confirming that yes, I was Evelyn Lau, no, I was not Kathy Wong or Susan Young. Then everyone unanimously and emphatically agreed that this child should remain in detention until arrangements could be made for a flight back to Vancouver.

My father called in the afternoon. I didn't want to talk to him, but the counsellor handed the phone over with a smirk and a 'Well, you better talk to him if you ever want to get out of here.' I can't deal with my parents! What was there to say? His voice was mixed with anger and bewilderment—anger that I'd taken off right after being brought back, that I was in detention; bewilderment about the way things had gone. He offered to fly over and take me back home, because otherwise I'd have to wait till Wednesday for social services.

'I don't want to go back home,' I repeated for the millionth time.

'Why?'

I sighed. 'I'll survive.'

'Okay,' he said heavily, and hung up.

July 30

The plane skimmed to a halt, and surprise, there was no one to supervise me through Customs. I followed the group of passengers, waiting in line, and then spotted Frank.

'Hi, Evelyn.' His blunt features were unmistakable. Arranging my face to hide the panic, I went through Immigration and headed towards the exit in silence. Then he stopped and motioned me to sit on one of the plastic chairs attached to the wall. Frank explained that my parents were waiting just beyond the two glass doors and that we were going to the social services office to have a nice big meeting together.

The group of us walked out to Frank's car, the sun beating down. It was a long walk, very quiet. Tentatively, I asked Frank where he was going to place me, and he returned sharply that I became more confused the more information people dispensed. My sister Karen ran to catch up and gripped my hand.

I was dumped into the back seat, stuck with my mother and Karen. The ride to the office went on for years and years; I stared blankly out the window. Frank glanced at me from time to time through the rearview mirror, but his sunglasses hid any sympathy there might have been in his eyes. Dad was silent in the front seat for the length of the trip, but Karen (prodded by Mom) made up for it. I smiled at my pony-tailed sister, who was exclaiming ecstatically about her friend's birthday party, her swimming lessons. The car ride continued. At certain points I had to clench my hands—otherwise I'd have leapt up and tightened my fingers around Frank's neck. Why was he doing this? Mom pawed over me, asking loudly if I had my period, until I ached to murder them all, promising myself I'd never go anywhere again without a hit of acid. Ever.

We arrived, but things didn't get any better. The meeting in Frank's office went on for a long time; thankfully, it was mostly between Frank and me, with my parents the bewildered audience.

First off, Frank claimed that running away to Boston and North Dakota wasn't the act of a normal person. I disagreed, arguing that I'd wanted to see Boston since leaving home (true), and that the second time I'd been headed towards Minneapolis, a bigger city (also true). Frank conceded sarcastically that perhaps these expeditions had been for the sole purpose of sightseeing, sprinkled with escapism. He ran up one side of me and down the other for using taxpayers' money and social services' money for transportation, phone costs—'You don't know how many people are involved when we have to get you back from somewhere. Do you realize that over five hundred dollars was spent in long-distance calls alone? And now everyone who knows you in social services is convinced that you aren't capable of making your own decisions, of handling your own life.' Ouch.

Frank declared that options only confused me, so he would decide what would happen to me. Then the phone rang and he stayed on it for a long time, while I turned white thinking about the psych ward.

Frank returned to his seat, regarding me with his straight, dark gaze, and began to lay out his plan (much too slowly; I agonized). First, I would have to see a psychiatrist. 'This is nonnegotiable,' he emphasized. This didn't bother me, though I pretended to be reluctant so it would seem like a victory for him. He was staring down at his lap, and I said impulsively, 'Look at me.'

His head rose slowly. 'I don't have to look at you,' he retorted sullenly, like a little boy. Seeing him this way made me want to laugh;

instead, I told him earnestly, 'I'll go to the psychiatrist. I know you can't trust me, that you think I'll take off again, and I feel like the boy who cried wolf, but ...'

'This is even dumber than the boy who cried wolf.'

I reeled back slightly, then shrugged. 'Okay, you're right. Going to North Dakota was stupid. It was really stupid. But I'll see the psychiatrist, I'll cooperate.'

He continued outlining his plan. He challenged my definition of a foster home, asking if there couldn't be just one parent.

'Yes,' I said, wondering what he was up to.

'Well then, isn't New Beginnings a foster home? Isn't the group home mother a parent?'

Frank asked if I wanted a family setting instead, to which I eagerly nodded, and he took my foot and steered it towards my parents. 'There's the family.' Okay, chalk up one victory on Frank's board. I repeated for the millionth time that I couldn't go back home.

I was delighted with the outcome of his plan. Frank said that if I wasn't going to go home, I would have to return to New Beginnings. It was either that or home. So of course I chose the group home.

At New Beginnings, Frank filled out the admittance form. He permitted my family to call and visit, but no friends. When he came to the section requesting a description of the child's personality, he wrote, 'Weird!' I couldn't believe it. Then he got up to leave, adding that he would come pick me up for the shrink appointment at 9:30 a.m. on Friday. Did he think I wouldn't be gone by then?

August 5

I don't remember the past few days. I can hardly remember names. The earth billows. I've been dropping acid daily, sleeping on the streets, doing downers. It's like I'm in a coma from all the drugs.

Granville Street at night. Men walk up out of the blackness; their hands dart out to grab my breasts; they lead me into their cars. Their apartments are empty, and they lock the door behind them. I'm too drugged to be cautious, although their eyes repel me so much and I need kindness and love, not this! It's so ugly. Afterwards they ply me with more drugs. I end up back in front of McDonald's. One night

one of the kids from the Changes group home, where I spent a couple of nights after I left New Beginnings, is there with her blond hair
around her shoulders, muttering to me out of the side of her mouth:
'Hash?'

She remembers me from Changes and we go into McDonald's, joining a girl hidden behind mirrored sunglasses, and a pimpled male
teenager. Other dealers wander up with Smirnoff in their Coke cups,
discussing the business. She wants me to go to Changes, get off the
streets. I buy more California Sun acid off her; she tells us that a guy
who bought a double hit off her the other night had a heart attack but
is all right now. My body is getting mixed up—with the acid and the
downers, I can be immobile for hours, my muscles lax.

At 5 a.m. I end up in Changes, though I can't remember how I got
there or why. The child care worker is lying on the couch in the living
room, his bright blond hair spilling over the pillow. He thinks I've
finally come home, so he lifts up his arm, squints at his watch, grunts
and falls asleep again. Don't you know that I need you to stop what's
happening? I weave around the house tearily and then crash on the
sofa.

Noon the next day; I swallowed some downers and left. There were
other experiences, though I don't remember what happened when.
There were a lot of cars, a lot of drugs; I was tired and drank in pubs.
Going to a gas station for coffee and ending up at the attendant's
apartment gone on downers. I went to English Bay and walked out
into the waves towards the mountain images and the peach sunset, the
sea rippling like a gown, slowly flushing pink. I lay on the cold, wet
sand alone and slept.

* * *

Today is my court date, but I didn't go. Somewhere inside I must still
care about people because it hurts so badly, what I'm doing. I've been
to Aunt Gayle's house a couple of times to eat, 'borrow' money and
leave my dirty dishes and clothes kicking around. It's just not like me.
But I can't get off the couch to do anything.

I was at a friend's this afternoon and fell asleep on the sofa while she
was talking to me. I had hot, horrible dreams about drifting through
watery highways where the traffic went on and on ... Later I met with
a child care worker from Seymour House and gobbled acid and

downers. We sat in a park and I withdrew into my little corner of the bench, wanting to alienate him, wanting him to hate me. He confessed that he really couldn't see me worse off than I was, that I needed help.

After he had dropped me off, I took the bus to Seymour House for no reason at all. I sat in the kitchen chewing vitamins, then stumbled to an open window in the dining room and lit up a joint.

'Hey, is that hash you're smoking?' The worker sounded uptight.

'No.' Maybe I just wanted him to be mad at me. And maybe he saw that, because he didn't come near me, just said tersely, 'Well, if you are, don't, because it smells like it,' and for a while I could hear him roaming around the house opening windows and doors. I stubbed out the joint on the windowsill and began shaking, then floated out on my very own cloud.

August 6

I'm going to deal with my problems alone and return healed, like those Indian youths who go into the forest to fast and consult the holy spirits. Well, the spirits are inside me and I have to unearth them. Nothing is simple, especially self-realization; a few of those native youths must have gone mad with the solitude. I am not exactly a shining example of emotional stability. But I'm trying. I must begin to understand why I'm running away, my feelings about people, my fears of attachment.

I'm writing because it's 3 a.m. and I'm cold, dizzy with exhaustion; things are beginning to waver. I'm writing to keep myself awake. I don't know who, if anyone, to trust anymore, because men take advantage of you if you're downtown late at night looking like you're not going anywhere. The male faces peering appraisingly at me from the passing cars are alarming. Who is looking for a good fuck and who is concerned about my safety? I'm wondering if any of those people would go out of the way for the latter. I hate having to be skeptical.

I'm able to write today because I haven't taken any drugs—I was really going overboard with them. Janet had fervently promised to fight for me and never, never let me return to Vancouver if things weren't going to work out. What happened? I lied to her by pretending to be okay. I kind of fooled myself, too.

If it means anything at all, now I have an understanding of what it's like to sleep on the streets. The chilling cold, the search for a place to sleep that dominates your thoughts day and night, the constant battle with fatigue, the dirt that embeds itself in your flesh and never really comes out. I'm not free, you know. Everywhere I walk I have to drag my thoughts and emotions with me like chains. You learn selfishness on the streets by beginning to understand how ugly other people can be, and realizing that the only way to survive is to take as much as you can get. Other people can take care of themselves, but you may not be as strong.

It's cold out here. What the hell am I trying to prove?

August 7

I stretched out for a while on the back seat of a bus last night. Other passengers drifted on and off, blurs. One native Indian guy in his twenties strode heavily down the aisle and shook my shoulder briskly. I groaned.

'Are you all right? I like to help people.'

The irony. Our roles were supposed to be reversed! Now I—who was going to change the world—was lying in the back of a bus, and someone was asking if he could help.

I spent the rest of the night drinking coffee in a donut shop and venturing outside once in a while to wave my thumb at the near-empty road. It was extremely cold. At least the shop was somewhat warmer than the night. I told myself that I wasn't proving anything except my stupidity, and that even if I had to be dependent on others, I was going to find a home. Sleeping on the streets while too drugged to notice is one thing; doing it while straight is quite another.

Why is life so goddamn hard? My clothes need washing. Am I still punishing myself for leaving home? It's hard to believe.

I'm so fucking tired I can't see straight, wishing for the nth time that Death would come and scoop me out of this scumhole. I'd like to go back to Boston, but LSD is difficult to get there, and right now it's plentiful in Vancouver. Despite everything, I still think it's an amazing drug.

Life is fucked. So is this brat sitting and writing here. Why is it always either too hot or too cold? Why don't fat men wear deodorant? Jesus.

August 8

'I'll help you with everything else, but I won't help you die.'

Dr. Hightower, the psychiatrist that Frank has arranged for me to see, smiles benignly at me across the white-walled office. I don't have an appointment with him today, but I don't have anything better to do, so here I am. The patient's armchair is soft, black, and I sink into it gratefully. The doctor is jovial, big, would look more comfortable in a Santa Claus outfit. Psychology texts line the bookcase; the mandatory box of Kleenex presides on his desk. In preparation for the annual air show, planes glinting like missiles dart outside the office window, trailing plumes of red-, green- and white-striped smoke, like toothpaste squirted from a pump.

'So, did you know that social services has lost their temporary wardship of you?' The doctor settles back in his chair. This was unexpected. I had knocked my head against a brick wall for months, and now it had exploded under the pressure. No more barriers between Evelyn and her parents.

'I don't know much about it, but apparently the judge decided that your parents should be your legal guardians again.'

I felt drained. The horned and spike-tailed specters of social workers, supervisors and their ilk that had been crouching on my shoulders, jabbing their pitchforks at me, were in one instant gone. Everything was suddenly discredited, meaningless. I wondered if anyone in social services was at that very moment wiping their brow and exclaiming, 'Whew! She's gone!'

We had a brief conversation because I didn't have an appointment, then Dr. Hightower shooed me out of his office. Downstairs I spread my raincoat on the steps, and slept for an hour.

I can't possibly be punishing myself for running away, because the real punishment would be to go home and pretend to everyone that everything was okay. Do you think that being on the streets is anything more than a physical flogging? If I wanted to wreck myself inside I'd go back to my parents, bring home straight-A report cards, do all the housework and smile. I could explain it so eloquently: how social services had been right, how much my parents had changed. Janet had called my ability to justify and rationalize things more of a disadvantage than a gift.

Dr. Hightower drove me to Vancouver on his way to the hospital. His noncommittal 'call me when you want to see me again' was disconcerting at first, but then, why not have a relationship for once that isn't a matter of life or death? In the car I said Frank didn't like me, and Dr. Hightower said that he did, like everyone else, but they were all just frustrated and angry with me right now.

Lately I've been getting on a lot of buses and riding them around and around. It increases my sense of irresponsibility, of being in limbo, of ... 'freedom.' This morning I delivered an apologetic letter to the social services office. Frank let me in, and his presence was so unexpected that I merely extended the letter. Afterwards I remembered someone saying I'd 'provoked' everything, and in reflection it doesn't sound so wrong. If Frank had sounded like an asshole, maybe I should have listened to myself.

'I guess you've heard you're out of custody?' He looked at me inquiringly, hopping onto a table and turning over the letter in his hands.

'What happened, exactly?' No use crying over milk you yourself had deliberately spilt.

'Well, we went to court to tell the judge that you didn't want to be in care, that you were leaving every home you were placed in, that we didn't know where you were and there was no use bringing you into custody. So the judge just said okay; now you're out of care and back under your parents' guardianship.'

Though shelter was unimportant, I did need protection. It had always been something to fall back on, having a faceless, gelatinous mass of government as one's 'parents.' A buffer. It must be hard being a social worker, being used as a shield between child and parent, child and world.

'Can I open this before you leave?' Frank gestured with the letter. He opened the flap and shook out the paper. '"Dear Frank," he read aloud, then looked up, improvising the first sentence: "You're a jerk."'

Had I been that antagonistic towards him? He folded the letter and said he would read it later.

We talked a little, and surprisingly it went okay. I left the office feeling all right, glad that he'd been talking to Evelyn, not a few blotters soaked in LSD and a couple of round white pills.

I called Michael, which was not quite as exonerating. When he picked up the phone he sighed, 'Oh, Evelyn,' sounding most exasperated. Which naturally brought on another fit of apologizing. Michael asked if I shouldn't try returning home. 'Hasn't this gone on long enough?'

Much as I hate myself, I'm not going back to my parents. Before Michael hung up, he ended with the predictable, 'Well, you know we're here if you need us for anything.' I laughed and said, 'That sounds like what a social worker would say.' His silence said, THAT'S WHAT I AM. There are no individuals in the government, it's just a glutinous mass. Bastards.

August 10

The days drift by, sultry, dandelion parachutes borne by an unsteady wind. Summer has claimed Vancouver, and I've been recuperating at my Aunt Gayle's. I'm not going to die, because I've decided to shape a book out of this journal and will see to it that it gets flung whole into the bowels of the world. The book that will redeem me, justify my existence.

Life settles back into a semblance of normality—waking up early, writing, spending long stretches of time on the phone with friends. I'm still aiming at getting my own apartment, though, and bury my nose in the Classifieds every day for that elusive job.

Things aren't perfect, but this journal is happening. It'll be about—well, my journal will be about what it's like to enter the world with shining illusions and end up with reality messy in your hands.

August 12

Dr. Graham, a counsellor who had been involved in my case since I left home, said that since I now realized there were no boundaries, I could begin to settle down, secure in the knowledge that I could break free any minute. Knowing that, I wouldn't have to physically do it. He recognized that the traveling had been a necessity, to prove that there weren't any restrictions on me. Unlike most people, he said, I had challenged the drudgery of everyday existence and so could never be oppressed in the same way again. I might go home today because I could leave instantly; no one could force anything on me.

That's the balance, between living 'normally' and 'extremely.' I'm trying to come to grips with it now. Dr. Graham thinks my decision not to go back to school is wrong, though, and when I tried to compensate by announcing my job-hunting plans, he snorted.

'That's wonderful. That's exactly what you need: to spend the rest of your life working for seventy-five cents an hour and paying rent.' It makes me strangely happy that he has hopes for and expectations of me.

There is a lot to do, between checking out job opportunities and writing. Which issue is the most important? Staying away from drugs? Becoming financially independent? Working on my writing? I only know that I'd give a lot to earn back the respect the system has lost for me.

August 18

Things are finally working out—I've found a job as a phone solicitor, requesting donations for blind athletes. I've only worked two days but am selling more than anyone else because the job means everything; it'll bring in enough for rent. Then I'll be able to move out in a few months and become gloriously, gloriously independent. It can't fall through.

Called my parents last night (epitome of bravery). We talked for a long time; my father was superb, handing out tips on renting, but my mother screamed that she wished I had never been born. Even talked to Karen for a while. So things aren't going bad—I'm going to enroll in a few courses in September, since work is in the evenings. It's an exhausting job; it pulls everything out of you.

August 20

Everything began fraying at the edges until the fabric disintegrated in my fingers. I came home two nights ago wiped out from the efforts of the job and slept till noon yesterday, waking up still exhausted. The four hours total in commuting left me no time or energy for anything else. The craving for drugs chewed at me constantly, even in sleep; I was always fantasizing about acid and kept having small flashbacks. I thought about the psych ward a lot, leaving the radio on to drown it out. I'd leave the job at night feeling exactly as though someone had reached inside me and scooped everything out.

Tonight I called a child care worker at Seymour House during work and talked to her for almost half an hour, waiting for someone to discover our conversation. Willing to lose the job and consequently my goals. The manager was making the rounds and reported me; I glared at him through my impenetrable cloud of smoke, juggling a spilling ashtray. Made very few sales tonight and ignored everybody, but fuck it, I only have one life and it shouldn't be populated with nightmares of jangling phones, pledge forms and sales slips, while I am constantly being harassed to make more money, bleed the unemployed for their last five bucks, assume a sexy voice for the men, plead, cry ... So I quit.

Tomorrow afternoon there's an appointment with Dr. Graham, and in the evening I'm dropping by Changes to visit the child care workers. Afterwards I'm going to Detox; my sanity is withering. The place sounds okay—patients aren't allowed outside during the first week of the program. It might be a reprieve; I don't want to commit myself, but I need some kind of shelter right now or I'll go nuts.

August 22

It was five months yesterday since I left home. Not bad; I'm still alive. Decided what the hell and dropped acid.

Got up late yesterday morning, packing clothes into a bag for Detox. By the time everything was sorted out, I was in a bitchy mood—how many times had I packed in the past few months? There was no particular reason for doing LSD, just that I expected a decent trip for once. After all, one more trip couldn't hurt—never mind that the acid on the streets lately is loaded with strychnine. Never mind the image of Janet resting her elbows on the tray above the hospital bed and asking quietly for me to stop doing acid.

'I don't usually tell kids not to do drugs, but I think it would be best in your case.'

An hour and a half later I was in Dr. Graham's waiting room, attempting to concentrate on a newspaper, tasting the drug. My heart beat quickly, and my eyes ached as though the pupils were straining to break free of their bondage. I was content. The room began to expand with sudden intense color, like a realization or an inspiration. Everything was brilliant, magnified; my eyes hurt with the intoxicating effort of drinking it in.

The session with Dr. Graham went well, as usual. At one point, I marveled, 'You know, I'm amazed you've stuck with me so long. Everyone else has gotten frustrated.'

'Well, you're soooo boring, Evelyn.' He rolled his eyes heavenward, but looked pleased.

He understands me, I think. He lets me do what I want and doesn't act surprised or judgmental. When I said I was headed for Detox, Dr. Graham did look at me and exclaim, 'Why? I thought you'd had enough of institutions!'

'I need to hide for a while.'

He took this in his stride, shook his head and sent me on my way, adding that it would certainly be 'an experience, and that's what you're looking for, isn't it—experiences?' He accepts me. Other people accuse me of playing games, and unfortunately sometimes I do seem to be pushing things a little too far. Yet I never was allowed to play much as a child.

The acid didn't affect our conversation, except maybe I was more relaxed and giggly, unsteady. Dr. Graham gave me strength in believing in myself. I felt good walking out of there; at the bus stop I unwrapped another hit of California Sun and moved it absentmindedly between my tongue and teeth until it melted into a pulp. I liked being happy. There was a pronounced and increasing sensation in my elbows of total relaxation, close to pain; I could barely move my arms. Acid and coke do that to me. It's like someone has jammed ice cubes into my elbows in place of bones.

On the way to Changes I settled in a park a few blocks from the house. The field before me had yellowed with the summer heat, patches of crumbly earth showing. A baseball game was in progress, the players shooting up clouds of brown dust as they skidded from base to base, hollering. The park was large enough to reduce the noise of the game to mere voices dissipated by the wind, mingling with the other sounds of summer.

I called my mother earlier in the day and told her about Detox. She was glad I was going but didn't understand, thinking I'd be going through withdrawal, that soon after I'd go home (her home), that it'd been drugs that had transformed her little girl into a monster. Then she became angry, screaming that surely the hospital had handed her the wrong baby; how could her own child leave her? But what upset me most was what she confided about Dad; the morning after my North Dakota trip and the morning of my court date, he'd washed my favorite mug, thinking I was going home. Sad, pathetic. I sat beneath the tree, looking out on the miles of dry grass, envisioning a broken-hearted man out there lost, washing his runaway daughter's possessions as if that could wash her life clean, as if that could bring her back. It hurt; he didn't deserve a kid like me, after years of unemployment, living with a wife who screamed at him, keeping his feelings bottled up. Fuck. Mom always knew just how to get at me. Somewhere out there in the fields was a man who had lost his child and was conducting a ritual for her return. He had gone out a few days ago (my mother related) and returned with bags of school supplies, which he'd stacked around the house because I was 'going to need them for school.' If the lot of them end up in the loony bin I'm going to make sure they don't have any unexpected company—in the form of their daughter.

I wandered into Detox past 3 a.m., but the place was tucked behind a maze of cracked walls and reminded me too much of detention or the psych unit. A chair blocked the doorway; I leaned against it tiredly, needing a place to crash for the rest of the night. The staff led me reluctantly into the library, handed me a pillow and beckoned me to the couch, turning off the lights. I lay sleeplessly for a long time, so hollow from the acid that I was past exhaustion.

They woke me up at 7:30 along with their patients, and then I knew I wasn't going to stay—if only because the people wore hospital-blue robes that brought visions of the ward tumbling back; if only because they sat at little tables compliantly eating plastic-looking breakfasts that reminded me of detention.

I talked to one of the staff for a while, then left. We both agreed it was pointless to stay anyway because I wouldn't be going through a physical withdrawal—they could keep me there for two or three weeks and I wouldn't freak out—but most of all because I had no motivation to quit drugs.

August 27

Unconsciously I'd managed to convince myself that Evelyn had only existed for five months, but small bits of my childhood are starting to emerge.

I'm in my crib, maybe four years old. It's after midnight. My parents are in their bedroom down the hall, fighting; the wooden bars to my crib are painted white, and the floor leading to their room is uncarpeted. Mom is screaming that she wished she'd married another man. I ache for my father, whose voice is lower, attempting to be rational. When I start crying he pads into the room, light from the street lamp through the window glinting off his glasses. He holds me for a while, and then I clutch the hand extending through the bars, huge and comforting, begging him not to go back. He spends a long time with me until Mom, her face pale and twisted, enters the darkness, and I shrink back. She screams that if I don't stop crying she'll walk out into the streets and never come back—then how would I take care of myself? Sniffling, I try very hard to stop because the vision of being alone and helpless is terrifying. They both go back to their bedroom.

As a child, when my father was always close and nurturing, I used to be terrified that my mother would hurt him so badly he wouldn't be able to take care of me anymore.

August 30

I don't think about suicide anymore. Once it seemed the best or only thing to do, but I've become a monster now, and monsters don't want to die, do they? They don't care.

I spend a lot of time reading, watching TV, looking for a job and organizing some sort of plan for school. Dr. Graham called this the next phase of my life, where I would do the reconstructing. 'The times of high drama are over.' He's my main support system right now.

I'm reluctant to enter the cycle of running, falling and being picked up again, yet last night I was determined to run to Calgary where I don't know anyone and would be without a place to stay. My plan was to find a job and live there for a while; if that didn't work out, I'd head east to Ontario, where all the publishing houses are. But there were the practical things to take into account; how could I be awake or healthy enough to find a job without money, food or anywhere to sleep? Besides, I've enrolled for three morning classes at a secondary school, and I'm not going to give that up. Won't it be wonderful, taking an English course?

September 1

Childhood events are becoming more lucid. I remember my fascination with small, bare, locked places—I would shut myself in a closet or bathroom and stay there, wondering, 'Would I rather live here, never to go out again, or continue the way I am (with my parents)?' The answer was always the same: I'd rather live in a closet.

Maybe this is why my memories of the Quiet Room have become obsessive; it was, in a way, a fulfillment of my earliest fantasies of freedom. I realized this last night while I was in the bathroom, locking the door and looking around: 'Would I rather live here …?' Then I saw what I was doing.

Other things are getting clearer, which is painful. When Michael and I were walking through the hospital parking lot, passing rows of dormant ambulances, footsteps quiet under the blanket of night, I had thanked him for staying with me.

He shrugged. 'I get paid for this, you know.' Perhaps I should have listened harder.

Here I am, sitting in Aunt Gayle's living room. She and my uncle are in the kitchen, making blueberry jam for the winter. A green fly explores the pages of a Jack Kerouac novel. The heat hangs heavy in the silent house.

September 2

Dr. Hightower says that my parents are two people living somewhere in Vancouver, that I will never have to see or talk to them again. My fears are of a husband and wife crouching at the back of my mind, following me everywhere, demanding, disapproving.

'The only people you have to deal with are the parents in your head. I'll help you get rid of them,' he promises. Another session in the roomy white office, the doctor a reassuring presence glancing occasionally at the clock on the windowsill as I talk tirelessly. It's been a troublesome week, because it's easier not to mature but to spin over and over in the same cycle. A few days ago I'd begun packing, planning to move to Calgary—what stopped me was that I'd run away before, many times, and as Dr. Graham had reminded me, things were changing.

September 11

Another day, peppered with irritations. Fuck everyone; how can they be so placid? Even Dr. Hightower is wrong this time, thinking my parents are what I must deal with. How can he watch me smugly across the bright office, thinking I can succeed with my writing, go to university with it? He has it all wrong; I prefer lying on the couch and watching television.

Yesterday Mom and Dad materialized in the school halls during the break, bewildered looks on their faces, swept along by the screaming, shoving teenagers. They were no more than shadows, emaciated. Horror welled up from a suppressed store inside me, and I ran to my next class; later the horror turned to anger. I never cry, Dr. Hightower, I just get pissed off; there's no reason why I should reveal my vulnerability. I heard from the counsellor that my parents had come to check up on my attendance and find out what courses I had in the morning. I was ENRAGED. I CAN NEVER BE FREE OF THEM IN VANCOUVER. How can two small human beings wield this much control? Last night my Aunt Mary called to say they'd brought over money for a bus pass, school fare and spending money—'as they'd promised to do if you went back to school.' I turned it down. Accepting it would be like going to school to please them again. I'm sure they didn't mean it that way, but that's how it makes me feel, okay? As if the money had been a carrot dangling in front of my nose so I'd hit the books.

School is shitty, boring. I want some acid. I want to tell Dr. Hightower to fuck himself. All psychiatrists are liars; everyone keeping me in Vancouver is a liar. I'm going to trash his office sometime, smear that benevolent Santa Claus smile off his face. Won't he and Dr. Graham leave me alone?

It's getting cold finally; it was freezing when I went out for a walk at 5 a.m., the scene like some freaky LSD trip. The sky was a whirl of fire and smoke, the streets black and wet.

I'm working in an office now under the guise of being seventeen, staring at a computer screen and typing letters. The kids employed here have all been on the streets, referred by social workers or street friends. It's pretty laid back, but the major problem is that I type eighty words a minute and the other kids are alienated by that.

Nothing has to keep me here anymore. I'd like to go somewhere where someone like Allan can read every feeling crossing my face, can motion me outside and explain things away.

September 14

I can't stand it anymore. It's time to travel again, to move not necessarily forward but away. It's going to be tough, with winter coming and having to find a place to stay. Well, I'm almost packed, and this time it's for real. Don't you see? This couldn't last; it wasn't meant to. I either run or go crazy. I wish I had some drugs—God, if I had megahits of acid I wouldn't leave! The boredom would dissipate. My days consist of waking up too early, rushing to school, rushing to work, coming home for dinner, submerging myself in television, then going to bed. What chance is there for creativity?

I don't want to go, but nothing's left in Vancouver, I have no real friends. I must stop hiding in a nonexistent womb. I keep wanting to stay, but for what? A roof over my head? Food? Why? There are other things of greater importance: I must get away from the nightmares about my parents. The smallest, most everyday things I do now remind me of them, other moments, times when we were a family.

Yes, I do love them, something in me loves them so fucking much I could crush them in my arms—Dr. Hightower, why did you have to unearth this? The sadness and guilt are piercing.

I'm going to see Dr. Hightower and Dr. Graham on Tuesday, then leave for Calgary. It'll be cold, but why not? This is the way it will have to be.

PART III

september 17 to december 30 1986

September 17

I have to repeatedly remind myself of my reasons for leaving Vancouver; it seems silly now. I shouldn't have left 'help,' in the form of a red-faced Dr. Hightower, who was sad that I was going, sounding angry for once. He gave me his home number and urged me to call. He thought that he had been too pushy during our last session in unearthing my feelings about my parents. At one time his caring would have mattered immensely, but I just sat in the office and watched him dully, thinking the world itself was a lie and he a fool to care about someone like me.

The bus arrived in Calgary this morning, just before six. It was raining in the flat city; you couldn't distinguish morning from night by the slate color of the sky.

I'm at the YWCA tonight, foggy headed, floating in some sea of unreality. There is a program here called Runaway/Homeless Youth, which shelters kids seventeen and under for two weeks until they can find a job or a better place to live—but first the workers have to contact the child's parents. I refused to let them call my parents, so I'll only be staying tonight. There is a great worker here who is obviously frustrated that they can't do more for me. I am truly what I wanted: on my own. Not as wonderful as it's made out to be, is it?

September 18

I've spent part of the night in a Dairy Queen, sharing a table with a derelict who was carrying a backpack and pillows. He was immersed in thought, but when I started talking he unleashed a torrent of heavily accented English that lasted without respite for almost forty-five minutes.

The man had grown up in Poland. He'd lived in Canada for almost twenty years but still hated it, having lost his wife and been forced into various 'crazy hospitals' by policemen. He reiterated indignantly that after having served as a sergeant in the war, he was now reduced to being a janitor. He was Roman Catholic and fervently anti-Communist. He showed his prejudice by assuring me every few minutes that he didn't mind talking with a Chinese person. Though I couldn't get a word in edgewise, I was quite taken with this crazy old man with his grizzled beard yet surprisingly smooth skin and harmless blue eyes. His rantings accelerated in both speed and volume until his arms and legs were flying in the air, and I became a little afraid that he'd have a heart attack and croak. Obviously, he hadn't had anyone to talk to in a long time. The other people in the restaurant stared as he jabbed his fingers in my face. Afterwards an elderly woman approached me and murmured how very, very sorry she'd felt for me, sharing a table with that man!

He was not so poor that he did not offer me as many cigarettes as I wanted; he was not so down and out that he did not hesitate to produce his wallet and push a two-dollar bill across the table, despite my protests. In a funny way, the old man completely won my heart.

Now I'm keeping warm by walking around downtown. The temperature is at freezing level, and it is growing dark.

September 19

Last night I called Alcoholics Anonymous, looking for new ideas. The monitor who received the call decided to bring me home for the night, after phoning several social services and receiving the same answer: No, she's fifteen, she's out of the province, we can't help her.

The woman's name was Sparky. She and her husband picked me up at a downtown corner where I stood, teeth chattering. Dr. Hightower was right; dying from cold isn't as painless as it sounds.

The couple lived in a house surrounded by miles of weeds, remote from the city. I was tired, but they kept me talking till 2 a.m., which was when I realized I had made the wrong decision.

Sparky ordered me to go back home, having gone through what I had herself and regretting it now. She spooned sugar into her coffee and got so worked up that her husband occasionally had to calm her down. She had wavy red hair, blue eyes and a bloated, bruised face that betrayed the ravages of booze. Her father had been an alcoholic and she had left home at fifteen to fend for herself. A guy had raped her; she'd worked the streets, dealt drugs. Sparky had come to Calgary without knowing anybody here, but she had been lucky enough to be picked up by a sympathetic cab driver who let her live with him for a year.

Finally Sparky took me downstairs, where I fell asleep instantly. But it was a disturbed night like it had been at the YWCA—bouts of wakefulness when I felt overcome with intense depression; fragmented nightmares about death and homelessness.

I woke up at 2 p.m. today, took a shower and waited for Sparky to return, meanwhile combing the papers for possible jobs. When she stomped into the house, stroking the cat and eyeing me expectantly, I told her that I still didn't want to go home but appreciated her advice and was very thankful for the night over.

Sparky regarded me stonily. She sat down at the kitchen table and raged for five hours without letting up, while I sat there numb. Would I ever learn? She shouted that whether I liked it or not, she would bring me to Emergency Services and make sure I returned home on the earliest bus to Vancouver.

I could understand her. It was kind of sad—she only wanted to give me a second chance at the teenage years she herself had sacrificed. But she was relentless, attempting to take my life out of my hands and make it her responsibility, which could only result in failure and resentment. She said that she'd gone down on hands and knees that morning and prayed that she could make me go home. She felt that I had come into her life for a reason, that God had placed me in her hands. It was hard—I was tired and hungry and couldn't think straight.

Still hoping that I could make her happy, that she would believe she'd passed her 'personal test' and done something wonderful for me, I consented to go home, with the intention of taking off from Emergency Services or, if necessary, getting off the bus before it hit Vancouver. I remembered what Allan had said about 'dirty ashtrays' (comparing my way of dealing with things with a woman who leaves her dirty ashtrays all over the apartment to let her roommate know that she's mad at her about something, rather than coming out and talking about it).

Sparky and her husband drove me to Emergency Services, which in Calgary is impossible to find. It's hidden in a building above a fitness gym and a flower shop, away from the downtown area. I turned and played one of my last cards, thanking them for what they had done and preparing to get out of the truck, but Sparky wasn't stupid.

'Oh no, we're not finished yet! I'm going to see to it that you get on that bus to Vancouver.'

We went inside Emergency Services. I began pacing in the waiting room, just as Sparky had done a few hours ago while drumming her demands like a row of bullets into my head. A social worker I'd spoken with over the phone before came out to see us—his blue eyes registered amazement when she pointed at me and proclaimed, 'This girl wants to go home.' He took us into another room and Sparky began screaming at him to hurry up and send me off; finally I asked to speak to him alone.

The worker was very composed, with slow, easy gestures, but was taken aback by Sparky's unprovoked shrillness. Alone, I told him what had happened, which was difficult, as I would rather have pleased everybody by taking the bus to Vancouver, then getting off at the first stop, returning to Calgary, paying Emergency Services back and trotting to the streets. At least it would have left Sparky with some satisfaction that she had done the right thing. Given me a new lease on life, so to speak.

Presently someone pounded on the door; the worker opened it and Sparky glared into the room. 'We're leaving.'

Without a word, the worker went after Sparky and her husband. So much for my new-found relief. He explained later that it was better for me to face these things. Resigned, I watched the couple sit down as the worker related some of my feelings. Sparky refused to look at me; her face appeared more black and blue by the minute.

It was her husband who brought tears to my eyes, his voice with its heaviness of caring, its pauses for thought. He apologized for his wife, said he'd never wanted to push me to return to my folks, and when Sparky began bitching at him he countered on my behalf.

'Look, dear, we're not talking about your feelings. Your opinions have nothing to do with this. It's Evelyn we're talking about.'

It seemed the nicest thing anyone could have said. If we had just understood each other better! They left soon, Sparky's husband wishing me the best of luck; Sparky stomping out the door, still not looking at me. The worker and I talked for a while longer, then he drove me through the rain to the YWCA again, saying I could spend the weekend there.

'You're not going to call my parents, are you?' I asked over and over, until I glanced at his face, which was reddening with irritation. I apologized. 'You must think I'm paranoid.'

'Very.'

He said that if I kept turning up, they would have to do something, whereas if I remained on the streets they wouldn't bother. Out of sight, out of mind.

September 20

Sitting again in the Dairy Queen, one of the few places in Calgary open for twenty-four hours, watching the hands of the clock creep towards midnight. I'm exhausted. Isn't the night going to end? It can't be even midnight yet. Tomorrow it'll be six months since I left home, and here I am waiting in the Dairy Queen for morning to come, yet realizing that it won't bring safety or shelter. It won't bring warmth.

My brain doesn't feel capable of functioning anymore. I'm scared. The streets are empty and black, and police cars comb the downtown area. Afraid of the aloneness, needing someone, somewhere. Afraid of getting caught. I miss Dr. Graham's jewels of eyes instilling strength, Dr. Hightower's good-natured chuckle spreading warmth.

There's just all this sadness, pulling me down and away from hope. Oh God, this can't be happening to me, can it? Too much pride and no money.

September 21

Autumn was sneaking into Calgary, breathing lemon over the trees, scattering carpets of leaves over the pavement. I walked and walked. Midnight found me shivering and trying to stay awake in a restaurant about to close. Two men came in and sat down near me, so I went over and asked if they knew which bus would take me to Emergency Services. They glanced at each other, chuckling—they were cab drivers, and offered me a free ride if I wanted to sit around while they had dinner. I joined them and we started talking. I didn't go into my background but admitted I needed a place to stay. This startled Henry into ruminating about times when he'd been poor and people had gone out of their way to help—a hippie had taken him in and dispensed bowls of Trail Mix; a hotel manager had given him a room for two nights out of the storm and made him meals. He looked thoughtful. I sighed and promised myself not to be drawn like a magnet back to the warmth of the YWCA. The workers there had made it clear that I should 'shit or get off the pot.' 'Sometimes you have to be cruel to be kind,' Sparky had stated bluntly, stubbing out another cigarette.

We got into Henry's friend's cab and began driving towards Emergency Services. Henry lifted the curtain of darkness by turning towards me suddenly, the street lamps illuminating his face, and saying, 'I wasn't sure before, but I'm going to take you home for a few days. It'll be my way of paying those guys back.'

I was really grateful—a bed! Sleep. Yes, there must be a God up there, looking after His kids. I was going to be safe.

The driver turned dubiously to Henry and asked if he really wanted to do this; he nodded resolutely. They began talking about where they could pick up some drugs, waving to several guys hanging outside a convenience store. Henry motioned me into his car, an old cab, parked in the lot. His friend rolled down his window and regarded me with big, serious brown eyes.

'Henry is a very good friend of mine, and I'm sure you'll be safe with him. But if anything goes wrong, talk to me about it, okay?'

I would have dropped to my knees right there and thanked God, except then I would probably have fallen asleep.

Henry was a different person when we drove home together. He had problems that were making him angry, but he wouldn't talk about them, despising people who unburdened themselves on others. So instead we talked about drugs—he dropped acid once or twice a year, snorted coke at Christmas, but drank and smoked pot and took downers a lot. Drugs had, I felt certain, fallen into their appropriate place in my life—as recreation, not escape.

Henry lived alone in a cluttered basement suite—Kurt Vonnegut novels were piled high on the floor, and cereal boxes spilled their contents onto the carpet. He pulled out the Hide-Away bed, switched on the radio, and speeded off to work. I unpacked some of my clothes and sank into bed, into a sleep undisturbed by dreams, waking only once. I was safe, safe!

Henry was shaking me at eight the next morning, after five hours of sleep. Pouting, I rolled over and attempted to hide under the pillow, but he was adamant.

'Get up! We're going out to look for a job for you.'

I crept reluctantly out of bed and splashed cold water on my face. Henry was hovering restlessly around; actually, it's pretty hard to describe a man over six feet and weighing two hundred pounds as 'hovering' anywhere. Henry was smoking, drinking coffee and combing the Classifieds, flexing his enormous muscles. Not somebody you'd pick a fight with. He waited for me to get ready, pacing.

Our first stop was Manpower. While he went to the bar for 'a few drinks,' I collected the necessary info for a birth certificate and SIN card and jotted down job possibilities from the bulletin boards. We met at the bar, where he was sitting by the window, gulping rye and beer. We sat there until he ran out of money, drinking and getting to know each other. The alcohol haze took the sharp edges away. We argued about politics—the theory of anarchism, white supremacy, poverty. When we started on the topic of suicide, Henry shoved his big, tanned arms onto the table. Both wrists and most of the lower arms were badly scarred. I stared out the window.

Our next stop was a youth employment center, where I made an appointment. Henry and I went back home, smoked hash and got more money for booze. After the appointment, I found him in a strip joint. Center stage was illuminated by scarlet spotlights; a naked woman gyrated to the music, sucking her breasts, spreading her legs. I shrugged, chalked it up as another experience and wove around the tables looking for Henry, finding him very drunk and depressed. He was singing loudly and smacking the tabletop, but he wouldn't talk about what was bothering him (at least it wasn't me).

The naked woman sprawled across the stage, holding out her breasts to the whistling men, arching and strutting, doing splits and spread-legged rolls. I wondered if she felt soiled, and wanted helplessly to change things.

As another girl, a blonde in glittering pink mini, high heels and tight blouse, began twirling and caressing herself, Henry growled in a slurred voice, 'Let's split,' and somehow he managed to drive us home.

September 23

Today is Tuesday. After we came home from the strip joint yesterday afternoon, Henry and I both went to sleep—the racket the people upstairs were making woke me up less than an hour later. Henry had set his alarm for 7:30 p.m.; when it rang for five minutes, I went in and set it to ring again in five minutes. I did this half a dozen times, asking him each time if he were awake, whereupon he'd murmur 'yes' and then be dead to the world. Realizing the clock wouldn't work, I alternated between talking to Henry, shaking him, and threatening to turn on the lights—in short, playing the role of too-nice group home parent or something. I was really trying. I spent an hour and a half attempting to wake him up—after all, he'd helped me.

Unexpectedly, a pissed-off man came stumbling out of bed at 9:00, claiming that it was my fault that he hadn't gotten up at 7:30 in time to buy dope from his friend before going to work. We got into an argument. I was hurt, but count on yours truly to end up apologizing and inviting Henry to share his feelings. He marveled at how he could kill me with one punch, then spun around and went back to bed.

This morning Henry kicked me out. I thanked him for the two nights over, said I understood and left.

Evelyn, you bitch. One thing's for sure: I'm not going to be nice like that again.

The Emergency Services worker blew his chance. He accused me of being paranoid about trusting him, then went right ahead and called my parents. He also filed a Missing Persons. No more understanding or empathy.

Henry. You think that pot is going to help me forget? (You knew, though, didn't you, that I would just toke and smile and say, I understand.) You know something, I liked you a lot. I liked your voracious

reading, your brilliant memory, your honesty. I liked your showing me
the scars on your wrists, and your drinking that made you vulnerable.
I liked how you looked like a teddy bear in your mustard-colored
sweater, how you looked responsible, fatherly and strong.

I came to Calgary searching for something better but found the
same things happening over again. I felt surprisingly close to someone,
and was essentially laughed at. God, I feel like shit. Henry, I hate you
for what you promised and then grabbed back. I hate you for pretending to be Mr. Macho Rescuer and then turfing me out on the
streets. I grew very fond of you in two days, maybe because under that
huge frame of yours you were a baby needing affection and were afraid
to admit that yes, you had a drinking problem; yes, just because you
could put a guy in hospital for six months didn't mean you couldn't
be hurt.

I went to the Food Bank after two days without food, hating myself
for it. Hated sharing a table with a block of moldy cheese, swatting
away half a dozen flies. How could people set up a food bank in an
unheated, boarded-up old store with shelves packed with bags of food
spilling onto the floor and still pretend to care about the broken people shuffling through its doors? What kind of respect is that?

September 25

I was clear on just one thing: going home to Vancouver. It wasn't a
matter of failure or losing face anymore. Aside from the Food Bank
stint, I hadn't eaten for days, or slept properly either. And I was very
cold. The cold seemed to have seeped through my flesh and be resid-
ing gleefully inside. I'd bottomed out.

The next morning I went to a drop-in center. I managed to march
in without running into the walls, set down my bags and proclaim
loudly, 'I need a place to sleep. Don't tell me you can't do anything—
I'm going to sleep now.' Go ahead, bastards, call the cops, do anything
you want. I added to the threat by surveying the dirty floor with las-
civious eyes.

The staff immediately brought in a counsellor, and the kitchen people hustled in tea, coffee and sandwiches. After listening to my story,
the counsellor called in a minister connected with a group home for

prostitutes. The minister was a cute little man, improbable in black preacher's clothes, with hair that frizzled below his shoulders. He was impatient with my story (I was rambling by now) but asked a lot of questions, mostly about drugs. The counsellor said how one of the girls she'd been seeing had a pimp who told her to do something she didn't want to; when she refused, he went straight for her face, slicing diagonally from left to right from cheekbone to chin.

The minister decided to drive me to the group home. We went out into the main dining area of the drop-in, where over a hundred people, mostly men, sprawled around tables eating handouts. They had stringy hair and bloated faces, puffed bodies huddled in someone else's discarded clothing. I would have reached out to them if things had been different ...

On the way the minister had to stop at a hospital to pray over a dying man; in the meantime I slept in the back seat of his car. He picked up the counsellor—when they got into the car they said I'd been talking in my sleep and had asked one clear, urgent question: 'Are we in Vancouver yet?' They thought it was funny, but I needed to go home. Rising out of sleep, discovering that it was still Calgary, I felt depression drop its cloak over me.

The group home, which had been in operation for only a few months, was in an old house that had been boarded up and had furniture collecting dust on its sagging porch. The daytime staff person (whom I later learned with astonishment was a volunteer), immediately gave me a hug, surprising me so much that I stumbled against him, extricating myself as soon as possible. I wanted a goddamn bed, not love or understanding.

The worker and I had a meeting in the living room, with the minister and the counsellor in attendance. I tried to make it clear from the start that I hadn't come here to live, just to sleep for the night, but the worker wouldn't accept that. Neither would the minister or the counsellor. More questions, then the girls who lived in the house filtered in. They hugged and kissed the worker, said 'I love you' to him and did the same to each other.

My jaw must have dropped a foot. The worker sat very close to me and explained that the home was run on love and spirituality—genuine rather than physical love, which had often led to pain for the girls. In answer to this I shrank into my corner of the couch, wrapped my arms around myself and stared. It had to be a put-on. A Jamaican girl in tight jeans climbed right on top of the worker and began hugging and stroking him.

The minister looked at his watch. He had offered to lend me the money for the bus ticket, 'if that's what you really want,' and the bus to Vancouver was leaving soon. The girls were sprawled all over the living room, on the couches, on the floor, comforting each other, asking me to stay. The minister watched with his liquid brown eyes; the worker squeezed my shoulder.

A native Indian with faintly simian features who was twenty-one but looked no older than sixteen motioned me to her and pleaded with me to stay.

'Come on, just try this place for a few days,' she offered, her brown eyes growing serious. The worker had described her as the life of the house, but she was quiet now. Panic gripped me and wouldn't let go. A voice droned: THIS IS YOUR CHANCE AT HAPPINESS. TAKE IT, EVELYN. Months ago these same kids had been prostitutes with pimps, getting knifed and beaten up. Months ago they had been angry and unreachable ...

GO BACK, EVELYN, TO WHERE YOU BELONG. GO BACK TO VANCOUVER, WHERE YOU CAN GET ALL THE ACID YOU WANT; GO BACK TO THE STREETS, GO BACK TO TRYING TO KILL YOURSELF AGAIN. WHAT HAVE YOU DONE TO DESERVE THIS LOVE? IT'S TOO GOOD TO BE TRUE. BE STRONG, EVELYN—YOU CAN DO IT ON YOUR OWN.

I shook my head. The worker's eyes sank into holes above his cheekbones and suddenly he looked very tired. The light faded from the minister's face. The counsellor simply looked pissed off. I felt somehow as if I'd failed, as we climbed into her car and the native Indian girl stood alone on the porch, waving to me.

We drove to the bus depot in silence. Then, standing in line for the bus, I turned back to the minister. 'Why do you think I've failed?'

He didn't smile or anything, just said, 'Maybe the girl made you feel that way. Maybe she knew what was in store for you—working the streets—and that's why she looked so sad. She's got knife scars all over her, and ... well, she doesn't tell many people this, but she's got a bullet mark on her too, from working downtown.'

Then he and the counsellor were gone and I was standing there holding my ticket and feeling more dead than ever.

You complain of being betrayed, Evelyn. You claim that Calgary is a write-off because people turned you in, disappointed you, failed you. How many people have you disappointed? Think about that, for once.

Reality is tough, isn't it?

So here I am, back in Vancouver—where's all the wonderful things you claimed to be coming back to, Evelyn? I don't see you rushing to the youth newspaper house, or giving your beloved doctors a call—instead, you're sitting penniless in a library, considering going to the Hare Krishnas for dinner and a bed to sleep in, after a day spent hunting for a meaningless and elusive job. What was it that the group home worker had said? 'I can just see you in five or ten years. You'll be a bag lady, wandering the streets.' At the time I'd scoffed, but just because I'm not pushing a shopping cart, what's the difference?

The world catches a person by surprise … No, Evelyn, that's not right. You knew what was going to happen all along, didn't you?

September 28

A devotee was at the door of the Hare Krishna Center. He wore jeans underneath his robes, had a big smile on his face and looked healthy rather than ascetic or withdrawn.

We went through two hours of chanting and reading in the center: Hare Krishna, Hare Krishna, Krishna Krishna, Hare Hare, Hare Rama, Hare Rama, Rama Rama, Hare Hare … The sky darkened outside the windows, but the small assembly continued. I closed my eyes and let the devotees' chanting overwhelm me, feeling very sad yet at peace. Incense floated over us. Someone came up from behind and placed a string of flowers around my neck. Their smell mixed with the incense, was intoxicating. I remembered missing a man named Father, who would read to me and rock me in his arms when I was a baby. Looking for a substitute, I opened my eyes on the saffron-robed devotee who was reading.

After the prasadam downstairs, I sat with several devotees on the mats and we talked. It was cold in the basement and everyone else had left. One of them contemplated allowing me to sleep overnight in the center. He went upstairs to talk to the others afterwards; I went up to get my bags and heard snatches of their discussion, heard the muffled protests.

He countered, 'She's not mad. It's our responsibility to protect her; she's just a young girl. We don't want to turn her out into the streets ...'

I stood poised over my backpacks, his words echoing: 'She's not mad.' How could anyone think ...?

I slept deeply that night in the basement, with the Krishna chant rising and dipping all night from the stereo. Dr. Hightower was in my dreams; we were in his car, talking, when a police car pulled up behind us. My psychiatrist was silent. When a cop approached us, he shoved me out of his car and roared off.

A devotee woke me up at 11 a.m., murmuring a firm, 'Excuse me, excuse me' above my ear. I got up, received prasadam and showered. The devotee ordered me to clean and vacuum the center, basement included, as a form of 'Bakhti Yoga, the highest devotional service you can offer to Krishna.' He paced back and forth, keeping an eye on me while chanting his mantra rounds. Sure, sure, I grumbled inwardly, hoisting cushions and mats back into place.

During the cleaning a man named Darryl came in. He was in his thirties, over six feet, with confident brown eyes and a moustache. He had a self-assured look on his face that was a real turn-off. After the devotee watching me told Darryl something about my situation, he appraised me casually and said he'd take me in for a few days.

While Darryl was running some errands and I was waiting outside the center, a man who'd been receiving prasadam that morning came up and we started talking. He was bundled up in heavy boots, ski pants and two winter coats, all of which were muddy. I liked him, though not his Krishna philosophies—the religion was starting to make me sick. He had been in the psych ward before and had done a lot of drugs—peyote, mescaline, speed—though he was trying to quit for Krishna.

After a while he pulled out a small bottle of tiny, oval white pills and offered me a couple. I took them greedily and swallowed them on the steps; they turned into distasteful mush in my mouth. 'People I've given those to say they make them real happy,' he said.

Darryl ambled by and we walked to his home. I listened, bored, while he talked about being a vegetarian and a non-drinker and how he was not into drugs but didn't follow the fourth Krishna amendment—celibacy—and had once sheltered a fifteen-year-old girl who was a hooker, 'a blonde and very, very beautiful. We had sex, but it wasn't just that, we loved each other.' Right. I paid little attention to him, knowing that if he made a pass I could ward him off.

We ate watermelon while Darryl asked about my drug use, then he took off his shirt and motioned me into the bedroom. The pills were starting to take over; I lay down compliantly on his mattress, and he began giving me a massage. I was totally relaxed and quite oblivious. After a while he pulled off most of my clothes. I hardly knew what was going on and didn't care. We got dressed and went into the living room, where his roommate had made platefuls of spaghetti and buttered bread. Those pills! Those pills made it impossible for me to think or to feel disturbed. I just sat there, unaware of the conversation Darryl and his roommate were having, then began bumping into things and weaving around until Darryl took me out into the cold and asked me what I was seeing. But I wasn't aware of anything being different, and his persistence was irritating.

Darryl and I went back to bed. Through the pills and everything I kept wishing he were someone else.

In the morning I saw for the first time what the bedroom looked like—it was windowless, and the wallpaper was a series of mustard-colored stripes. The bed itself was a mattress on the floor. I felt like I was in an empty gift-wrapped box. I left quickly, without telling Darryl (who was expecting me to pay a share of the rent immediately), popping a pill that his roommate had dispensed and that made me so sick I rode for hours on the bus clutching my stomach. I called Dr. Hightower, who breathed a sigh of relief, knowing I was back in Vancouver; he offered to let me sleep at his family's house tonight and work things out in the morning because 'I'm your doctor, I have to look after you,' and that's all, isn't it? Everyone would be on your case if you didn't 'save' me, right, Dr. Hightower?

October 2

'Suicidal people are boring,' Dr. Graham said, his presence transfixing. Good to be back in that office, together with the one person in the past half year who has always been there, who won't give up. 'Personally, if someone told me he was going to kill himself, I'd open the window for him. Obviously I can't do that professionally, but, you know, they're so boring.'

Yes, being suicidal isn't very creative or productive after the crisis has passed. Come on, woman, you're going to be stuck with life whether you like it or not.

'That's how we first met, at Emergency Services,' Dr. Graham reminisced. 'I told them then, just as I'd tell them now, that here is a girl who's intelligent—troubled, yes, but someone who has the makings of a warrior. I know that you are a warrior in the making.'

Home again; even if home is only a softly lit office with a doctor, it's enough. Though I miss parenting. Watching little kids with their moms and dads, a pang of remembrance goes through me.

Lana's father said that my friends have petered out, because they see me going through the same things over and over, throwing their offers of help back in their faces. I asked her family to give me a place to stay for a few weeks, promising to pay them back once I had a job. Dr. Hightower suggested a series of group homes for emotionally disturbed kids.

'Will you be disappointed in me if I decide to live there and then take off?'

'Evelyn, when have I ever been disappointed in you? Tell me, when?'

'I don't know, maybe you don't show it, but you must be.'

October is a funny month to be in. I could be self-pitying and point out that at Thanksgiving I won't have anything to be thankful for except being alive, and is that such a wonderful thing after all?

October 4

I've spent the past week writing at bus stops and wandering around. After two nights at Crystal's, I bumped into my friend Art from Changes while he was visiting there, and he invited me to come over to his new apartment sometime. Yours truly took advantage of the opportunity and arrived unheralded that same evening.

Seeing me waiting, shivering, on the front steps, the tenants on the second floor—a single mom on welfare and her six-year-old daughter—invited me into their kitchen. The mother had left home at fifteen and was now overweight, with a bloated face the color of raw meat, blank eyes and hair that jumped around her face, crying out for shampoo. Their apartment was strewn with armfuls of clothing from the Sally Ann, their broken vacuum cleaner sat in a corner, and the kitchen table groaned with the weight of week-old leftovers, donated by the Food Bank. The place should have been preserved as an art piece. I brushed off the unidentifiable pieces of food on a chair and sat down. The daughter was adorable and seemed bright, but as Art put it, the mother 'wasn't normal.' She got a kick out of sharing a bathroom with a teenage boy, and her biggest fantasy was to take a bath with him—'to conserve energy.'

She liked me enough to lend me her spare bed for the night. I studied the sloppy remainders of the woman in front of me, scratching herself, thrusting leftover oatmeal in my direction, enthusing about my friend, and thought: SHE LEFT HOME AT FIFTEEN.

The next morning, the object of her affections stumbled sleepily into the hallway, his hair to his shoulders, wearing a black hat and black sandals run through with gold thread. Art was on Independent Living—his rent, college education and bus pass were paid for each month. Couldn't I manage as well as he, living on my own? It's the only thing I haven't tried; maybe it would work.

Yesterday a woman from the First United Church persuaded me to see a street worker. He drove me to Emergency Services to be apprehended and placed for the weekend; even if I AWOL'd, my being in care and labeled a 'street kid' would open up the services of the Outreach program—a small allowance, food vouchers and clothing even if I stayed on the streets. I looked away from him and out the window, from my position in the office seeing nothing but gray sky.

Kristin and I talked at Emergency Services, then she placed me at Changes for the weekend. The alert at Emergency Services read that they should put me somewhere social services could hang on to me, which we both laughed at, but even more ironic was the note from Frank and May's regional office to send me home if I came back.

October 5

I called Kristin to let her know that I'd probably be gone from Changes for the weekend—she was annoyed but confident that they had a grip on me since I'd have to be at the group home Monday in order to connect with the Outreach worker. 'Someone here was asking about you the other day,' she added brightly.

'Who?'

'Michael. He's here right now. Do you want to talk to him?'

I glanced around. A man at the other phone booth was grinning oddly at me, and the place was full of derelicts from the downtown eastside, drinking coffee and staring emptily.

'Hi, Evelyn.' Michael. I pitched a smile back at the other phone booth, then leaned into the conversation. 'How are you?'

He had finally completed his degree in social work and was for the most part sitting back and enjoying it. I found myself musing about how things had changed. 'I guess what I'm seeing now is that you have to do certain things to get what you really want, like the Outreach program. Like, I guess what's changed is that I'm not so stubborn and unrelenting anymore about what my wants are. I guess there has to be some sort of compromise.' The man at the other booth had taken a seat and was waiting, smiling with a horridly suggestive look in his eyes. What I'd said came out blurted, surprising me; I started laughing.

Michael was delighted. 'Hey, that even sounds like maturity! I'm really impressed!' Before we hung up he added, 'I do think about you a lot, wonder how you're doing,' and it made me feel good. Besides, the creep on the bench had taken off.

October 6

Spent last night at the youth newspaper. When I got to Changes this morning, May Wong had left a message for me to call her. Throughout the conversation she maintained that she was still my social worker and could delay the Outreach worker from coming if she wanted. May also demanded my appearance at the court date on Wednesday, challenged my wishes for apprehension and asked for innumerable explanations till I was left fumbling. The child care

worker at Changes swore and promised that it would be all right, she'd work things out about May. I felt defeated, though.

'Don't take off on me now,' the worker warned. 'It's kind of embarrassing trying to be someone's advocate and then not being able to even find that person.'

For a while I sat in a bedroom, then left. It would mess up what Kristin and the child care workers were trying to do, but when I picked up the phone and called May again, she confirmed my suspicion that I shouldn't have returned to social services. She agreed that it was my fault for getting everyone excited about nothing, for wasting people's time and energy, for not living at home.

October 8

Yesterday I found out that Outreach had accepted my case, that I would be in care for forty-five days, and that either May or Frank would be at Family Court. Kristin insisted that a street worker accompany me, to be a go-between with May/Frank/my parents, and to intervene if the judge decided to place me at New Beginnings.

At first I balked at the idea of someone 'holding my hand,' but as she went on it made more sense. May had proved that I knew little about Outreach—'stepping blindly into something you know nothing about'—but the street workers were aware of the program and would be able to help me out.

I was really worried about seeing my parents in court. Therefore, yours truly was drunk when she tottered into the street worker's office in the afternoon.

Demanding money from him, I raced to the nearest pub and gulped a few more beers. Some guy bought me another drink and made some proposition about fifteen minutes of sex in the bathroom for money. I giggled and said I had my period, whereupon he instantly withdrew his arm from my shoulders. After the booze I was just about ready to puke.

Don't remember much of the cab ride, nor the exact moment when things went wrong. All I wanted was to be able to face my parents. Instead, when the street worker took me inside and I caught a glimpse of them sitting there, heads bent, something broke. The next thing I knew we were out in the parking lot and I was screaming and he was massaging my back, murmuring, 'Hey, Tiger, it's all right, you don't have to go in, you can't go in like this.'

May was behind me, patting my arm. I couldn't raise my head. The street worker tried to get it through to me that I didn't have to be in court, but don't you understand? How can I go through life being a baby? I needed to face my parents, deal with their presence.

I wanted to return to court and be cool and okay. I wanted to show them (but most of all myself) that I could deal with things and be strong. As it was I fell out of the cab and had to be steered into the street worker's office, apologizing and insisting I was fine the whole way. The walls were spinning.

Even though you-know-who fucked up, my social worker is Jennifer from Outreach, who's going to see me tomorrow.

A hangover is already setting in. I've managed to break into a friend's house ... maybe she'll let me spend the night here.

October 12

A child care worker calls Kristin 'the only good worker at E.S. She never seems to burn out, and she's been there forever.'

Kristin laughed when I told her some of the things people were saying. 'Oh, it's not always that way. Take the other night—every phone call I got was from furious parents who said they held contracts on my life for taking their kids away! It's hard sometimes; it gets to the point where I can't take it anymore. But you have to get beyond the parents' frustration and make sure the kids are okay.

'And there's so many things that upset me. I was walking in the downtown eastside a few nights ago with a friend, and suddenly a couple comes staggering out of the darkness towards us. They were really drunk. The woman dropped her pants right in front of us and urinated on the sidewalk, then struggled to pull them back up but she could only get her underpants on! It was gross. I mean, you wonder how people can humiliate themselves that way. Then later on there was this one guy who got kicked out of a seafood restaurant, and he stumbled back and chucked a bottle through the window. The front window smashed and there were pieces of glass flying everywhere, landing in the fish tanks. The worst part of it was a couple of Expo tourists who started yelling, 'Look! A free sideshow!'

I liked Jennifer when she came to pick me up after the night at my friend's. She was like Kristin in some ways, and I sensed that she would do her best to help me.

I couldn't find a place for the night and so was out on the street. Walking around the downtown eastside, I passed a man slumped outside a pub. He was wearing bright blue pants and a yellow cap tilted over his face, and wouldn't respond when I shook him. I stalked into the lobby of the pub and was greeted by a drunk manager who swaggered by the unconscious man, sneering. I didn't know what to do— this man was more drunk than I'd ever seen anyone. He was too vulnerable to be dismissed—it was after midnight and he was alone.

Someone had punched him between the eyes, leaving a black and blue lump oozing blood steadily into his mouth; the back of his neck was a widespread pattern of bruises; blood was running into his right shoe from marks on his calf. The people who walked by kept walking despite my appeals, and the pub's manager watched and snickered. This went on until Frannie's ex-boyfriend came by.

He was with another woman who was walking a bike. We managed to revive the man, who blinked up at us with bleary eyes and told us to fuck off. He was in rough shape, too much so to be physically violent or even verbally abusive in any convincing way. He was certainly in no position to walk home, wherever that was.

Frannie's ex gave me a piercing look. 'Are you staying anywhere? Do you need a place to sleep?'

That just about made me cry. The man couldn't be left, though. So I shook my head and the couple walked back into the darkness.

The guy tried to tell me to fuck off, over and over, but he could barely move. I sat cross-legged on the sidewalk beside him, touched him, and then did cry. It was all so sad, how nobody would care, even if he was some stupid pissed asshole. Eventually he stopped gurgling 'Fffuck off.'

I took off his cap and he looked up at me. His eyes were like lost blue clouds. 'You've got nice eyes,' I said, inadequately. Everything seemed worth it when he slurred, 'You're … a … lady' with great effort before slumping back against the wall.

In the meantime a car had pulled up in the alley and the driver got out and approached us. He had glasses and curly hair, and a concerned smile. He was a social worker who worked occasionally with Emergency Services! I was so glad when he arrived. I explained the situation and he was sympathetic—he was someone who cared, who was willing to help.

'I thought I was the only crazy one,' he laughed, giving me a light hug, which was reassuring. 'It was so incredible when I drove by—it was just this guy lying on the ground, the darkness, the wall, and you. I had to stop.'

He confirmed that the man was in bad shape, and after half an hour, we agreed to call an ambulance. I didn't want to, but he was too heavy to lift and we couldn't leave him there either. While we stood by him, one vulture actually stopped and went through his pockets. Right in front of us! He straightened up with a pleading grin and opened his palms.

'Hey, man, all I want is a cigarette.' Someone had probably already gone through the man's pockets, as he didn't have anything in them. While we watched he pissed his pants and lay in his own urine. It was very depressing.

While we were waiting for the ambulance, another drunk man writhed and contorted on the ground at the end of the block. Leaving the others, I approached him; he suddenly reared up and tried to hit me. He was foaming at the nostrils, his hair wild around a gruesome face. I took off.

The ambulance men came to fix the man up and almost shoved me aside—the overreacting female, the good samaritan. I was falling apart, wishing something more could be done for the man, yet remembering how I'd hated it when others had done things for me— i.e., the psych ward. No one should have to go through something like Detox, even, if they didn't want to; if he was bent on self-destruction, who was I stop him?

The social worker took me away and then started hugging me tightly and getting an erection. He forced my face around and kissed me. It was disgusting. Then he locked both his arms around my neck and ground out between his teeth, 'I'm not letting you go,' but after a few minutes he did. God.

October 14

The one person who knows that I've sort of been wanting to go home is my one-to-one worker, Fred, who works with Jennifer by seeing the kids in her caseload more frequently than a social worker has time for. Of course I won't go home; it would be ridiculous, right now anyway. But I've been missing it a lot, even if it's only the warm bed and the meals that I took for granted. Running away is never easy. Wouldn't it be good not to struggle for a change? To go back to hiding my writing under a math textbook, cleaning the house, helping with dinner. I don't know, but there's definitely something magical and irreplaceable about a family.

I should go to New Beginnings tonight. Maybe the past month has been good after all—Jennifer and Outreach came of it, anyway. There's also been Kristin's support, which is genuine—and around here when you find something genuine, you hang onto it.

Life is a gift, somehow. It's too early to die.

October 18

'I go insane for a few hours sometimes.'

Dr. Hightower had laughed. 'Well then, you're the only person I know who can accomplish that.'

It's true, though. Last night nobody had provoked the mood I'd gotten into. The housemother's fill-in for the weekends looked confused while I fidgeted, snapping at her and wanting to hurt someone, anyone, for no reason.

I called up Dr. Hightower, and my one-to-one worker Fred. Two people who might be hurt. Dr. Hightower sounded pleased to hear from me even though it was dinnertime; I snatched at that and told him to cancel our Tuesday appointment.

'Why?'

'Because I don't want to go.' I might have added, 'And because I don't want to see you,' but couldn't.

'Well, it's your choice. No one is forcing you to do anything.'

'All you want to do is make some dumb psychiatric assessment of me!' I wasn't going to fall for his games anymore.

'No, Evelyn, I just want to HELP you.'

Help. What made him think I needed help? I hung up, then phoned Fred and canceled our plans for Sunday, venturing that maybe Outreach and being in care wasn't the right thing anyway. He countered with, 'Well, now you've got my phone number. We went out once and proved we could get along together. It doesn't matter whether you're in the program or not, we can still talk.' The line started buzzing and he began taking his phone apart to see what was wrong—before he could put it back together I hung up and marched upstairs. He called back and I told the fill-in to tell him I didn't want to talk.

'Evelyn?' She motioned me, sullen, to the top of the stairs. 'I told him. He says he's sorry for taking so long to put his phone back together.' It seemed very sad all of a sudden that he'd be the one to apologize. This was how I'd wanted to feel, though: rotten, hating myself. I didn't want to be at New Beginnings; didn't want to be anywhere.

I tried calling Dr. Hightower back to tell him I didn't ever want to see him again, but his wife said he wasn't home.

Ordering the fill-in out of the living room, I turned off the lights, cranked up the stereo and huddled on the sofa for half an hour in the pale darkness. It was eight o'clock on Friday night, so I put on my makeup and stalked out the door.

I hitched. The darkness wasn't solid yet, just a light blanket flopping restlessly over the city. The guy who picked me up, G., was in his late twenties or early thirties, nice build, with wavy brown hair that brushed his shoulders, a moustache and a really charming smile. He wore jeans, and the car was a mess of cigarette butts and Coke cans. G. said he was an ex-junkie; we smoked some pot from a packet under the car seat. I wished quite a bit that we'd get killed as the car swerved back and forth across the bridge and we passed a joint back and forth.

We went to his apartment on Davie Street. I was starting to feel better. The apartment building was a dump; in the lobby the overhead lights ejected mysterious streams of water into garbage pails set underneath them, and wire casing crept above the suite doors. The elevators were wooden boxes; a Christmas bulb lighted up above the entrance to announce the arrival of each floor.

In the apartment, G. took off his sweater and went to get some booze. I called up both Dr. Hightower and Fred to apologize and confirm the appointments. I sat back contentedly until G. came back and we drank and toked for a while, then I gave him a hand job for some drugs.

I left soon after and hitched partway home. The man who picked me up was Oriental, in his late forties, wearing a black leather jacket. He was solidly built and tanned, and wore a leer on his face. He claimed to have a wife and kids, but in the next instant he reached over and squeezed my breasts.

'You've got big boobs, eh? Very big boobs for a Chinese girl.'

He didn't get in more than a few squeezes because it was a short ride. I crossed the street to New Beginnings, amused at how it was like a bubble bursting when someone Chinese, and therefore 'safe,' did something like that.

October 21

'I wasn't angry with you last session. Just—irritated. I felt irritated at you for days afterwards.'

Dr. Hightower looked at me thoughtfully, speaking very slowly. 'Sometimes ... I think I make you that way by not giving or showing you the—affection—you need. I'm telling you it's there, but not giving it. You need parenting. I can't afford to play that kind of role, because I need to be everyone for you.'

'Omnipotent?' I sneered. The truth was that he'd uncovered probably my greatest need, because he looked so fatherly, and it was scary that he'd recognized it.

Went on another healthy dose of acid today. 'Medicated,' Dr. Hightower said. Yes! I feel numb and a little euphoric as well as somewhat sick to my stomach. No urgency for life to proceed, or for the world to touch me.

I'm not even hallucinating—the last trip was too recent—but I feel very drugged.

Only now, after the session is over (spent for the most part silently, as I didn't feel inclined to discuss things), do I remember that for the past few days I'd yearned to talk stuff over with Dr. Hightower—making me feel very lonely.

* * *

I told Dr. Graham I'm not going through with it anymore. I'm going to veg out on drugs and booze for the rest of my life. The down of the acid is even better than the high. Smoking dope in the mental health bathroom. Numb. Dead. Who's Evelyn?

He was furious at my paranoid, drugged, edgy state. 'I don't want you here on drugs! What if I say something that bends your mind completely out of shape while you're on acid ...?

'I was really proud when I discovered that article of yours in that peace magazine. You're going to be a warrior, Evelyn!

'"Well, she's seeing a private psychiatrist, let's close her file," they said. A file. That's what they think of you as, a file! To me you're a person. I want to share your frustration and disappointment when things are bad, to love and kiss you when things go well ...

'You mean they were right? That you're nothing but a disturbed, wayward adolescent? Come on, Evelyn! You can do better than spend the rest of your life standing around downtown ... thousands do that ...

'So what do you want to be? A teenybopper? A preppy? A street urchin? What? Come on, pick from the three!' Dr. Graham pounded his desk and glared.

Yes, you're right, I thought, then tried to form the words aloud. Yes, I do want to be a street kid. I want to be anonymous, I want to be without thoughts.

'I don't want my potential!' I finally burst out.

'Oh. Okay, so we were wrong, were we? You don't want to be anything better than the thousands of others! It took me thirty years to discover my own path, but you chose to do it now. You saw something more.'

Don't you understand? I want to be without this 'perceptiveness' and 'insight' blah blah blah, which are all euphemisms for struggle. WHY CAN'T I BE A MINDLESS TEENAGER?

Dr. Graham pelting his words through the acid was too much. He sat there in a gray sweater looking beautiful like a father, the unrelenting glare of his eyes shooting like flashlights through the fog, trying to find me. I felt sad and angry but mostly just drugged. How could he show so much caring, more than he'd ever done, today, when it felt too late? When he MUST NOT get through to me.

'I'm glad we had this session,' he said at the end, trying to smile. 'I got a lot of things off my chest too.' He only 'tried' to smile because I wouldn't accept it. Couldn't! So I went out and hitched, landing a big Italian guy in a van who offered $120 for sex and $20 for just some smooching, and I thought, FUCK YOU DR. GRAHAM. PLEASE DONT CARE ABOUT ME and I let the big stinking bastard chew my mouth and lick my face and damn near pull my tongue out, thinking all the while of my doctor and how he was trying to get through to me. How he really did care. How he looked like my father, love shining through the rage, the accusations. ONLY BECAUSE THEY CARE DO PEOPLE GET ANGRY.

Well, I don't know; I for one am going out tonight with A., who's been frantically trying to make another date. He can get me drunk—well, is that so wrong? Men only have one purpose. Don't they just use me as well?

October 22

I think I've just learned an important lesson.

We went drinking last night, you see. I mean, major drinking, more in two hours than I've ever consumed at one time. A. brought me to an isolated park and watched me get more and more drunk, as I defiantly thought of Dr. Graham and how he cared. The sky was dark, outlined with city lights, turning pink at the horizon. The park too was dark, lumps of pale sand the only illumination. Booze shut off the pain. 'Medicating yourself,' Dr. Hightower had called it. Isn't it ironic how I'd be willing to take anything now to make it stop. 'That's all the street kids want,' he had added. 'They want it to stop.'

A. offered to be my pimp. 'I've got lots of friends who'd love to do it with you. Then you'd have money to buy nice clothes, anything you want.' We began making out while I continued to drink and pretend his fingers and lips were Dr. Graham's. What would it be like to make love with the silver-haired man with the magnificent eyes who had sat with me across a table for over half a year?

A. half-carried me to the bus stop, and I fell in. 'She's okay,' he assured the driver.

'I'll bet she is,' he retorted. Everything began swimming. Faces staring meant nothing; they were all lakes of emptiness. I passed out, then woke up at the bus depot, got off, passed out on a bench in the cold, then woke up to find myself throwing up over and over on the cement. I didn't care that other people were watching; pride is a silly thing when one is in pain. Vomit gushed out and I was doing breast-strokes in a pool of black water—a woman's face on the other bench was blurred as if seen from underneath an ocean. I began pleading for someone to help. A woman called a taxi and someone else called an ambulance, so an ambulance attendant approached and tried to get me to go to the hospital, but I wasn't that far gone. A taxi driver supported me to his cab and drove me back to New Beginnings. I fell on the couch and the housemother stayed with me while I screamed and things kept spinning. I really thought I was going to die, it hurt so much. Everything was a tangled mass of blackness and pain.

I threw up at least half a dozen times during the night while the housemother slept fitfully on the other chesterfield. Apparently I kept whimpering, 'It hurts, it hurts,' and it did. It wasn't fair that there could be so much physical agony and still a person is resilient enough to survive. I wasn't able to move up off the couch till this afternoon (only then did the walls stop rotating), to hobble cautiously to the bathroom and douse myself with cold water.

Never again, I'd told the housemother and myself. I've been home all day and night, missing my job-training class and dinner with a friend. The thought of booze turns my stomach. How long can this resolution last? Perhaps it was meant to happen, to prove that it's not worth it. Dr. Graham was right; I was meant for something more. I'm not going to throw my writing away! Nothing else matters except my writing.

October 26

Lounging around today like some bum sustained by the state. I told you, group homes aren't conducive to contributing towards society. Living in a group home is too easy. It's too easy to give up fighting against barriers (real or imaginary) and to do fuck-all but lie on the couch watching TV, going out at night. It's called being a teenager, I guess. Then what? A repeat performance, going on welfare after a few abortions or a few unwanted kids, dying of something like a car accident if not a drug overdose? Waking up hungover in the morning, blitzed out on drugs. I think it might have been healthier for me to run, and emphasize my differences.

October 27

You know, it's difficult distinguishing between lies and truths when the lies are simply gross distortions of what actually happened. One kid here boasts about her ten-thousand-dollar-a-month cocaine habit, how she spends several hundred a week on LSD, how she works the streets and nearly got knifed the other night and how she is, yes, a junkie. Another kid brags about her seven boyfriends, how she can't walk down the street without being propositioned, how she plays pimp for her girlfriend. Another kid tells us that she's had two abortions and that she's been raped 'a few times' (casually spoken) in a parking lot. But I don't care about your pimps and johns and your boyfriend's sugar daddy who gave you a houseful of stolen furniture. I don't care about your multiple dates grabbing your crotch. I don't want to hear you imitating everyone else's drug problems and sexual assault histories when you haven't even been drinking for a year and the housemother has no idea why you're in care.

And there's me and my acid trips. It's stupid, really stupid. How many people gather their life into one armful and cast it away? I wish someone would help me find myself. Is destiny inevitable? Will Dr. Graham help me?

'I don't think people realize what a burden it is for you to have talent and potential,' one of my friends from the youth newspaper had mused as we walked under the growing dark, Hallowe'en firecrackers popping off around us. I hadn't even realized it myself till recently—how much responsibility a vision can be.

Last night I went out with a guy who thought he could shove people around, including me—he threatened to blow my brains out if I told anyone where he lived. And touching me all over, instigating furious self-hatred. But it was an exchange, for a gram of coke.

Lately I never go anywhere by bus, hitchhiking with a fury, especially after dark, hoping Death will be behind the wheel and will pick me up.

Jennifer's taking me to meet a potential foster parent tomorrow. Can I hang on till then? Why is it so hard?

October 31

'Please help me.' It is 6 p.m. and the sky is dark outside Dr. Hightower's office.

'I'm here to help you, any way you want me to.'

'How?'

'By being here once a week to talk to you. I can't bring you home with me, Evelyn. It's important that I'm not your father; I'm your psychiatrist.'

'I want to die. I wish I were dead.'

'If you keep saying that, Evelyn, I'll have no choice but to lock you up. You know that. Don't push me to do something I don't want to just to hate me, to feel as if the world has betrayed you. Look, if you walked out the door and felt suicidal at ten o'clock tonight and did kill yourself, your parents could sue me and they'd probably win. 'Why didn't the psychiatrist do anything?' people would ask. I'm taking that risk.'

'Is there any medication you can give me?'

'Well, no. You're not psychotic, you're not manic-depressive ... I could probably prescribe antidepressants, but you'd just end up eating them all at once. I'll still care about you, no matter what you turn out to be.'

'Even if I don't write? That's so important to Dr. Graham ...'

'Even if you never write another word.'

'Really? But my writing is me. How can you care if I stop writing?'

'I will, Evelyn. It's your basic humanity that I like, your need to help people.'

But is that enough? Who am I if not a writer? It's all I have—this pile of crumpled paper that follows me everywhere in my backpack, words breathing life, my existence.

Dr. Hightower met with my parents on Tuesday and says they're doing better than I am.

* * *

'Why are you sad?' Dr. Graham looks at me curiously.

The clock ticks loudly in the silence. 'Because—because I've failed you somehow. Anger and disappointment, those are the two things I can't stand when they're directed at me. Yet I can't live my life for other people.'

Dr. Graham's retort is swift. 'But you're doing that now, more than you ever did. When can I expect to see you standing on Seymour Street in fluorescent net stockings and high heels?

'I feel like I've failed too,' he continues, his face older without the smile, the bright eyes. 'Failed in mattering enough so that you don't trash yourself. Failed to help pull you through all this so that you won't be completely lost in the street scene. I'll always be here, Evelyn, years and years from now. I'm your friend. Who can you talk to if you can't talk to me?'

Two sessions in one day was too much. The rain fell with the leaves and they could have been tears. In a restaurant an old man picked up the rose in the vase on his table and smelled it. I promised never to be old like that, alone and smelling the flowers. A law professor picked me up and afterwards plastered me with vodka. Of course his position didn't stop him from taking working girls to his place. Came home at midnight and cried myself out on the couch in the housemother's arms, cried over Dr. Graham and everything I wanted to do but was destroying.

November 3

I spent the weekend at the foster parent's home and am moving in. It's better than following the urge to take off from this province again. I didn't like Melanie, who was cool and remote when Jennifer introduced us, but I'll ride it out. Melanie lives with her friend and her friend's kids. I told Melanie I didn't think I was capable of making a commitment, but she cleared things up by saying she didn't expect one.

It's hard because there's still so much I need to prove to people; it's almost all I live for. Kristin is going on vacation tomorrow for two weeks, and can I keep up the act until she returns? I have to prove that

I'm doing better, that I can grow without first fucking things up. It's imperative that I don't linger in people's memories as another teenager who used her potential to manipulate others into caring for her, then turned around and threw it back in their faces.

I want to stay alive. Help people. To take my mind off things, I'm doing as much as possible for the Food Bank. Once I seemed to have all these huge, huge dreams. Where did they go? I can see the months unfolding: living at Melanie's, watching television, sleeping, perhaps attempting to go back to school in January and then dropping out after a week. One could ask: If she can see all this, why doesn't she get off her ass and DO SOMETHING? But it's not as simple as that.

November 9

I went out with J. last night and it was disappointing. We drove up to Chilliwack (I love pretending I'm escaping), parking in an isolated area beside the river. The sky was a deepening blue and the only other sign of life was the occasional logging truck barreling past on the bridge, out of hearing distance. I had come to trust J. as a friend who was helping me out without expecting anything sexual in return; he was witty, fun to be around. Then without warning he reached into the bowels of the van and pulled out a bag with half a dozen huge joints in it, and we toked up. Even before he had taken a toke, though, he was already all over me. That ruined it. Sometimes I wonder, isn't there a single guy in the world who is willing to be a friend without eventually wanting something sexual in return? In order to get more pot, I had to put up with the groping. I won't go out with him anymore. Is that unreasonable, not wanting sex with someone you don't love or feel physically attracted to?

November 18

It came out during today's session with Dr. Hightower that in fact I hated Melanie and was 'barely hanging on by my fingernails.' I haven't been writing about the foster home enough—the days seem busy, yet tedious. Can that be possible? Sleep has been dominating at least 50 percent of my time since moving in—it's the first thing I complain about in the psychiatrist's office. Oversleeping, but never managing to feel rested; constant dreams filled with faces, not making sense. Usually these faces are of friends who keep their distance, excluding me from their activities. Miserable to wake up with eyes that ache as if they'd been blinking nonstop during sleep. The sky is gray; everything looks dead. Dr. Hightower attributes the sleeping problem to the drugs, which don't feel as if they're a problem.

There's nothing to do. Both elections, civic and provincial, have swung to the right. I pound away at the typewriter twice weekly at the Food Bank and have just taken on a three-week phone soliciting job run by a left-winger; the employees are mostly left-wing. I spend the rest of my time sleeping, eating, watching TV. It's difficult to read because my concentration appears to be have been fried by the acid.

Life looks as gray as the walls of this bedroom. Melanie pisses me off with her fastidious house rules. Sometimes I just want to pound her face in, yet as I asked Dr. Hightower, how does one express anger? It'll only make me feel guilty and therefore be more harmful to myself than anyone else. When will this change or stop altogether?

December 4

I finally kept an appointment with my former high school counsellor about enrollment for the second semester. It went well. She remarked how even the sound of my voice was different: 'Your syllables are tighter, more strung together. The last time we talked your speech was very vague, drawn out sort of, as if you were looking at everything from a great distance. You were in really bad physical shape, too—I felt certain you were going to die, whether it was from malnutrition or drugs or prostitution or even suicide. At least I have some hope now!'

Jennifer and I also met today. At first I resented her, resented the whole idea of being back in the Outreach office wondering where to go, but she was very encouraging—pointing out that I hadn't been AWOL at Melanie's or New Beginnings for two whole months and had behaved reasonably during that time. I couldn't understand why she wasn't judgmental; May would have flown off the handle with exasperation. Jennifer said that she would look for another placement, but it would take weeks and during the 'in-between' time I would have to choose between New Beginnings and Melanie's.

How could she not give up on me when I've just about given up on myself?

December 25
Christmas Day.

Christmas Eve was hard. Art, my friend from Changes, came over, but it was awkward. We hadn't seen each other for a while and didn't have much to talk about. Eventually we escaped the gray confines of my bedroom and wandered around the city, telling empty jokes and laughing very hard. The streets were deserted. I kept wishing Art would go away. It was a mistake; being out on Christmas Eve just increased the isolation. Everyone else, it seemed, was warm, loved and at home.

Today I got up early and fled the house. The buses were empty except for one or two people; the streets were pearly gray and silent except for Skid Row, where the street people nodded on their benches like pigeons on a line. I spent the day at Lana's house, where we fooled around, accidentally broke some glasses and had a good time. She's still the one person I can be a little kid with.

I called my parents on the spur of the moment tonight. Dad answered. He wasn't terribly excited or thrilled that I'd phoned and took the opportunity to launch into a lecture. Melanie's friend claims that I'm a sucker for being lectured by people.

Well, merry fucking Christmas.

December 30
I know that much of my writing is immature and self-absorbed, and that alone is enough to depress anyone. Depression is a brick sitting on top of your head, weighing down and compressing your thoughts into nuggets of lead.

I am scared to let anyone know how much I love them because then they would understand how lonely I am.

My mother in her kitchen, a thin woman rushing back and forth to clean cupboards, sweep floors, make meals, wash dishes—it was never-ending. There was always something that needed to be done! None of this is pleasant to bring up. She kept everything in order while each of us disintegrated.

I remember how, in the very beginning after I'd run away, Michael watched us from his chair in the family conference room, a smile twitching the corners of his mouth upwards when she came in and clutched me. Unable to deal with touch from previously aloof parents, I found it an effort not to recoil. Why did he come to me in the hallway, anyway, to offer me another opening: a few more days away from family? Though I never thought I might blame him.

Of course Dr. Hightower's right. Of course I wish none of this had happened. Even Dad was right, to predict that I would regret it one day, even as I sneered and flaunted my new life at them, baiting them, pretending to be so tough and free. What an elaborate scam. Of course I was wrong, wanting a glimpse of life, yet social services had ended up accommodating me after all. Why? Why is Jennifer catering to the confused whims of a child who wants nothing but to go home?

I won't be going back to school. I eagerly listened to Joe on the coast when he declared that school was bad and that he knew what he was talking about; he'd been an anarchist for twenty-five years whereas I'd been one for only two or three! Every other person in the world is convinced that I need to go back to school in order to make it in life, even perhaps in order to become a writer, but I will listen to an aging hippie hidden in his cabin, collecting welfare, smoking pot, drinking and dreaming about the sixties.

Here I am. I want to go home. I want to have friends. I want to be loved by someone. Is that naked enough for you?

PART IV

january 16 to april 26 1987

January 16

I want to ask myself a few questions tonight, here at my Aunt Mary's house after deciding to take a sabbatical from Melanie. Over the past few days a mass of doubt has been burgeoning in my head. Be honest: can I make it as a writer?

Or has this been ten years of self-delusion, struggling towards a goal that isn't anything but a mirage? As a kid it never occurred to me that becoming a successful writer might he too much to expect, not with my determination. You begin to believe it, after years and years of convincing yourself—just as after fourteen years of my parents telling me I wasn't good enough, I believe that now. I resent that, just as I resent not knowing where I'm going, where I am in fact. I'm too full of thoughts to be a hooker/junkie who dies in some back alley or hotel room; too full of excuses to get an education and go to university. I'm doing dick except bumming around, bouncing from place to place, to whoever will take me in with pity in their eyes. Not working, not going to school, not really doing anything with my life. People are right, I do have potential—I could become a bag lady in five years. Like Aunt Gayle pointed out, 'Social services is only going to support you until you're nineteen.' Then what? Welfare? She adds that my cousins in the States are getting straight A's in school and, at my age, already deciding which university they're going to attend. There. Talented, motivated, up and coming young adults. Model youth. Where do I fit in?

Maybe my writing has never been more than a pipe dream. My former English teacher, now working as a home tutor through the school board system, tore into my latest short story, 'Working the Corner,' when he came over for our twice-weekly class together. Who says I can

write? Me, of course. Thinking I could do so much, become so many
things. Maybe I was wrong. Maybe I'll become a frightening old lady
fanatical about something or other, ranting to anyone who will listen.
There are people like that out on Skid Row, their garbage bags full of
could-have-beens.

Don't you see: I don't fit in anywhere. All I have in the world that is
precious is my writing, which I clutch and shove in front of my vulnerabilities like a shield. Evelyn isn't alive at all, it's always her writing,
her writing. Well, isn't it about time someone told her it's trash? That
it's not worth dick? Isn't it about time someone told her the truth?
She's floundering in some kind of murky half-life, some swamp where
she still spins fantasies about seeing her books on shelves and people
actually reading them, books that would make people think and feel.

I'm tired of running after a dream, so foolishly. I'm sick of not
belonging anywhere. What if I'm never going to make it as anything?

January 17

Nothing has changed, has it? I took a bunch of aspirin around 5 p.m.
(it's 8:00 now). Thirty of them went down my throat; I couldn't swallow another without gagging. Picture this: standing in the kitchen,
pitcher of orange juice in one hand, clusters of white pills spilling over
the counter. Remember? I was laughing. Everything around me
became very sharp, a polished white.

I'm not gonna die. I'm just going to be really sick, telephones jangling in my ears, white mush oozing from my mouth, stomach
screeching. Oil will start leaking out of my hair and skin and continue
for the next few days. I'll sleep and sleep. Temporarily, life will be put
on the back burner, less relevant than the hurting.

But this time there's no Tommy to rap on the bathroom door.
Where are the social workers, the ferry, the night—the promise of a
brave new world? Am I a welfare bum who cannot write, who sits
watching television all evening and sleeps till three in the afternoon?

It's not going to work. Dr. Hightower said that if I haven't passed
out in the next hour, I'm not going to die.

Everything's disintegrating, worthless. I am not even a good writer.
That's all that's important. I can't love myself or feel equal to anyone.

Nothing but the motionless TV, and the couch. Everyone else has plans, is moving farther and farther ahead.

I want to die, but instead I'll go sleep this off, keep it a secret. Relatives, friends and the government support me, each grudgingly. Everything throbs ... the house looks long and white, full of corners and corridors. You make me want to cry.

January 19

Jane was my best friend in high school for a while; she's the only one out of that group of people who will still talk to me. I almost cried when she came to the phone, demanding to know what I'd been up to. What am I missing out on by not returning to school? What have I so carelessly tossed over my shoulder—running off into a fake sunset as it were—as though it were worthless?

Jane's going out with a guy in university. He's her first boyfriend and they do everything together; they study together, go out. He doesn't demand sex from her, either. How come I never got a boyfriend who was half-decent, a friend more than anything? What's wrong with me?

January 27

The phone rang, twice. Guess who it was?

Daddy dearest.

I fought off an impulse to slam the receiver down and instead listened to his hesitant, bitter voice. He must have been standing barefoot in the living room, wearing pajamas with gaping holes, the furrows between his eyebrows deepening. The TV was chattering in the background; my mother was yelling at Karen. Nothing changes. I felt overwhelmed with gladness at having escaped.

He announced that tomorrow they were having a dinner for Chinese New Year. Every Chinese person, he said, attended this dinner no matter how busy they were. He expected me to come home and help make the meal.

It was one of those times where I thought, 'Dr. Hightower, help!' I told my father that I might or might not come, depending on what was happening Wednesday night (as far as I know, nothing). Karen grabbed the phone and babbled about school and her Christmas presents as though she had rehearsed it many times. Then my mother came to the phone and chewed my ear off when I suggested I might be doing something else tomorrow evening—after the past ten months, my parents are still incapable of understanding that I have my own life. That I could breathe on my own, go to the bathroom by myself, even (holy God!) walk out the door on my own two feet!

'Going out tomorrow night? Where is there to go?' She was genuinely puzzled; surely there was no world beyond the walls of a house. What I had stepped into was unreal, mirages she could poke fingers through.

They expected that I would transform back into the dutiful daughter for the occasion. As Dr. Hightower had said, if I went back they would think that 'God had dinged you on the head and made you their compliant little girl again.'

All right, if you're feeling sorry for them, think about my side of it—Mother screaming all evening, Karen reaching up pathetically to grasp my hand, Father scowling. Mother will rant about my shoes, my jean jacket being too thin for the cold outside, my perfume smelling funny, my hair looking wrong, my painted nails and above all my weight. It's only recently that I've told Dr. Hightower about my eating problem, which Mom and Dad never understood, though I sat them down several times and explained for hours about bulimia. The doctor said that bulimic children often come from controlling families, that developing the disease is their way of asserting control.

Tomorrow night my parents will go on and on about my lack of schooling, lack of a job, lack of everything but bumming off people. I don't need it right now! To them it's my fault that I was fucking born. I'll get dick out of it, except humiliation. Are you telling me that it's not their problem, that I'm being unfair and stubborn? That I never talked to my parents, never gave them a chance to understand? Listen to this. I've spent countless hours explaining to them about bulimia—the horrible binges, sneaking food, stealing food. If you think that was easy, you're crazy. I told them about the insecurity, the month-long bouts of depression, the frustration, the anger. They looked at me and said I was 'a greedy pig.' Their glances said, 'We've bred a pig for a daughter!' My mother's reaction was to watch every morsel I ate, keep better track of the food in the house, examine me naked and force me onto the scale every Saturday.

A letter from Dad arrived today, and I stormed into Dr. Hightower's office, waving it. My father had lectured about school, social services giving me money ('It isn't fair') and my smoking, saying that even though I didn't smoke very much, it was going to kill me (if I thought it would, quickly and painlessly, I would spend every waking minute puffing my face off). They have finally agreed to hand over my bank account, which has about two hundred dollars in it, which happens to be my money. 'This amount of money took a long time to save; I don't know how long it takes you to spend it,' my father wrote ominously. He didn't once congratulate me for quitting drugs; in his letter it was 'the first step to correct your "wrong things."' He also questioned whether or not I was lying. How's that for faith? *Nolite te bastardes carborundorum*—yet it doesn't matter when the bastards are already winning. My father kept emphasizing that I had an 'easy life.' Oh? Where is it, then? I must search for it among my possessions ...

Okay, stop crying. Boy, I'm mad. Dr. Hightower pointed out that my parents were like the Ford sign outside his office window—no matter how much he talked to it or yelled at it, the letters would never change. 'F-O-R-D. Never, never, never!' But that seems impossible. I wish life were like a TV show; at least things get resolved at the end.

February 1

I don't know if staying here at Aunt Mary's will work out, and I get desperate thinking that there is no workable place. My aunt is disconcerting. I feel as if I'm home again, home with its frightening connotations. Aunt Mary sits there and looks at nothing. She carries with her a cloud; I can't predict her moods. Her impending outbursts are settled like dust in the gray lines of her face. I'm terrified. I feel as if the house won't let me leave, although today the air is spring—and the air presses close!

Aunt Mary doesn't trust me with money for fear I'll spend it on drugs. None of my relatives trust me with money for the same reason—without seeing that it drives me up the wall.

In many ways I've been cast out by the whole family and for some reason that bewilders me, forces me to see them as people, so it becomes a personal rejection.

I feel a little nostalgic for Melanie's home. It was home for two long months, you know. A few days ago I thought about going back, but maybe it only looks attractive from afar. I'm a lot like that; I only get fond of people and places after leaving them behind.

Last night I read E.L. Doctorow's Lives of the Poets in one sitting, devouring several pages at a time and then surfacing like a diver to suck loud gulps of air before going back down. It was fantastic to be able to read with such absorption again.

The past few weeks I've been going through spells of feeling strong and then feeling crazier than ever. Sometimes I can smile at everything and feel as if I'm a whole human being, as if Dr. Hightower is standing directly behind me, so that if I looked over my shoulder he would be there, smiling benevolently. Those times, I am a part of the breathing world.

Other times, pieces spin inside me. My head breaks up into fragments that threaten to consume my thoughts, to suck them up and spit them out; inside, I'm broken mirrors gleaming with color. Those times I am dizzy; I can't sit still.

February 3

Today I went in search of my weekly Dr. Hightower fix.

I resented him because we never seemed to get anywhere in our sessions; he never seemed to do anything except sit there and look familiar; I got to see him just once a week and had to share him with other patients; and he had a life of his own that was separate from mine.

You know.

I carry that annoyance with me to each of our sessions, though usually it's not a factor. Today was different. When I walked into the waiting room there were seven minutes left of his previous appointment. I stared at the white walls separating the two offices, then realized that every word being spoken inside was audible.

A couple was in there. Ordinarily a waiting patient wouldn't be able to make out more than a few words at a time, but today the couple was arguing. I got steadily angrier. The man and woman were yelling—the woman saying it wasn't her fault if he didn't like chicken for dinner, that she had other cooking and cleaning to do; the man yelling that no, he didn't have intercourse with so-and-so—and there was Dr. Hightower, the almighty shrink, chuckling in that understanding, involved way that I'd previously found endearing. Now it was maddening. Was that all he did, sit there and chortle like Santa Claus? Dr. Hightower pointed out that the husband knew his wife got crabby a week before her period; the husband exploded that he shouldn't have to put up with a week of hell. I could hear everything. I was angry at myself too for that sudden feeling of protectiveness that had risen in me—Evelyn, who always needed to protect and care about people. I wanted to save Dr. Hightower from the shit flying around in his office, even while knowing that he was strong enough for it, hundreds of times stronger than me.

Presently Dr. Hightower wished them a happy marriage, laughing, and they came out into the waiting room. Everything changed once the couple emerged from the shrink's office. They were smiling, the husband was cracking jokes with Dr. Hightower. It's too beautiful, the masks we construct for ourselves.

Brushing aside my rage at what had happened, including Dr. Hightower's incompetence in not discovering the problem sooner, I told him that the patients' voices carried into the waiting room. He looked concerned, apologized and promptly brought a radio in to drown out the noise.

I proceeded to tell him about my week, about Aunt Mary and my worries about where to live (what else is new?). Take it out of the parentheses, take it out of the closet, and it becomes WHAT ELSE IS NEW? I talked about choices, which are funny things; it's not like I'm without them, but they're always the same in that none of them are desirable.

'You've hated every place you've lived in,' Dr. Hightower observed.

True. (What does that say about me?) Sometimes the choices change a little—they narrow down, or a few more are added—but so far that hasn't made them any more attractive. We agreed that the big choices are relatively meaningless; it's the day-to-day ones that determine our lives.

From then on we talked about my anger towards him, but it was fruitless. There were long silences, and he infuriated me further by not interrupting them, by repeating that he 'understood.' I wanted him to ask questions, but he wouldn't. I mocked him for choosing his words carefully, for the frown of concentration settling between his brows. I was angriest, I said, 'because I come here every week, expecting something to change, but it never does. I'm just really sad now because after this session I have to go back and go through another week, and nothing's different.'

At the end of the hour Dr. Hightower mused that he didn't think we'd gotten very far that day. I said, 'It's like a drug. I feel as if I've taken something that has always worked before, but nothing happened. I feel cheated.' On that note, our session ended and I was herded out the door, my little daddy shrink courteously holding it open for me.

February 5

I began an entry yesterday but threw it aside in exasperation. 'I feel as if I have lost my jolly-bellied psychiatrist ...' Lost him, yes, actually I have. You know how easily I lose things—what's one more therapist? He could, after all, have been no more than a pen or an earring or a book of matches. Perhaps it is even easier to lose people.

My tutor stayed for an hour and a half and we had a marvelous session. He comes over twice a week; we're studying James Joyce and a poetry textbook. Sometimes lines of poetry run through my head at the oddest times, like while I'm doing the dishes. Those times, I fool myself with the misconception that nothing could tear me away from my destiny as a writer.

Yesterday this brilliant idea formed in my mind: I would write a story about my first visit to the psych ward, detailing everything from the moment the main character sauntered into the waiting room to three days later, when she is released. I lay down on the floor under a blanket, with a cup of coffee, and began to write. Several hours later I transferred to the couch and continued writing. By mid-evening I had forty pages and still a day and a half to cover. Every detail had come back to me, stripped of sentimentality or what my tutor called 'special pleading.' But it was forty pages of worthless scribbles. It was such bad writing it made me furious.

So the masterpiece is lying incomplete and scattered over the floor, together with 'Working the Corner' and my (I swear to God) thirtieth revision of 'The Waiting Room.'

There is nothing more disgusting than a heap of unfinished stories, none terribly good, many oft-revised yet still repulsive … And me sitting in the center of the floor, smoking disconsolately, watching TV and wondering if maybe I shouldn't poke my head outside for just a teensy breath of air.

February 12

One of the men I hitched a ride with to Dr. Graham's office this morning was middle-aged, drove an expensive car, and wanted me to turn tricks. Sooner or later it'll start getting hard to say no. What are we trying to protect here, anyway? If these men with their rough, salivating mouths and pouches of fat weren't so repulsive, it would be easy. Why is there that remembered feeling of worthlessness when they move closer, when their eyes don't register your face, much less your thoughts?

If I were a man, I'd never entice a kid into working the streets, even if she were low on money and bumming rides. I'm starting to hate men except for fatherly fantasy figures who are gentle, comforting, and couldn't possibly have real penises.

Dr. Graham emerged from his office more than half an hour late. 'Sorry. There was an emergency—this pretty eighteen-year-old Indian girl. They brought her in and she was having a crisis, she was suicidal.' His office was brightly lit but intimate; I felt exposed. To my relief he immediately took charge of the session, then I told him what had happened over the past few months and we talked at length about depression. He felt that my mood swings were environmental; it was difficult for him, he said, to determine just how much was biological. At this point I eased in the possibility of antidepressants.

You see, Dr. Hightower won't prescribe medication, and so far I haven't had any luck in acquiring sleeping pills. I've decided that if a decent magazine won't accept my writing or if I don't win a contest soon, I'll allow clusters of pills to slide down my throat, and watch the life some confused Maker had given me evaporate. The thoughts in my head are beginning to clamor again, each getting louder till my brain reels with the competing voices.

Dr. Graham promised to talk to Dr. Hightower about my depression and ask if medication would be suitable. I wanted to kill myself so badly! Dr. Graham had returned to his masterful self; his eyes were clear and his steel-colored hair made idle waves around his face. He was still there and didn't ask why I'd disappeared for several months, seeming to understand that I'd thought I wouldn't need him anymore and had been wrong.

Dr. Graham felt that living with my aunt was inducing my current depression and that a group home would be a better alternative. We had spent an hour together, but a social worker was waiting his turn with me. He had been with the other psychiatrists who had shipped me off to the psych ward last April.

'He's a jerk,' I informed Dr. Graham.

'Well, he's not,' he replied, tight-lipped. 'He met you in the beginning and still wants to be involved.'

The social worker motioned me into his office. It had been nearly a year since I'd been led into this same place, with May patting me daintily and confiding that the hospital would he a wonderful place to rest for a while. I'd been fourteen and just born into the world. Life had been a drama then, with Evelyn the wronged heroine.

'Have a seat.' The worker smiled kindly. The skin on his face sagged. When he spoke he emitted a whistling sound, as if the air were being sucked in sharply through a gap in his teeth. But these things were misleading, for after a while I saw that his eyes were stronger than mine and that he wasn't the wimp his appearance had led me to believe he was.

I asked again for antidepressants. Actually, I was begging to be hospitalized, describing my latest overdose of aspirin. Outside the window the gray sky was swimmy; across the street a woman dangled her kid out of the apartment window. For me, the barriers of suicide were eroding—lots of people killed themselves, all the time. Pretty soon suicide would become as ordinary as the common cold, for the taboos were disappearing and it was on its way to acceptance.

The worker thought that I needed some close friends. All right, then, shall we go shopping for A Best Friend? I spoke passionately about my writing and my worries about it, and my major problem: where to live. He thought that Jennifer would be willing to put me on

Independent Living since nothing else had worked, and offered to speak to her. In the three weeks when Aunt Mary had left for a business trip I'd managed on my own. I told the worker that I would even go back to school if they gave me my own place.

He made another session for the Monday after next. How do you like that, there are three people taking care of my head now. If I do succeed in committing suicide it won't be just poor Dr. Hightower's failure.

February 16

Aunt Gayle calls: a package has arrived at her house for me. Alberta Poetry Yearbook, the return address says.

The puppet strings jerk and I discover myself bent against the wind under a sky newly washed with rain. Did I win the contest? There's no use in preparing oneself for failure—no matter how hard you try, the foolishness persists. The rain has left water diamonds hanging from each bare branch.

Somebody else's fingers tear open the battered manila envelope. I examine her hands curiously, the chewed painted nails. Like a drowning person my eyes beseech the blameless pages ...

There it is. Under the youth section—third prize, Evelyn Lau, with 'Bobby-Pin Scratches.' A poem about child abuse. I walk home, clutching the magazine, jealousy and relief battling inside. The words I have stuck onto the magazine page are hopeless, inadequate; in a year they will peel off and the page will bare itself to a more promising writer.

February 23

A couple of days ago I began wondering if my feelings weren't because Dr. Hightower's leaving for his holidays. Tomorrow's going to be our last session, and it's supposed to sustain me for a month. My dreams are frantic, full of fragments in which he is abandoning me. Before this, I'd looked forward to his vacation—it would be great for him and would give me a chance to manage on my own. But what will happen on Tuesdays? Without him, I'll become a jellyfish washed up onto the shore—spineless, exposed.

My tutor came this morning just after I woke up and stumbled into the gloomy living room. He might as well not have arrived, since I couldn't participate, could only thrust my homework at him and doze on the couch.

I described my sleeping problem to Dr. Graham this afternoon and he instantly prescribed twelve Rivotrils, which are sleeping pill/muscle relaxants found helpful in therapy. He didn't like dispensing medication, and when he capitulated I lost some respect for him. A dozen sleeping pills couldn't hurt and I do need them, but a sickening sensation settled in my stomach. The pills were the beginning to something; a barrier somewhere had been broken.

Dr. Graham said that he'd talked with the social worker, who had in turn talked to Jennifer about the possibility of Independent Living. He had good news—if they could get the cooperation of Dr. Hightower, social services might be swayed. Dr. Graham was prepared to write a letter stating that I should be living independently for medical reasons. Now that the idea sounded feasible, I was reluctant—what if I screwed up? What if the depressions persisted? Dr. Graham warned that I would have to cooperate by enrolling in an educational program full-time.

I went to collect the medication downstairs. The pharmacist bustled behind the counter, calling over his shoulder, 'You're in good hands with that doctor.'

'He's cool,' I conceded.

'Dr. Graham's a real person.'

I suppose, then, that real people are generally pretty bizarre, and fallible.

Once outside, I felt better. The twelve orange pills rattled uneasily in their bottle, but the sky ignited into blue fire, and the sun's rays strutted as if to say: How could Death possibly equal this magnificence?

February 27
Things have been tumbling apart for a long time and now they can't be ignored, now that my Tuesday appointments with Dr. Hightower have disappeared. The sessions never had to be miraculous; they just had to exist. I can't talk to Dr. Graham because then he'd take away

the Rivotrils and they're my one path out of all this. The past two days have been disasters. There's very little to hang on to. I keep talking to myself out loud, a running monologue—Hang in there, you can kill yourself after you finish writing this story, after you have a good cry, after you catch up on your homework—but it halts the process only temporarily. I tried to arrange an appointment with Dr. Hightower's partner; he called back today and I just asked if Dr. Hightower had left yet, then hung up. I called the pharmacy beneath the counsellor's office to talk to the pharmacist. I said I was writing a research essay on the too-little-explored topic of teenage suicide and needed to know about the effects of the drug Rivotril. He teased me, saying he often got calls from patients upstairs who wanted to know how much of a certain drug taken would attract attention but not remove them from this world, but I was so convincing, so obviously sane. He said that ten two mg tablets would 'make you pretty spaced-out for a while' and that fifteen would probably be 'approaching a dangerous level.' Rivotril, he explained, was a fairly unknown drug, originally used to control epileptics, but it had recently been discovered as effective in psychiatry—controlling panic attacks and mood swings.

'Are you sure you're writing an essay? The world isn't coming down too hard on you?' he asked kindly.

Oh but I'm not going to take twenty mg of Rivotril to attract attention. I must hoard them, obtain another week's ration and then another. Two of them are already gone and worked well; they gave me two nights of deep sleep. Wednesday night I fell asleep naturally, exhausted, but woke up with the most intense feeling of sadness … fragments of dreams spinning into lonely wakefulness … Do you know what it's like to be sad like that? As if your best friend had just died, except the sorrow is worse because that's not what happened, because even while people are leaving you you've always been alone. Their existence kept you alive a little longer, that's all.

March 2

I took the wrong bus to a local hospital to see one of the staff psychiatrists. It stranded me in Burnaby; it was already the time of the appointment. Panic struck; the sky was a bright gray with clouds, and then it started raining.

A couple of thumbed rides brought me to the hospital. Finding the clinic shouldn't have been hard, but I circled in the downpour for half an hour, sliding on mud and grass. The rain kept coming down and I got more and more disoriented; nothing looked familiar. It was like that dream where you're trying to go somewhere totally ordinary, but the scenery has changed so you can't find it. I used to always have that dream as a kid. I'd be coming home after school on a summer day, and suddenly all the houses would change. I'd know I was walking in the right direction, and that home must be near, but how could I find it with the landmarks gone?

Finally I took a correct turn somewhere and landed in the clinic. In the bathroom mirror a teenager with dripping hair stared back at me, her cheeks an accusing red. She stayed immobile there for a while, then fell into the psychiatrist's office.

The room held a stillness that was extraordinary. The psychiatrist was a shrivelled brown man with stringy hair. I thrust my story, 'Prologue to a Therapist's Vacation,' at him, but he didn't comment on it. He stared with beady eyes and asked about my feelings; over and over I said I was stupid and inadequate, I was very depressed, why was he scrutinizing me, I hated him, my feelings were so typical they were ludicrous, he couldn't let me walk out of there in the same shape I'd walked in. He must have thought his time was being wasted because I couldn't express anything. I couldn't say how much I wanted to die and how crazy I was and how black the days had become. I couldn't cry or slit my wrists or break the office windows ... WHAT THE FUCK DID THEY EXPECT?

The psychiatrist called Dr. Hightower's partner, requesting that he see me, then stood up and expected me to leave. I felt like the worst disaster that had ever been created. God, if He existed, made the biggest mistake of His career in letting me get born. I looked at the skimpy shrunken psychiatrist.

'Isn't there anything you can do?'

'Well, I'm not authorized to give you medication. The only things anybody can do is provide you with more therapy, prescribe drugs or put you in the hospital. I think if I were giving you drugs, I'd try some phenothiazines.' Phenothiazine is a powerful tranquilizer, an antipsychotic, which is often used to treat schizophrenia.

March 5

The three of us—Dr. Graham, the social worker and I—proceeded into the worker's office. We sat in a triangle and they looked at me. I could feel a panic attack starting—they had accelerated to several times a day recently. I had had them for as long as I could remember, though they had been more sporadic before, and nameless—my hands and feet would tingle, I'd break into a sweat and feel like I couldn't get enough oxygen into my system, my mind would blank out with fear and I would be incapable of listening or sometimes even talking. Dr. Graham and the worker aggravated this with their simultaneous presence. Dr. Graham's face loomed large and uncomfortably close, while the worker watched placidly. I realized I was gripping the arms of my chair.

Dr. Graham exchanged a look with the worker. 'The panic attacks are from hyperventilation.' The worker agreed, saying I breathed even more heavily while talking about Dr. Hightower. There wasn't much else to talk about, except that I'd been having a lot of colorful dreams about living at home and being screamed at by my parents. Only I would be the one to start the fights, and my father would be doing most of the yelling. I said I had replaced my father with Dr. Hightower, and my usual behavior with anger at him for 'abandoning' me. Dr. Graham nodded, smiled and said it was a good insight.

Neither felt that medication was appropriate, though Dr. Graham wrote a prescription for twenty Rivotrils with little prodding. A sick feeling persisted in my stomach—what kind of death would it be? Now I had enough; death would be guaranteed and not tentative, as with aspirin.

Later I went to the Outreach office. Jennifer came in after me and flitted about, flinging off coats and scarves, then motioned me beside her. She had met with Melanie, and they, along with a resource worker, had agreed that if I wanted to move back to her home I'd have to remain there for six months. During those six months, if I hoped to be placed on Independent Living afterwards, I would have to go back to school full-time and demonstrate that I was 'super-together' and capable of handling my own place. Even with the doctors' letters, going back to school and behaving, it was 'still a big gamble' whether social services would approve Independent Living. In any case, once I enrolled in school and social services received the letters, then Jennifer could proceed with the lobbying, and the decision would arrive in a month. She warned that it could very likely be no. If they did agree, I'd still have to remain at Melanie's for the six-month period, and if I ran away then obviously there wasn't enough responsibility on my part. Then, too, Melanie's would become the only placement social services would approve for me.

'So if you ran away and came to me after a while, every time you came here I'd have to tell you, 'Melanie or nothing.' I know that sounds disappointing.'

The other alternative now would be to go to a group home that held six other kids. I wouldn't have to make the six-month commitment there but would still have to go back to school full-time.

I smiled at Jennifer, said I'd call on Monday and fled. I've got enough pills now. The chasm is widening, and it is entirely black and bottomless. What I'm writing now won't mean anything, ever. I've pinned too many hopes on Independent Living. Over the past six months I've more or less been stable; will that change again?

Wasn't life supposed to be a realm of choices? Wasn't that what was going to make it the growing, learning experience it's exalted to be?

I walked in the rain to the first session for depressed adolescents at a local hospital, arriving an hour late. There were a dozen kids seated around one long, rectangular table, with a social worker at one end and a psychologist at the other. Suddenly I hated them all. Would you believe how much I hated them? Their faces were young. They peeked at each other and darted out hands for the chocolate chip cookies lining the table, nibbling furtively. The psychologist limited himself to two-syllable words, and both he and the worker kept asking, 'How do you feel?' The teenagers snuck glances at each other with wide eyes, giggling and chattering about what they'd done at school: how they'd been detained at recess for whispering. Then at the end everyone spent fifteen minutes discussing what kind of food they'd like on the table at the sessions, since the government had blessed them with some extra funding.

When everyone had left I told the psychologist that the group probably wasn't going to help me.

I'm going to get drunk tonight. My head is sort of spacy, hurting. Aunt Mary's coming back tomorrow, and something will have to be done. I've never felt quite this way before; the observant part of me is astounded that it is possible for someone to feel they have nothing.

March 6

This morning the social worker at Dr. Graham's office remarked over the phone, 'I've been interviewing people for a new position here. The new staff person will work with families. Saw one of them this morning; he was from Emergency Services. Actually, you might even know him.'

'Really.' I toyed with another drink, drifting somewhere blank and buzzing.

'Michael.'

Funny how our paths keep crossing. The worker had been impressed by him; Michael wanted to leave Emergency Services' irregular shifts. The worker has to do more interviews before a decision can be made by the board, but he sounded pleased with Michael's attitude. Imagine me walking blithely off the elevator into the waiting room and smack into Mr. Caring and Concern himself.

I went to see Dr. Hightower's associate, an emaciated man like a wire hanger draped with a cream-colored turtleneck and brown corduroy suit. He's filling in for Dr. Hightower during his holiday. His hair brushed his shoulders; he had hollow cheeks and his eyes were cloudy behind spectacles. Absolutely steady eyes; I swear they didn't move at all. It was only when he smiled, his face sliced open, that he looked halfway human.

He motioned me into Dr. Hightower's office and sat down in my shrink's chair. There was no warmth in his stare as he perched a sheaf of paper on his thigh and began to take notes. The more notes he took, the faster I talked, until it became a competition and he didn't have time to look up. The doctor began to speak with agonizing slowness, his eyes unwavering; finally I asked why he was talking so slowly.

'Because you're talking too fast, and I'm trying to slow you down this way.'

He was straightforward, with little of Dr. Hightower's gentleness. He threw my own words back, reading from his notes. I sounded immature and self-centered. I would have laughed if someone else had said those things. When I talked about suicide he was annoyed that I'd be selfish enough to do it.

'From what I've heard, you're a person who cares about people, who's politically active, who wants to help other people,' he accused. I rolled my eyes. People change, don't you know? It's confusing because it seems all I do now is hate people, but caring is exhausting. It absolutely drains you, especially of anger that is justified. And men are pigs. All men, even Dr. Hightower.

The psychiatrist said I could be normal if I wanted to be, and should get outside of myself. He said bluntly that he didn't know what Hightower would do if one of his patients died: 'He gets worried even when they're sick. If you committed suicide, I don't know what he'd do. I think he'd be devastated.'

Was he saying a shrink could care? I didn't want any doctors or counsellors or social workers to be human anymore. It makes me too vulnerable. To love someone on a pedestal is fine; to love someone as they are is torturous.

March 9

Death is so close. It's just not scary anymore. What is there to be scared of? Sometimes I look around and think I'll miss this little bright world, with its sharp corners you can cut yourself on too easily, its colors and fragments of love … But I'm trapped in its policies and regulations. Things aren't panning out for me, that's all; what else is there to say?

The Rivotril had better work. If it doesn't, social services will probably render me unfit for Independent Living for emotional reasons and I'll be doubly screwed. I never thought about that before. It just makes me more certain that I have to succeed this time. Third time lucky?

There wasn't much to discuss at today's meeting about where I should live, just when to move into Melanie's and how long I should stay there. They insist on six months. I'll have to go to school before they start processing the request for Independent Living. I'm too depressed and numb to achieve that crazy, excited energy that one has before and during a suicide attempt. It's a mad spurt of adrenalin that floats you way above where anybody can catch you.

Prism International, UBC's literary magazine, has bought two of my poems, 'The Quiet Room' and 'An Autumn Photograph!' I picked up the acceptance letter gingerly and dangled it, disbelieving. That's an achievement I've spent two years waiting for, and I'm going to die? What sort of crazy thing to do is that? I must be out of my mind. Gee, any more acceptances or prizes and I might ... what?

It's unbelievable. I suppose this means I have promise, worth as a writer. It seems sacrilegious to bury that with death. I wish more and more often that I could kill myself but that the part of me that has the potential and determination of a writer would live on. It has so much to do—so many books to read, so much to write, you wouldn't believe.

March 10

Michael got the job at Dr. Graham's office!

A social worker called to congratulate me on being one of the winners of the Alberta Poetry Yearbook competition. How did he know?

'Kristin told me ... most of the people in this office know, yeah, and we were really happy.'

'So, I heard that Michael was applying for a job at Dr. Graham's,' I said, embarrassed.

'Yeah! He got it! Do you want to talk to him? He's right here, at the desk beside mine.' It was like they were a family there or something, all sitting together in the glow of their offices. I missed them.

Michael grabbed one of the lines and his voice came over the phone. Musical, an unusual voice, sort of wimpy. Things change ... feelings. He asked a lot of questions; it's been six months since our last conversation. I told him things were going well—we all need to pretend sometimes; I do it a lot. Otherwise nobody would talk to me. Things haven't been going bad at all, on the outside: I've been stable, have a tutor, go to a short-story class at night school, am hoping for Independent Living and so might go back to school full-time. Michael's looking forward to starting at Dr. Graham's the week after next, to do family counselling. 'He's good at that,' another worker had said. Yep, hands clasped between knees, nice green eyes, smile—what more could you want?

March 11

Just to prove what pigs men are: In our writing class, there's this one guy who looked caring and sensitive, and tonight he joined me and this other woman who was going to give me a ride home.

The first thing he said was, 'Did you see that hooker standing outside this campus?'

'Oh?' He sounded so enthusiastic.

'Yeah!' He was smiling a wide, boyish smile. 'Did you see her? She had this skirt on that was way up to here, and she looked great in it.'

The point is that I had created this nice little fantasy about him—that he was artistic and creative, with potential—and those were the only words we exchanged.

Lately I've been having a tremendous sense of unreality—nothing matters, nothing has any substance. I have to reach out and touch something to make sure I'm still here, and even then it doesn't feel concrete. I step back in my mind and look about me, notice little things about this world I hadn't noticed before. How mundane they are; death could hardly be less exciting. Also I've been getting spells of déjà vu that are pretty intense, transporting me back into certain scenes or memories of people. It's like a perfume that evokes a past event; it's like being back there. You know what they say about your whole life flashing before your eyes before death? It's happening like that, except in slow motion. My world is suspended in a state of flux, and I've let most things go. What's the point of doing anything now? Although I hope to manufacture a few more pieces of writing first, and do some volunteer work for Amnesty International.

March 12

I have never wanted death as much as I do now. I want it lasciviously; I crave it; I need to get away from this world. I need to get away! It presses closer and closer, preparing to choke me. Dear God, when I take the pills make it be the last time. Either way you can't win, you know. If you're too sensitive, you can't survive; if you're not too sensitive, you can't write.

I think I'm hysterical. Is this better than being depressed? Times like

this everything looks bright, like with acid; things take on a round-
ness. There is no point to life. Here we are, these trivial scurrying creatures called human beings, searching for some meaning to our
existence, yet there is none.

Trapped. Things rush back at me, old memories, days, parts of my
life. Everything has been cut into small squares of wall, which are
pressing in from all sides. There is nothing. Try to comprehend. Try
to see what is happening. Nothing is three-dimensional. Everything is
translucent. The floor can hardly support me, even when I sit down
hard on it ... Oh God, I can't even write. The shelves here in this
kitchen are white and round; they bulge forward, curve. Distorted,
candy-colorful. The stove stretches wide and matronly, a stuffed stove,
a fat mother in her apron ...

God I've just gone crazy. I had an appointment with Dr. Graham
today but didn't go because I thought, therapy sucks; the more I go
the crazier I get; why not just forget about it? Shrinks screw me up
more than I can screw myself up. I rely on them too much and as a
consequence explore and analyze myself too much, thus getting
involved in my problems and less with the outside world. So I didn't
go. Then I began to panic in the afternoon, but by then everybody in
the office had already left ... evading me. Everything keeps evading me.

Tonight I was on the couch and began to write, listing different
ways to go about getting my own place. It is a fucking OBSESSION! It
goes on and on and on. I was very logical, pretending I had the money
and budgeting with it. When people have asked what if Independent
Living isn't the answer, I've said, 'Well, then I'll let you stick me in a
mental hospital for the rest of my life.' I wasn't being totally facetious,
either. My own apartment might not be the cure to most of my problems, but I'm betting it would. If anybody would just give me a
chance! Why isn't Dr. Graham writing his letter? Why does he pretend
to be magnificent and human, and extend hopes so carelessly?

Six months of therapy and no further with my parents. I called
them tonight. During the conversation with my father I suddenly got
weak-kneed and it hit me, just like that: WHAT IF EVERYBODY IN THE
WORLD IS AS ROTTEN AS MY PARENTS? WHAT IF? That's the most
impossible thought to entertain, but why else am I starting to dislike
people this much? Why doesn't somebody tell me what's happening.

My mother screamed in the background and at first I was able to handle it, but then it got worse and I couldn't stand it. They would pay for my own place only if I pass math, don't go out at night, study hard and get A's and B's in the other subjects. Why am I taking that so hard? I'm so bloody unrealistically sensitive. What's wrong with my head? What did my parents do to me, if anything? My mother screaming, my father lecturing and criticizing my existence ... But what if there's nothing wrong with that? I can't stand it. Those pieces of the wall are cutting into me now, drawing out evil things. Oh God, please help me. Please get me away from here!

March 14

There is so much that I still dare to want to change. Everywhere I turn there is somebody who is innocent, who is doing good and who is being crucified for it.

I see myself going nowhere, running constantly, wishing to hide in a different personality, behind a different mask. Moving, but in circles. Trying to run away from life and from its eyesores that only the truly brave can face and attempt to change. It will go on and on: somebody being battered by rain down on Skid Row, on any street in any city, and people walking by. You give up after a while or else you go crazy.

Some people do beautiful things, once or twice in their lives, and create something for somebody else—a freedom, a glimmer of hope. Each of us measures happiness differently. If all of us could just be brought down to the lowest rung of existence, wouldn't we understand better what happiness is about?

Another move. Barren walls. Going nowhere, leaving behind (now it seems, as it does each time) everything. The ashtray sitting lonely on the windowsill, smeared with ashes. The closet with one T-shirt hanging. Suitcases and backpacks waiting for morning.

I want to do something good in this world. I want a life for myself, a life not chosen at random and too easily disposed of, but a life that will create something concrete for people. It isn't enough just to have visions but nothing in my hands to give.

I don't know how to live reasonably. I don't know how to stop from being hurt at the most insignificant things, from being overresponsive to people, except by shutting and locking doors firmly, checking them twice to make sure no one can penetrate. How does one manage?

I want people to be good to each other, but I don't know how to begin changing anything because I myself can barely cope with other people and with being alive.

March 15

The Chinese have a superstition: Hail is the sign of bad luck to come. When Melanie drove me away, it was hailing. The sky, pouting with clouds, spat derogatorily on the windshield. The streets were riddled with bullets; woodpeckers tapped busily at the puddles.

No goodbye to Aunt Mary; she crawled back into her shell, and her last words were, 'Shut the gate behind you.' Her silence. I felt a tenderness, a regret and a guilt for leaving. You might say I'm repeating the act of running away from home over and over. Sad this time, as though I were leaving a sanctuary, irretrievable. Something silent and clean, something that had been my very own for five weeks. It is the same now as when I went there first, except there are more smears on the walls, pen marks on the cushions. My bedroom is once more a room with covers tucked around the bed and covered in plastic. At the head of the bed are three stuffed animals again, wrapped in plastic also. Mummified.

March 25

Dr. Hightower didn't look rested; his face had gone a shade darker, lending him a vaguely menacing appearance. His eyes were alive but less hazy; perhaps he hadn't been crying as much. I had survived his absence, and now he was back.

I dutifully asked about his vacation, and he said that he'd spent two weeks adjusting to being a person again and another week worrying about coming back to work. 'I need a vacation.' He smiled briefly and obscurely, and asked me about the past month.

Surely by now the titles of the texts on his bookshelf have been committed to my memory. During a session it is easier to face straight ahead and pretend one is talking to the air, to the wall or to the object in one's line of vision—in this case, the bookshelf. Psychology texts, bunched together, a few of the spines sticking out like crooked elbows. When a difficult issue is being examined, I stare at the titles fervently. If I come in one week and a few of the books have been rearranged, withdrawn or replaced by others, it becomes quite disturbing. The bookcase is as much my psychiatrist as Dr. Hightower; it is after all what I talk to.

About fifteen minutes into the session I wanted to leave, extraordinary for someone who gouges into every minute of her therapy, digging her nails into the hour as though it were her one and only connection to life. My calm was dismantled only when love for this doctor flooded impossibly over me. It is such a pain, loving or even caring about someone; I've been eliminating those people from my life.

So there was Dr. Hightower. The last person left. I sketched my feelings of the past month, asking for the hundredth time for antidepressants. They were more than justified. Dr. Hightower didn't want to prescribe medication under any circumstances, though, and he kept insisting that the depression was circumstantial, that he could list a dozen reasons for it. What if it is even a little biological? Isn't there something I can take? I would even opt for major tranquilizers; they're better than feeling like this. But he said that one of the most effective ways of committing suicide was by overdosing on antidepressants. That's useful information, but irrelevant right now.

I took the plunge and asked if any of his patients had died on him. Yes, he said, and it had been painful; he'd wondered if there was anything he could have done, or should have done, if he could have stopped them somehow. I knew he meant it, but it didn't matter. I wanted to spare him that, not out of any compassion, but because it was unnecessary. It didn't seem proper for him to care so much. If I could do it over again I wouldn't have started therapy; maybe I'd have isolated myself completely, contaminating no one.

I told him I thought that it would be a good idea for us to terminate; he disagreed. Dr. Hightower insisted on keeping our upcoming appointments and hoping I'd show up. While I was adamant during the session about the advantages of discontinuing therapy (after all, nothing was happening; I didn't have anything to talk about), his availability was disconcerting. How to resist the Tuesdays? I'm collecting more sleeping pills from Dr. Graham next week. How hard it would be to paddle and flounder through the days, to give up even an imagined salvation. But I want to disengage Dr. Hightower from me; he mustn't think in any way that he should have done something differently. The only way to absolve him from this is to make that break, to paw out a gulf between us and become totally responsible for myself. If I don't see him, there would be nothing he could have done.

I went to the Zen Center and meditated. The quiet filled a purpose of sorts. The living room and dining room of the house had been opened into one space, carpeted golden brown; the air, smoky with incense, was almost tangible.

Six of us participated in the zazen, or 'sitting meditation.' This consisted of twenty-five minutes of meditation, five minutes of walking, twenty-five minutes of meditation, five minutes of walking, twenty-five minutes of meditation, five minutes of chanting and bowing. Holding one position for almost an hour and a half was torture. We were supposed to keep our eyes half open, regarding the carpet through slits, but I closed them often, drifting into inertia, concentrating on the pain in my crossed legs. My mind wandered and attempted to focus on Dr. Hightower in order to release him, but his name had been buried and would not come forward. My singular thought concerning him was that he was reliable, an okay person, so why stop seeing him? The contentment of this thought flowed in and out with my breathing. The monk had dimmed the lights and the air swam in a soup of gold. Across the room were three still, black-clothed figures. Dazed but curious, I widened my eyes and cautiously examined them, not as a whole but as sharply defined individuals.

The five-minute walking meditation consisted of following one another and weaving circles around the room. We were idealists trying to unite the world; we thought we could make peace and happiness with the circles of our hands and arms. The robes of the man behind me brushed against my ankles, soothing.

After the chant, we sat around a small Japanese table and drank tea. I was far more relaxed, more clear, although nothing had been resolved. Perhaps the meditation had buried things further, obscured them entirely. That wasn't so bad, if it were true.

Dr. Hightower's pull is too strong to resist. 'I won't abandon you,' he had said cleverly. 'You can't stop me from caring about you.' He cares too much about people for those words to be false.

March 27

It all began with hitchhiking. After a few minutes of standing on the curb, I heard a small voice peck from behind me. 'Where're you going? I'll take you there.'

A woman sprang out of the corner of my eye. She was short and sparrow-thin, with thick brown hair terminating in split ends around her shoulders. She had a wide smile and what struck me as enormous eyes, but that was because her face was too thin, unable to accommodate her features.

She was going to Mission. I said I'd accompany her there; it was a long drive through the clear, hard darkness. We swam in shadow along the highways. She needed somebody anonymous to talk to, somebody who would absorb at least a little of her pain. She told me her life story, talking nonstop the whole way to Mission.

When she dropped me off, I got back on the highway towards Vancouver and an East Indian man picked me up. He was in his twenties, well-built and good-looking, with a smooth face and neat moustache. He initiated a conversation about sex, and by the time we'd reached the main highway he had asked me several times to sleep with him and received no for an answer. He pointed out how late it was getting and that I'd be welcome to stay at his place for the night, in a spare bedroom. I agreed, after a while.

On the way back K. bemoaned his dilemma. He wanted to 'get his rocks off' before going to bed, but if I wasn't going to suck or jerk him off, what was he going to do? One of his girlfriends was waiting for him at home but would freak out if he brought me back.

We pondered this, I with amusement and he with apparent anguish, while driving around the outskirts of Mission. The sky gleamed, littered with stars. I advised him to tell the truth, that he'd picked me up hitching and because it was late decided to bring me home. He countered that his girlfriend was very possessive and would storm out, and that the one solution would be for me to meet him halfway by at least jerking him off.

'What's the big deal? It's only your hand.'

How can I explain the revulsion? I asked if he had any coke at his place, since he'd done a few lines before coming out.

'Sure. Only it'll have to be afterwards, because I have to get rid of her first.'

Gullible Evelyn who still sometimes, once in a long while, believes in people and looks for warmth and compassion in them, jerked him off, and not five minutes later he dumped me off at a gas station and when I turned around he was gone and I was in the middle of nowhere.

It's been too long to still feel betrayed and abandoned by humanity at every little incident. It's just a game, really. An unfair one, but you learn after each spill to understand it for what it is and go on from there. Otherwise it'll eat away at you and you'll be destroyed.

The cashier wouldn't let me inside the station. He gestured at the sign that forbade entrance after midnight and, looking uncomfortable, scurried back into the bowels of his store like a startled animal retreating into its burrow.

There was a bench around the corner. I straddled it and looked about, resting for a moment and dismissing the greedy cold. The crisscross of highways swam uneasily, as if they didn't know their destination.

'Missed your bus?'

A man emerged from the shadows where he'd parked his car. The fluorescent lights cast a pallor over his ruddy features. His eyes were hard but curious.

'No, I was hitchhiking back to Vancouver, but my ride made me jerk him off and then dumped me out here.' I surprised myself with this honesty. There it was, the reality of my life imprisoned in that one sentence.

The man considered me with a smiling curiosity in his eyes; he seemed to like my answer. 'Okay, kid, I'll take you as far as Pitt Meadows. It's better than sitting outside in the cold.'

We got into his car and nosed out onto the tangle of highways. In the soupy light I saw that he had dark brown, bristly hair, a moustache, curling lips and nostrils that flared obnoxiously. His features were crude and unapologetic.

The car lapped up the gray sheen of the highway, an endless thread that blurred and wavered in front of me. I told him my story through yawns. The driver grunted with apparent lack of interest, but just as I leaned my head against the window and prepared to go to sleep, he started talking.

'Yeah, I was a real messed-up kid too. I was moved around from group home to group home, and by the time I was fifteen I was a junkie and busy selling my ass downtown. So you're in a foster home, and you like drugs. They give you ten dollars a week there? All right, if you can survive on ten bucks a week, fine, but I personally have never met anyone who could. So you've got a choice—either you hustle, or you forget the drugs and anything else you want and go back to school.

'Some girls think they're sitting on a bloody gold mine. False pretensions. But they can MAKE it into a gold mine. I might sound cold and callous, but at least I'm not playing games. I've gone through the whole ten yards. I've slept with a lot of people in my life—banged a lot of pussy, sucked the occasional cock. It all depends if you think you can become a part of that scene, how much of it you can take. It's like any other job—you want to be good at it so that when you're on that corner people will come to you and give you money for your services. Who's to say that's right or wrong? If you want to get what you want in life, you have to make it an obsession, and you have to do whatever you have to to get there. Later when you look back there's no shame, there's none of that shit. It's all water under the bridge, what you did to get there.

'You've been on the streets for how long now—a year? And you haven't really gotten into hooking yet? You should know people pretty well by now, darling. If you don't now, you'll never learn. So people aren't what you thought they would be. Nothing ever is. But you do what you have to to survive, because sad as it sounds, this world is made up of dollars and cents. People grab what they can from strangers, every little bit. Instead of working at a four-dollar-an-hour job, you can make fifty, sixty, seventy dollars for a twenty-minute poke, you know what I mean?

'You've just got to make a choice or you're sunk. You can't go through life with morals, prying every little thing open, analyzing and dissecting it, 'cause then when you get down to the nitty gritty it stinks, it's not worth Jack Shit. You've wrecked it. You just have to let each situation come, and deal with it. Treat sex as a purely physical thing. That's all it is—a business exchange, a physical act for money. It's not a big invasion, you can't say, 'Oh, you're touching my body, you're a creep.' People all have their wants and needs, and if you can supply those, well, then you've got it made.

'I'm not telling you to go downtown and sell your ass. I'm just telling you these are the choices you've got to live with, and you better make one soon. If you want to get an education instead while living in a foster home on ten dollars a week, then fine, go through six or seven years of school, if you think you can handle it. But if you like your drugs and, as you say, want your own place, and you want to get these things as fast as you can, then you'll have to hustle.

'I go downtown now and pay my money and get my ladies, because I'm only human. I deal coke. And everything's fine. I don't fall in love, I don't get emotionally involved with anybody. I've been in love before and it hurts too much. You go through too much pain and you get too fucked up. When I make love to a hooker downtown, I make love to an illusion. I don't let myself get emotionally involved anymore.

'You're young still, you've got lots of time. Sex is only a part of life. I never hated any of the johns who screwed me when I was a kid; they helped me get where I am now. After a while I found that a few of them kept coming back. And then I found that we were spending more time rapping than we were screwing. Then they became people. But they had to be objects first—you can't have it the other way around.

'All the people I identify with are street people. I don't know anybody else because people who are straight hide behind false values, and I'm sick of that; there's no time to play those games. The street is where it's at for me, that's where I understand people and they understand me, we each get what we need and go our separate ways. I'm satisfied now. I've got everything I want. But in order to get where I am today, I had to go through hell. In order to find heaven or happiness, first you have to fuck the Devil.'

A nudge, and I saw we were on the Trans-Canada Highway close to Vancouver. It was 3 a.m. and there was little traffic. I got out, his words heavy inside me. He had been more practical and straightforward than anyone I'd ever met. I stood, looking down; through the mixture of light and dark his expression came close to warmth.

'What will you do?'

He lifted his shoulders. 'Go drive around for a while, then maybe head downtown and get myself a lady.' He smiled wryly. 'You've talked and been with an old perv for long enough. If you don't go, I might do a whole bunch of things to you that you wouldn't like.'

And with that, God left me stranded on the Trans-Canada Highway.

He had explained it all and I had understood. I'd been floundering for too long, postponing choices, running away, hoping naively for something better. But nothing was going to get better.

It was black; sky and earth were indistinguishable. I walked and waited, the bundle of his words inside my chest. He had been right. I had to make a choice about my life, based on what I could handle.

The man who picked me up next was maybe seventy years old. He had a shrunken body and a face like putty that had been sitting in the sun for too long. He was drunk. We weaved back and forth along the highway, and in Vancouver we stopped and made a deal. He pressed a button so that his seat fell back, undid his pants and murmured, 'I love it ... I love it ...' while I jerked him off. I smiled and looked into his eyes, knowing it was all right. It was purely physical, my hand and his penis; he wasn't stealing my soul, and that was what I'd feared for so long, that I would lose myself doing this. But even if I did, it wouldn't make any difference, because things couldn't get any worse. Nobody could punish me more than I had already punished myself.

He grabbed my head and shoved my face down on his cock, but that too was all right because he was old, drunk and helpless. His skin was as smooth as a baby's. In five minutes I had made an easy twenty dollars, and when he came onto my hand I wiped it off on the seat of his car.

April 5

Every movement is an earthquake. So these are the ups and downs again. The downs delve far beneath the surface. A blind date with death. It's not a crime to be high and then low; it's the in-between nothing that's bad.

I spent a couple of weeks getting together two short story entries into the Burnaby Arts Council high school competition. The film of life has been set on slow motion. It takes a day to lick the stamp on the envelope. Another day to find out that the government has raised the price of postage by two cents. Two more days to buy a two-cent stamp. And so far a whole weekend to locate a mailbox.

Every movement is an occasion, an avalanche crashing. My head feels like a sack full of rocks. Why should I be disappointed that there's no mail when it takes as much psyching up for me to write a letter as to write a final exam?

This can't be very interesting. But lots of people get born and die and lead unremarkable lives in between. I meet them on the street every day; they are looking for something, something to alter the truth of their lives. I'm going to roll myself a joint, enough journal scribbling for a year.

April 10

It's one of those days where I'm in love with everybody, and almost with life. But it's dangerous—every time I've entrusted myself to someone, they've screwed me around. Maybe my expectations are too high. Maybe I'm associating with the wrong people, people who have few values. But where could I fit in, without putting up a front? Should I go back to school, giggle in the washrooms, checking to see if every strand of my hair is in place, talk in rapt whispers about clothes and boys and s-e-x? Should I dive into politics again, bearing scarlet banners through the streets, yelling obscure Marxist slogans at the passersby?

Got stoned before going to the Zen Center last night and smiled dazedly at my friend Roy, who was already there. During the first sit I was still high; time expanded and swallowed me. The giggles were irrepressible during the walking meditation—I hobbled around the room, interrupting the sacred mood.

When it was over I was down and would have run out of the house if I'd realized then that there were four men around the table and no women except me. I was a silent river with grains of sand running smoothly in it. I was calm and deep. We got into the topic of sex; one man asked why women were allowed to meditate with men, or become monks, since they created a distraction. This woke me up enough to retort that the whole aim of meditation was to merge into a whole, not be separated as males and females. Roy shot out that the man wasn't putting women down.

After tea I hurtled down the steps of the Zen Center, burnt out and feeling horizontal with the sidewalk. Roy was behind me, peering with mock concern into my face. We started walking, and he apologized for snapping at me about what the man had said about women, conceding that the guy had been aggressive. He agreed that any sexual urges that emerged during meditation should be accepted rather than suppressed and that one should continue from there. He added that he'd gone through a period during the zazen where he'd felt turned on by me and had let it pass.

I was vaguely triumphant that he felt something for me but also confused. Roy reminded me of Michael, and that was where the questions began: Michael, you're a social worker, you're not supposed to feel this for me ... And maybe Michael becomes a bit defiled in the process, because he's superhuman, devoid of something as base as sex.

We had a few drinks downtown; momentary waves of longing and love swept over me, but were they only for somebody who was faultless, who could save the world? Roy had morals, at least—he said he was sexually attracted to me but would never come on to me unless I started it, in which case he'd try to refuse but likely couldn't.

The room was getting dizzy. A rose-colored flush crept up Roy's cheeks. 'You know something?' he said impulsively. 'I like you.'

We left around 1:30 a.m. and walked back to Granville Street, under an umbrella in the rain. I felt warm and loved and buoyant. He was close to me, and I accepted him then for who he was, for who he might be.

I took the bus up to Broadway, then stopped. I'd decided to turn a trick, because I couldn't even afford a pack of cigarettes, and what could a kid do except steal, deal or trick? Out on Broadway, in the rain, thumb out. A sadness in the downpour, in the night. Two guys picked me up and we went to their place in Kitsilano, smoking a couple of joints and drinking. I got really out of it. The living room spun, spun.

I forgot I had to work. It was 3:30 a.m. I showed the younger guy, M., some of my writing, which I carried with me; he turned around, looked at me and said, 'This is GREAT!' The way he said it was so fucking beautiful. The two men wanted sex, but they began to respect me as a person after a while, especially M., so it was all right.

April 19

At Melanie's there is a fire in the fireplace, flames licking and sputtering. I begin talking to her about my parents—the fights, their blows, living at home. I think of Michael and the others who tried to help but could not find one gigantic bruise or one long scar they could point to triumphantly and say, 'This is what they did to her, take her away.' No, it was much more insidious. My parents screamed and hit me when I cried. My mother couldn't deal with the possibility that for just one minute, one minute of my existence, I might have no more homework, nothing to study, no more chores to do—a minute of my own. There was never that. If after five hours I had done my homework inside out, then for two more I would have to study for some future test that would never materialize. If that was over, I would spend another hour hunched over the piano. And if by then it wasn't late at night and therefore bedtime, well there were always kitchen floors to be swept and washed, dishes to be done, carpets to be vacuumed ...

The fire dies out. Melanie goes to bed. I struggle with a sleeping pill that at last tumbles into my stomach. Approaching reality.

April 21

On Broadway, watching the traffic. It's early yet, Monday evening, men coming back from work, looking for a piece of some woman and not realizing that sometimes they take all of her.

The guy is thirty years old, driving a van, has a childishly cute face, a moustache, brown curls and an easy smile. We talk, and he likes me. I know he will be gentle and flattering.

Here we go. There's even a mattress in the back of his van. He wriggles out of his jeans, sprawls there waiting. I laugh away the tension that rises, putting my mouth to his penis, sucking it, feeling it grow hard.

No, I will not throw up over him.

His mouth covers mine, tongue exploring, hands pulling clothes up and down. His prick probes into my throat, but somehow with great control I force down the nausea. Licking, sucking, holding his balls, licking his balls, holding the cock that is thrusting and thrusting.

'You're beautiful,' he exclaims, over and over. 'You should be a model. Or at least a dancer.' I can't help laughing, wondering what he's seeing.

It's an endurance test for me—how long can Evelyn keep going without puking. I imagine I'm in my P.E. class at school, doing sit-ups. Just keep going, keep going, soon the stopwatch will buzz, soon you can collapse gasping against the wall and collect a decent mark for your performance.

It's over. Come spatters back onto his stomach. He gives me a huge hug; I like hugs. We feel our way back to the front of the van, smoke a joint together. He takes out a battered wallet and shows me pictures of his family—his wife's teenage son from a previous marriage, their little daughter with a dimpled chin like her father's and the same cute curls. His wife is holding her, smiling into the camera, a good-looking woman in a suit. She used to want sex 'after work, before dinner, after dinner, at bedtime. Now it's only once on Sundays, and out of duty at that. We've been married ten years. Marriage hasn't cracked up to be what they say it is.'

He drops me off at the youth newspaper house, where there's a newspaper meeting in progress. Tommy opens the door with a big smile, hugs me joyfully. I hang on to him, feeling the strength and love in his body. He lets me go but holds on to my hands for a moment, and I don't want the moment to end. I grab both his hands, almost crying, 'Tommy, I just turned a trick, I hate it, please hold on to me,' but with some bewilderment he pulls his hands out of mine and hurries into the kitchen to answer the phone, and Don and other people are watching, waiting, and Tommy's gone, and finally with total sadness I realize it's not my right to tell him this or to demand his comfort.

April 22

Walking to the corner. A man in a blue Cadillac leans sideways to inspect me walking slow. Will he come back? I reach the corner and wait, and he does, rolling down the window.

'Hi.'

'Hi. Are you working?'

I smile through the night. For the first time, instead of hopping into the car and letting the driver initiate (or not), I lean forward and say, 'Want some good head tonight?'

Evelyn?

Into the car. The guy is French Canadian, from Montreal. I strike up an earnest conversation, my one protection against getting hurt. He used to be a drug dealer, although he eventually quit drugs, booze and even cigarettes. Sex is his remaining addiction. We talk about how hookers get hurt, and he says he respects women too much to ever hurt them. When he goes downtown he only picks up native girls because often they need the money, and not to support a cocaine habit. He fantasizes often about Oriental women and that was why he picked me up. He only cruises the street to look for head, because his girlfriends won't do it for him.

He insisted on looking for a quiet, romantic spot, so we chose somewhere around Jericho Beach. It was a few minutes past my curfew; I was relaxed and less abashed. Maybe I was right, maybe it does get easier every time.

It was cool; the guy didn't even touch me. He told me calmly how he wanted his blow job done, and I obliged. He was undemanding. I did what satisfied him; he handed over paper towels so I could wipe my hands off, and drove me home.

It was all right. He'll look for me again on Broadway. I wonder what part of me is so stubborn and so disgusted that it would insist on insomnia afterwards, then dreams filled with rows of penises waiting to be sucked on.

April 24

Main and Hastings. It is evening, just before the Zen meditation. I look around for somebody to save me, but nobody sees anything wrong. The man who picks me up is past middle age and overweight, driving a Cadillac. He's wearing a gold watch and belt. I ask for thirty dollars for head and he laughs in my face.

'I get head for ten dollars in this part of town.'

I shudder thinking of the girls in the downtown eastside, mostly native, turning tricks for whatever the john will give them. Hiding my contempt, I try talking to the guy, persuading him, but he is rude. Finally I tell him to let me out.

But now he's horny, will go for more money if he can shove his hairy knuckles in me. I've already said no. He argues, 'My hands are clean. See? Fuck. You're supposed to be selling love, not hatred.'

The laughter wells up bitter. 'No,' I try to explain. 'I'm not selling love. Love can't be bought or sold—how can you say that? Can't you understand?'

Evelyn.

It's over his head though. He lets me out with an angry, 'Fuck it.'

Zen meditation, the monk's voice echoing in the chambers of my mind. Tears ooze out of my eyes. I can't stop the sadness crouching in me. Together with these people in one room, each of us meditating— but separate. I have lost the will to merge with them. How could they know what is happening, how could they be expected to share it? Or even to understand. Watching their faces, I realize that expecting even one of them to help me is too much.

Roy, my friend from the Zen Center, and I meet on Commercial Drive afterwards for coffee and talk. He shrugs nonchalantly at what I'm doing, telling me that it is a joke that I think I'm superior to my customers.

'You're no better than they are. Nobody's asking you to stand on that corner; it's your choice. You're providing those men with the service. No one's forcing you to do this, Evelyn. You're selling yourself; they're buying it. It's just two sides of the same coin.' He reaches into his pocket and tosses a nickel into the air in front of my eyes.

All my brain cells scream to ignore or deny what Roy is saying, but then it sinks in that he is right. The possibility has never struck me before; I'd always assumed that the men were the evil, disgusting crea- tures, that they were the ones hurting women, and especially prosti- tutes. But the money I earned on the street wasn't for basic survival anymore, so who was I to call myself pure?

In that one moment I realized that I was trash. I was a slut.

To be considered one and the same as the men who picked me up was for me the last straw.

I beg Roy to let me stay at his place for a while, knowing that otherwise I will turn a trick because Broadway pulls at me like a drug addiction. Never has anything been harder to understand.

* * *

Running up the steps after a night's work. Banging the door, kicking my shoes off, stomping into my bedroom. Melanie screaming, 'STOP!' and inside something wilts and dies and echoes, yes, stop, please, someone, stop all this.

Emerging out of a sleeping-pill sleep, dreams of rows of men's faces, different features and nationalities, moving past in an assembly line. Some pop out and beckon, and I willingly follow.

I pass a young prostitute on the street exuding perfume, wrapped in white. I wonder how she goes on. Men are leering and examining her. Sitting downtown, smoking and watching the drug activity—lots of people peddling LSD and of course hash. 'Hash?' they breathe from the corners of their mouths; sometimes it comes out: 'Husssh.' Hush, world, stop this. Stop! Watching the wheeling and dealing.

* * *

The worst thing happens on Broadway in the sunny afternoon. Women going by in high heels and long bare legs. Men looking, though the wait is long, longer, longest. I am becoming more frustrated, my thoughts and emotions are pounding their fists inside me, fighting to get out. I cannot stand this, and yet I am standing here.

A blue-gray van slides to a stop. I can't see the driver because the passenger window is broken, replaced by a sheet of plastic. I open the door. The man inside looks like Michael. So much, like you couldn't imagine—the expression on his face, the decency, the desire to help, the cleanliness. I stare at him, a part of me hot and irritated that I've been waiting and haven't made any money.

'Do you need a ride? To Granville?'

Unbidden, the proposition flew out of my mouth as I continued to absorb that beautiful face. 'Into some head this afternoon?'

'What?' He hadn't heard me. I had been given a second chance. 'I can drop you off on Granville.'

'You want some head this afternoon?' Oh my God, my tongue has a mind of its own while the rest of me continues staring at him, hoping my eyes are conveying something better than the cheap slutty words issuing from my mouth. Sinking and sinking ...

Immediately he understands. Unlike any other man that has stopped, there is no hesitation, no consideration, no is-this-too-much-money or will-she-give-me-what-I-want. While I continue looking at him, mute, he says, 'No, thank you.'

The words come without a change of expression on his face. No anticipation, no judgment, no mockery. He looks back quietly—as though I were still a human being.

I want to say 'Don't leave me here. You're the first decent man I've met, please,' but in despair I hear myself say, 'Well, bye then,' in a disgusted voice, then watch as my hands slam the door shut.

He drives away.

Tears try to battle their way out of my eyes, right there on Broadway. I want to die. There isn't anything to live for; I cannot get out of prostitution.

A man in his thirties, in a suit, picks me up. He's in the computer business. He's only got ten dollars. I remember how just yesterday I'd recoiled in sympathy and horror at the idea of girls in the downtown eastside selling head for ten bucks, but as we drive along I find myself saying yes.

Into an underground parking lot. He takes himself out; I begin sucking. His fingers probe as far and as hard as they will into my ass. The guy comes in less than a minute; I am unprepared when he exclaims, 'I'm coming' and forces my head down on his penis. I jerk up abruptly and he utters a strangled cry of fury and helplessness as—though he immediately grabs his prick with both hands—come spurts over his underwear and onto his pants.

He is furious. I cower in my seat, making sure the money is in my bra and the knife in my bag within reach. I think he is going to hit me, but instead, after he's cleaned up, he says in a deadly voice, 'Would you mind getting out of the car?' I split.

What is happening? My head is fucked up. It's not like I need the money desperately; besides, I know how the money was made and loathe it. Believe me, prostitution is the worst sort of hell; there is no way you can convince yourself you're even human anymore.

April 26

Saturday morning yesterday, the annual Walk for Peace. I wake up
early, but not to join the throngs of marchers.

Out on Broadway, in the brilliant sunshine. The traffic is heavy, but
nearly every car going past is full of families or couples. The buses are
loaded with the peace marchers. Friends had called me several days
ago, hoping I would help organize a youth demonstration inside the
Walk because they felt that young people weren't being represented
properly. They also felt that the Walk was apathetic, and that there
were larger issues at stake such as discrimination against women,
racism, etc. I agreed perfectly, but I no longer felt comfortable with
politically active people. I belonged on Broadway more than at the
Walk for Peace.

The dazzle of the daylight is sickening. There's no business here. I
even move to the downtown eastside, looking for a cheap trick, but
the streets are spilling with Chinatown shoppers, and among the shuffle of cars and passersby I am lost.

My head is packaged wool; after a while I go home. The exhaustion
of just standing there is incredible. The struggles that are tied into
hooking for me are enormous; my thoughts churn like crazy all day,
and there is no time or energy left for anything else. Even writing in
this journal doesn't feel right anymore.

I go home and rest for a while, commanding the sky to hurry up
and darken, the peace marchers to return to their apathetic lives, the
shoppers to settle down to their meals. Saturday night creeps forward.
I start dressing, and for the very first time dress unmistakably as a
hooker.

Drowning the bedroom in music, and myself in perfume, I climb
into shimmering purple Spandex tights and a thin sleeveless top that
wraps around my hips. The other foster kid gawks at this change and
gives me a pair of white heels that don't fit her. Feverishly I do my hair
and face, grab my bag and totter into the living room.

Melanie's eyes pop out, but she gives me the benefit of the doubt.
'Are those your clothes?'

'Yeah, except these are the other kid's shoes.'

'I've never seen you dressed like this before. Are you going to a
party?'

'No.' I can't look at her. She knows I'm going to work.

'You don't even look like the same person.'

Staunchly I march out into the evening. I feel exposed and glittering. I am confused, and my mind is so overwhelmed that it thinks maybe nothing is wrong.

A curious thing happens when the bus comes. Watching it stop, I wonder for a split second if the driver will let me on, knowing I'm a prostitute. The sudden degradation is tremendous. The passengers stare as I find a seat near the back entrance; there are no more seats on the bus except the one beside me, yet the people that file on ignore it. The man who eventually sits down hesitates, standing and approaching, then stopping, then sitting and shivering. I want to put my arms around him and console him, chase the cold away. Two boys hopping onto the bus grab the seats behind me, and to my horror I hear one of them saying, 'No, she's not,' and then the other laughing knowingly, 'Yes, she's a hooker,' and afterwards when I turn around they are staring at me.

* * *

I walked back out to Broadway at the end of the evening, towards the nearest bus stop, knowing I was too drunk to work any more that night. I hadn't taken more than three steps before an old, ugly man in a silver van stopped and wanted me to trick him. I climbed in, but after we'd driven around for awhile I said I couldn't do it; the motion of the car was too much, tossing me like driftwood in a raging sea, over and over and over.

'No,' he whined, 'no,' as I lurched out of the car. We were near Broadway and Fraser. I staggered a few steps in the semidarkness. Two men passed, looking at me. They said sympathetically, 'You'll make it through the night, baby.'

On the inner edge of the sidewalk there was a high curb that dipped down in front of a store. I swayed, looking down at the curb, wondering if I could step over and sit there. Somehow it was possible, and I put my head onto my shimmering knees and cried.

There was nothing romantic about it. I was crying because I was too drunk and it didn't feel good. And there were too many women out there; I couldn't help them. There were so many men, they all thought I was a hooker, and most unbelievably of all I was a hooker. A man came up to me. He was maybe in his forties, not too tall, wearing a black leather jacket. He said his name was Hank. I thought he was going to proposition me too, but instead he put an arm around me and asked what was wrong. He said that he would help, that I should not be working, that it would soon be all over. Through my sobs I mumbled that he shouldn't be seeing me this way, that there were lots of kids like this and I should be the one helping them instead of him. My emotions were too strong for words. I needed him so badly to understand, to understand that even through my drunkenness and shame I was strong and capable of helping others.

Hank went off, presumably to call a cab. He stopped another man to stay with me. Somebody was shouting from behind; the old guy in the van was back; he had the passenger door open and was actually waving money in his fist, yelling, 'See, I got the money. See, I got the money,' and in the futility of it all I just muttered, 'No, there's other women out there working, there's other girls, just down the block, just up there, pick one of them up,' helplessly horrified at the words that were coming.

And then Hank was back and he had his arms around me, supporting the glimmering exposed me across the street. I was half-crying still, and it was very hard to walk. There was a cab waiting. He pushed me into the back and said to the driver, 'I think she's been abused. She says her foster parent will pay for the ride. I tried talking to the cops, but they said there was nothing they could do.'

I realized then that if I was looking for the police to rescue me, I would be disappointed. They wouldn't help. There were too many fifteen-year-old girls who were out there every night, who hustled for a pimp, who had criminal records, who were runaways or lived with sugar daddies. Needier people.

Stretched out on the back seat. Crying with the sickness of the booze. Finally I gasped to the driver to stop and, opening the door, threw up onto the curb. Shamelessly; was this Evelyn? What was happening? He handed me some Kleenex, silently. I rambled on about the other working girls and how horrible this life was. He remained ominously silent. Then we were home, and we climbed the steps up to the porch. The cab driver knocked several times, but Melanie didn't answer the door. He turned around and his words were angry and abrupt.

'I think you're full of bullshit. I'm giving you a free ride.'

He stamped down the stairs, back into his cab, and took off before I could say anything.

I woke up this morning at 6:00, after a dream in which I'd been working. I couldn't go back to sleep, with the booze sour in my mouth, and my clothes a loud reminder of the night before. My stomach felt torn and ripped, and the bedroom was still spinning. Turning on some music to drown the heavy, whirling thoughts. Every morning now, the first thought that comes to mind is, 'You're working today,' and instantly I'm awake with emotions churning. I took a bath, threw up and went back to sleep.

It is evening now. I went and read 'The Window' and 'The Waiting Room' at the Burnaby Arts Gallery this afternoon. The judges awarded my two short stories third prize in the Burnaby Arts Council contest, but I didn't feel the same way about my writing. My head was filled to overflowing with thoughts of working the street, and with them the growing dread that maybe I'd do it again today. My stomach was still actively twitching.

The other people who read were terrific, and the guy who won first prize was remarkable. I listened and yet it was superficial because I couldn't identify myself with the kids or the adults—the writers—in the room. I realized dully that writing was something you worked at and devoted your life to, and I couldn't do any of that at present. I was just a dumb hooker.

It's almost 8 p.m. I've stayed away so far. Will I don my frightening outfit and go back to the corner? What will happen to me if I do? Broadway clutches, seizes me. I don't know which is worse, the physical risks or these emotions that I can't see through, like fog. I am terrified. The days and the hours tumble together, and I haven't done anything this week except work and recover from working.

PART V

may 1 to august 11 1987

May 1

So Jennifer arrives, wearing an expectant smile: Independent Living has been approved for September. She didn't get the hugs and thanks she deserved so much. For one thing I was stoned and somewhat incoherent, and for another I no longer believe that Independent Living will be the magic wand that will turn my life around. Reality isn't easy; each day you uncover more of the illusions.

I've been working, on and off, and trying to come to grips with it. I might round up some regulars, which would be safer. One wealthy john wore a condom slathered with butter inside—my job was to lick his balls while he looked at pornographic pictures and periodically jacked himself off. You should have seen that engorged penis, slick with the yellow butter, making mushy sounds in the plastic. He carried a hatchet for protection and brought it out for show and tell—the blade was impossibly sharp, glittering as he turned it over and over.

A man named Larry picked me up last night. We began talking and he gave me money not for a blow job but for conversation, touching and kissing.

Of course he didn't want to see it as an exchange of money for services. We smoked a joint and he gave me two pills that helped me relax. Larry is an ex-junkie. He is separated and has a teenage son, so he is desperately lonely and insecure. He looks like Bob Dylan. While we were talking he clutched me, tears brightening his eyes. I couldn't stop the compassion from welling up inside me. He couldn't bear to let me go, wanted me to feel something for him, wanted love and not cold sex. His slim smooth fingers stroked me gently in the darkness of the car. I didn't know what to do for him, but his enormous need sucked me in. Larry said that he wouldn't be able to stand it if I rejected him, that he had to be special: 'You haven't sat and talked like this with other guys, have you?' he asked fearfully—when of course I have, striving just as desperately to be accepted as a person.

We're supposed to see each other Saturday night. All I could do was spend the afternoon looking up the names of psychiatrists and therapists who might be able to help him. Some people in this world are so full of emptiness and need that you could destroy yourself for them.

I honestly believe death would be a better world than the one we have here, the one I don't have the ability to change. Maybe I could do something for people, given time, but their cruelty crushes me.

It's hard to think; the days whirl past and I don't do any writing except in this journal. Maybe it's the pot, my sleeping patterns and the fear and stress of working the street. I spend a lot of time sitting on my bed drowning in music and cigarette smoke, or dressing to go to work, or else trying to stuff this hell into oblivion.

I fantasize I'm off in a hippie commune anywhere, surrounded by music and drugs, babbling about peace and change while frying my mind on LSD. That's all. I would prefer to do something like that than participate in people's suffering, exposing myself shamefully.

Here I am, entertaining thoughts of death again. But I am emerging from the long frost of depression into the spring that is exploding so unexpectedly around the city. The mad energy isn't there, the crazed surge of Death-Death-Death that has to precede a suicide attempt. The Rivotrils are still waiting in the desk drawer beneath this typewriter, speckled with silent but knowing eyes.

May 2
Last night I went back to my corner on Broadway and Commercial. It was cold; the wind cut into my arms like small knives and ran through my body like fear. I was having a hard time getting picked up and considered migrating to another corner, as I was sharing mine with an experienced and very eager-looking blonde who peered voraciously into each car and swivelled her hips unabashedly. She soon walked off with a john. I deplored standing there, exposed to the stares from passing cars.

A brown car drove around the block several times, then stopped. I trusted its driver on sight; he wore steel-rimmed glasses and had whitening brown curls and a beard. He looked friendly, an ex-hippie probably. We settled on a blow job and drove off to an isolated area.

While we were driving, he lit up a joint and passed it to me. I smoked nearly all of it, rapidly sucking the skunkweed into my system, looking for redemption. I should have remembered that dope is really bad when I'm working. When I finished the joint, we were in some sort of construction site, a huge sand pit surrounded by tall grass, railway tracks and trains.

The nausea hit me suddenly and mercilessly. Dimly I realized I was shooting overboard, fast. I climbed and climbed up the waves of sickness, rolling, swimming in circles, trapped in a whirlpool, paddling in the sky ... and then I fell and spun around faster than you could imagine.

The trick was talking about music. During the climb I was able to nod and murmur with simulated interest, but I couldn't even talk. I got out of the car and tried to throw up but couldn't. The air was cold; the sky, velvet blue. I wrapped my arms around myself, noticing the bareness of my skin, trying to let the silky air soothe me. Tears lodged somewhere in the back of my eyes.

I re-entered the car and managed to say that I couldn't work tonight, I was sick. The explanation could have been better, but the effort needed to expel words out of my mouth sent me tumbling deeper into the sea of nausea. The john was amused at first, then impatient, and finally angry.

'We came here for a blow job, didn't we?' He undid his trousers and guided my hand to his penis. I shrank against the side of the door, battling with the sickness. He grabbed my arm painfully and made me start jerking him off, but I needed to throw up. Then he grabbed my neck and tried to make me start giving him head.

He threatened that if I didn't perform he'd screw me instead: 'I haven't fucked a Chinese broad in a long time.' I shrank further into the mazes and unrealities of my mind. He was hurting me. My hand darted for the door handle, managed to pull it towards me, then I was tottering out into the night.

But there were no people here, in this sand dune, this other world. He was calling after me, faintly. I kept plodding forward in my ridiculously high heels, through the mud, clawing at the tiny winking lights of passing cars in the city. Then I cried out. The long thick grass ended in a cliff; down below were supply trains humped on the tracks. I was stuck. Something in me started praying viciously to God, shaping Him out of nothing all at once, as I swivelled around, searching for some fucking way out of the blackness, any way.

He was coming out of his car, towards me. I looked back at him, then at the cliff, helpless. He called out that he was sorry and would drive me home. Without any other choice, I went wearily back to his car.

'Jesus, you're one fucked-up little girl,' he observed, as I swayed with the movement of the car, voiceless, ice-skating in infinite circles. Halfway home I begged him to stop and I fell out and vomited over and over. It kept coming up. I bent there in my heels and glittering tights and puked my guts out.

We went on; the journey was interminable. I appeased him by promising to screw him another day, and he let me go.

There was no one home when I got back. I wound my way through the too-bright lights into the washroom and threw up until convulsions racked my body and there was nothing left inside. I wondered if maybe I were going to die but knew somehow that it wasn't over yet, that my pale corner would still be beckoning.

May 3

Larry called; he'd been waiting for over half an hour. His voice was heavy with disappointment. I thought, well it's Saturday night, and if I'm not going to die I might as well not sit at home and mope.

We went out for coffee, then back to his place in Burnaby. I swear Larry is a walking pharmacy. He dumped a handful of pills into my palms—'They'll make you tranquil'—so I swallowed them. Immediately I was nauseated, and the snaking highway receded in and out of focus. But it got better and I was calm, rather careless; my initial intuitive apprehension about Larry vanished.

We sat in his apartment and talked; he touched me. I liked him, and he wasn't as screwed up as he'd appeared at first. Larry just really misses having a girlfriend, and he said that instead of moving out on Independent Living I could live with him—he drives a cab and is hardly home, there's a spare bedroom, and he could provide whatever drugs I needed. I asked him if he wanted sex, but the best answer he could come up with was 'I don't know.' He probably thinks I'll fall madly in love with him if he treats me nicely for a while.

Larry gave me forty dollars. We didn't get back to my place till 5 a.m. I was attracted to him, strangely enough—his gentleness, his insecurity and his pills too. He's not stupid, either; Larry's widely read, and his comment on my poetry was 'not bad.'

May 6

Wednesday. Brilliant sunshine. One of my customers just called. but it's going to be a busy day today. I'm jittery, took one of the tranquilizers Larry gave me because I was so down this morning I could hardly climb out of the bathtub. Tried to act mature last night with Larry by telling him I wasn't what he needed, that we shouldn't see each other. I didn't want him to get hurt, because he seems to be a caring person. Yet Dr. Hightower thinks he just wants to be my pimp, with his promises of drugs and a place to live. Larry wants to spirit me away to Mexico. Dr. Hightower is always right and I love him, but what can he do? He says he knows Larry's type. There's five black guys along Broadway who would love to be my pimp, and all I've got to do is work every night and they'd give me my apartment and all sorts of drugs.

This is heavy. I'm supposed to meet a regular—the man with the buttered safes—tonight at nine. Larry doesn't want me to do this; he says he'll give me the money I'd otherwise earn. But once he vanishes and I've lost my regulars, it'll be back to the street, and then what? I don't need a replay of that night, stuck between an angry man and a cliff. I thought today that I wouldn't mind going back to school, getting married, having children—boring, but I'd be alive and not screwed up.

I really tried last night. I wanted to save Larry; he thinks he's falling in love with me, and I'm not what he needs. I want somebody to slap me around and hurl abuse at me. I can't hurt myself enough—why?

Dr. Hightower cares about me, and that's tremendous. If it weren't for our Tuesdays together, where would I be? What man out there could be like him?

I'm ready to climb the walls here. Pot doesn't do anything for me anymore, it just brings me down and makes me nauseated. Larry tells me to hang on and he'll meet me at the bus stop this afternoon with 'something that'll make you warm inside, relax you.' He says he will give me all the drugs I want, he can be my Mr. Tambourine Man and get me through the jingle-jangle mornings. Dr. Hightower's right— he's no good; he's going to screw me around. He's clever too; he can play on my sympathies and needs so well. Larry's hinting at wanting to be a customer as well as a friend and drug supplier.

May 7

The pills that Larry is feeding me obliterate chunks of time. There is lots to write about, but I don't know if I can assemble it all.

I spent yesterday afternoon and most of the evening with Larry. He had just been to his doctor, and from his hands sprouted an array of pills. There were heavy tranquilizers and narcotics, of all shapes and sizes and colors. Glossy creatures some of them, capsules gleaming in my palms, married to round pills with oval children.

I swallowed eight pills, several of each. We went down to the beach to lie in the sun. I liked Larry and felt comfortable with him, and the time raced, courtesy of the drugs. I felt relaxed and without history, no past to color the moment—little future, either. That was all right.

I pulled out a joint and we smoked it together. Instead of enhancing the moment I was experiencing, it made me dizzy and spun me through hoops. The sea and the ships were a postcard I was gazing at. I could hardly scramble out of the shallow grave of sand I'd dug for myself—Larry had to support me off to a spot sheltered by tree stumps and rocks, where I sank into the coolness and retched. There wasn't much food in my stomach, so at first nothing came out. I closed my eyes, but colored circles twirled. Looking down at the broken pieces of shells littering the beach was fine, but if I raised my eyes to the ocean the sickness welled up. I started hearing voices and thought I was writing a children's book; I got sicker and sicker. The ocean chattered and roared. I threw up several times. Larry sat out of sight and came by every ten minutes to hold my hand and ask if there was anything he could do, but talking increased the nausea. In my head I was recreating the scene with that trick and me running through the mud to the edge of the cliff, so I cowered from Larry, thought he would hit me or take advantage of my helplessness. He would be crazy if he didn't, every other man did. At the least I expected him to spit out, 'You're disgusting,' and leave. But he didn't. Larry held me, though it didn't help, and remained gentle. I told him to leave after a while because it wasn't going to get better, and he slipped forty dollars in my bag to make up for my spending time with him instead of the trick with the buttered safes. I couldn't even thank him.

I stretched out for awhile, then managed to pick myself up and walk home, aware that I couldn't walk a straight line. At home the nausea was over and I was happy, miraculously happy. The pills were racing merrily about in my body, and the air was soft pillows around me. I was walking on clouds. I couldn't even sit up but the happiness was delirious. I called Larry and told him how much it meant for me to be sprawled on the kitchen table, stoned out of my mind, rather than being on the street. Larry told me he loved me.

May 10
My life is becoming very bizarre.

Today is Sunday and the sun is shining. This person sitting at the typewriter is a stranger, not Evelyn. I have a sense that something horrible has taken place and that there's going to be a lot more to come.

I can't remember anything clearly, but I spent the past few days and nights with Larry. He popped pills into my mouth to get me up or down or straight. We were in bed together much of the time, making love. I thought I loved him. I wasn't eating. We spent a lot of time touching each other and didn't venture into the heat and sunshine. I drank methadone for the first time (he didn't know it was the first time) and was uplifted into bliss and love. There were always more pills. I gave Larry his first triple orgasm.

But something was wrong. My eyes kept shutting and I'd hallucinate. It was like being very tired when you start seeing things just before you drift off to sleep. Like, you start dreaming, but you're still

awake. I couldn't control it. I was seeing mailboxes, people in white
... other things. I can't remember. I couldn't read or move. Although
I wasn't sleepy my eyes kept shutting and these visions kept material-
izing and walking around, doing their thing. About once every hour
my body would be seized by a spasm of intense loneliness and fear,
and I would have to clutch Larry.

Last night on the way back to Melanie's we drank methadone again.
I can't describe what it's like—the first time it was like coke, but with
a kind of detachment, as if you're floating a bit outside yourself. But
this time instead of feeling happy, I got angry. Larry kept on talking
about Mexico and how we were lovers, and I was getting angrier and
angrier, and by the time we were in Stanley Park I was shouting. I was
furious that somebody had given me such a raw deal in life, that I had
had to be a prostitute, that I was perhaps still prostituting myself with
Larry, that I was going through a creative period after so long and it
was being obliterated by the drugs, that I was begging for independence but would probably end up dead or on welfare. The rage
exploded. I hated men. Larry was crouched down, near tears, wanting
me to give him my knife so he could cut up his arm to prove how
much he cared about me. I was furious that I'd spent several precious
days with him and drugs when I could have been writing, and that the
creativity was dying. It is dying.

I feel that I can't write anymore. There's this fury attacking me from
inside, but I can't get it down on paper! The frustration is real bad.
Larry gave me some money last night after much prodding. Of course
I don't love him, though his gentleness is exceptional. He's a jerk like
the rest. But he says he'll fix me with heroin if I really want. A boy
arrived at the door just a few minutes ago, hired by Larry, to deliver a
badly written poem saying he loved me. There is increasing reason to
die here; my body can't handle the shit that's going on. I don't know
where I am or what's happening.

May 14

Larry called yesterday saying he was confused and disturbed and had
to see me. We arranged to meet at the bus stop, and I was so nervous
I was shaking and bumping into things, which is becoming a habit.

The bruises on my legs are amazing.

Larry picked me up and told me what had happened. He had gone to see his doctor, who supplied him with his weekly prescription of pills, and told him about us. Fear raced through my body. The doctor warned Larry that he could go to jail for having sex with me and that we were living in a dream; this was real life and not a movie.

Larry's friends had advised him to be careful or get out. They told him that I could be 'unconsciously manipulating' him since I'd worked the street, that other people they knew who had gotten involved with young girls had ended up in court if not in jail. They were also convinced that our relationship couldn't last.

We drove to a McDonald's parking lot and Larry said that he didn't want to see me anymore, except occasionally as a friend if I brought an adult female along. He explained his calmness by saying he'd bought methadone and that he was high.

Over the past week, Larry has kept me alive. He's seen me every day and occupied most of my time; because of that I've come to depend on and even love him. I've enjoyed sex with him. Perhaps it hasn't been love at all; perhaps the drugs created those feelings. But whatever it was I can't do without him. I have no real friends. He's all I have, besides Dr. Hightower.

'At least you've got your drugs. What do I have?' I was crying. It was terrifying that there'd be no more methadone, no more pills to make me happy and forgetful. And there'd be no Larry. He had taken me off the streets when it was getting dangerous, and now I would have to go back. But now that I couldn't smoke pot without throwing up, what was left that could get me through working, or even through each day?

The rain fell through the branches of the cedars. Larry said quickly, 'I thought you might need this' and handed over the methadone. I recovered while drinking but could feel my loss/abandonment complex (as Dr. Hightower called it) working up. Larry was just another person; who would have guessed I'd trust and love so recklessly? But I'd promised myself he would be the last person I'd care about. Larry's friends and his doctor were right, he could go to jail. Dr. Hightower thought he was 'walking a tightrope.' But I was too. A lot of us are; our emotions and our lives are always precarious. But I could let Larry go so that I could be abandoned by another person, so that I could go home and eat the Rivotrils. This kind of pain hurt. I had enough energy to commit suicide.

Larry changed his mind at last. 'Oh fuck, my feelings aren't telling me to leave. I love you. Fuck the rest of them.' We went into McDonald's for coffee, and by that time the juice was working. I was really happy. Blissful.

We walked back to the car underneath the rain and drove around, talking. I was all over him, ecstatically happy and peaceful and wanting to be with him. The idea of returning to Melanie's was repugnant; I've been growing increasingly furious about where I'm living and want to move out.

Larry put conditions on our relationship. I heard them, but then I was too high to be angry. He said that we couldn't have sex anymore, that I couldn't phone him, that we couldn't do methadone again, that I would have to edit out everything about him and drugs from my journal. Of course I don't want him in jail, but there's no way I'd edit anything from these pages. He said that I'd have to be home by curfew every night we were together, that I couldn't talk to anybody about us except Dr. Hightower, that he had to tell his friends that our relationship was over.

He also said that it would be over between us if I started working again. At the time, cozy in the car with the rain plinging onto the roads, these conditions were just words, but now I am angry. He's imposing one rule after another on me. Haven't enough people done that?

May 17

There's been a lot of shit going down over the past few days. Larry allegedly called Emergency Services to speak to a social worker about our relationship and the legal implications (hypothetically). By some freak, the phone rang miles away in the Outreach office and he was connected to Jennifer. They talked for half an hour before she realized it was me they were discussing.

When Larry told me I exploded. I called up Jennifer and began yelling at her; she said I was undermining my chances for Independent Living. Art happened to be over and took the brunt of my rage. A lot of things happened that I don't remember in order; the drugs of the past two weeks have blotted things out. Anyway, Larry sent his son Kirk over to apologize for him, and then we spent a few minutes together during which I almost hit him. The anger overflowed from nowhere. I could have killed somebody. I got out of Larry's car and slammed the door, saying I didn't care if we never saw each other again. Melanie called Jennifer to ask what the hell was going on, and she said that I wanted to move out but that would screw up Independent Living and Larry couldn't legally have me living with him anyway. Larry had said that I'd told him Melanie was mistreating me. A lot of shit went down. I went out that night to Larry's apartment to hunt for drugs or to trash his place. Along the way some guy picked me up and gave me twenty dollars for watching him jack off.

I spent the night at the apartment, sad and drained of anger. I still couldn't forgive Larry, though, because he had come across to Jennifer as a caring, concerned man who loved me. He'd told her that we'd never gone beyond hugging and kissing.

This is very hard to write. Melanie says she's worried because I've changed drastically over the past two weeks, that at times I act strung out and desperate. I've been trying so hard to conceal it! I haven't taken anything all day and it's evening. I'm scared. Larry wants to beat it to Mexico; his face lights up in anticipation of the narcotics available there and the nice Mexican woman who will bear his children. So in essence I am no more than a fifteen-year-old foster kid he's having a fling with. And he doesn't want to continue giving me so many pills. I'm really scared. My enormous obsession with Larry is largely the pills, but it's him too. I've come to rely on him, as well as filling up his hole of necessity for love and companionship. But if he stops feeding me drugs I don't know what I will do.

I don't know how serious the drugs are becoming, but I'm forgetting a lot of things and everything is falling into disrepair. I don't care about anything or anybody except Larry and his pills. I don't have time for my friends, don't do my tutor's assignments, don't think about Jennifer's feelings or about Independent Living. The social workers think I'm behaving this way because I'm scared of Independent Living. It isn't true, but I don't have the will to argue otherwise, especially when I know I could work and get my own place right away. I don't even think about Dr. Hightower. I am glued to the phone when Larry isn't there, waiting for him to call; it's like I don't have my own life anymore. And here he's delighted that he's leaving for his heaven on earth in Mexico, expecting me to be happy for him. He says he loves me and wants to help me, yet he doesn't think that once he's gone I'll be working the street or dead. I'll be terribly alone without him or his drugs, because after one or the other or both are gone, there will be nothing. I can't face the prospect of going without the Darvons, Valium, methadone and everything else he's been giving me that I forget the names of.

I don't think Larry is infatuated with me any longer. His friends have convinced him that he's playing with fire and I'm manipulating him. Maybe I started out doing that, but whenever. you do that to somebody you're the one who ends up getting hurt. I could have deliberately set out to seduce Larry for his drugs, but now I'm attached to him and can't stand a waking moment away. Once he finds somebody else, or he leaves, I won't be able to take it!

I'll never survive like this. Mornings are the worst. The days are like the faded, shapeless dresses of overweight women. Dr. Hightower says he's standing at the edge of a forest while I'm trundling down one of the paths, and he's cupping his hands to his mouth and hollering, 'It's the wrong way, Evelyn!' But what am I to do? I can't talk about this to anyone because I'm supposed to be together, with my writing and the short-story course and my tutor, and Independent Living waiting in September. Nobody has noticed that these things are held together by the slimmest of threads, ready to snap at the merest breeze.

Larry says he'll call at 8:00 and it's 7:30, so I'm not moving. He's working today, but he can spend half an hour with me. I'm becoming more blunt in my demands for drugs, and he is becoming more blunt about refusing them or cutting down on them. I really need something now, Larry. I doubt that I could love him without drugs, considering my feelings about men, but his drugs loosen me up, make me happy and loving.

I haven't been with another human being except Larry for almost two weeks. I don't talk to Melanie anymore because there's no point; this afternoon she suggested that I go into Detox and straighten out. I didn't realize other people could see I was out of it. She thinks from my behavior that I'm using needles. Oh God. I'm trying to avoid bumping into things, but today I noticed another big bruise, on my wrist. How do they happen? Funny how none of the bruises and cuts hurt, either.

It sounds trivial compared to the other things, but I have to take a Rivotril every night now to go to sleep. What am I, a walking pill? But—I might as well go into everything—it's so insidious; I thought I was only taking Larry's pills for fun or escape and didn't expect by any means to feel this desperate. Now I understand a little how somebody could go and rob a drugstore for what they need.

There's no fucking way I'll go on any drug-withdrawal program, because without drugs life would be a desert. I don't have anything otherwise except my writing, and it's not anything compared to the pills. It isn't. When I take Larry's pills everything and everybody disappears and I'm in a secure world of contentment and fulfillment. I feel like a success; I belong. Isn't that a great deal?

But the fear creeps up—that Larry will cut short my supply, that he's going to leave, that I will lose both a lover and a world at the same time. Where do you go from there? I've never been like this before— at a loss, knowing the inevitable, yet too far down the path to turn around and pay attention to Dr. Hightower's calls.

May 19

Back from Dr. Hightower's. It wasn't good; Larry left a message on my psychiatrist's answering machine several days ago, saying how much he cared about me and how worried he was. Unlike Jennifer, Dr. Hightower didn't believe this for an instant and, staring into my eyes, said several times that if he ever found out Larry's name, he would put him in jail immediately. At first I thought he was joking. No matter what anyone thinks of our relationship, I do like Larry. He's a human being—an intelligent, sensitive human being who I believe is doing me some good. Not much good in anyone else's terms, maybe, but no matter how impaired my judgment might be, I'm the one accepting the drugs and asking for them, and I'm the one hanging on to him. I could dismiss him just like that if I wanted to, except for his pills. He's probably been lying to me about many things, but he's a human being who in my eyes hasn't done any wrong, and it would be criminal to put him in jail.

The whole session was disturbing. It's like my psychiatrist and Larry are facing each other from opposite poles. Who is going to win? Dr. Hightower doesn't seem to matter so much anymore, although it worries me when he says that since I've met Larry, some of the progress we've so painstakingly made together has disappeared down the tubes.

I think it's sadistic of Dr. Hightower to want Larry behind bars. I may be a minor, but I don't need to be babied, and much of the time I'm fully conscious of what's happening in my relationships and the things I decide to get into. The thing is, there's nothing wrong right now—the drugs make me happy, and they're fun.

There's heat coming down, too. Melanie suggests that I should check into the psych ward, and I think Dr. Hightower is toying with the same idea. This worries me. I'm exhausted all the time, sleep like crazy but can't get enough; it's this thing with drugs. Does everybody think I don't know what I'm doing? Perhaps Larry is consciously manipulating me, setting out to hurt me, doesn't have any feelings about me. I am aware that this is the way it could be. Does that change anything? Not for me, not right now when I'm so hell-bent on destruction.

May 23

The meeting with Jennifer and Melanie went on for over two hours. Jennifer's clear, pale face and blue eyes pained me. We talked mostly about Larry and the drugs—she's coming back next Wednesday to look for changes. If I don't stop taking drugs, both she and Melanie will escort me to Detox. Jennifer is used to serving restraining orders to older 'boyfriends' of her clients who have provided the kids with drugs, acted as their pimps or used them sexually. One man just got out after six months in Oakalla. Jennifer wants to see Larry in jail if our relationship continues.

I asked about Independent Living. At least Melanie said I was making progress with the curfews and the house rules, but Jennifer seemed not to hear this one piece of good news.

'What if I leave now and go work the streets to get my own place—where would that get me?'

Jennifer said that Outreach would then alert the cops in the Mt. Pleasant area to look for me, which would make it difficult to be out there.

Of course I'm still seeing Larry. This is Saturday morning and I look like death warmed over. Methadone is anything but a beauty drug. We agreed that I would tell Melanie, Jennifer and Dr. Hightower that our relationship was over. It wasn't easy making this choice; I could feel Dr. Hightower trying to guide me onto the right path. I've already told Melanie that the relationship's over, that the prospect of going to jail frightened Larry because it would mean surviving without his pills. At first she believed me and was proud, but my drugged state is becoming harder to conceal. It will be much harder to lie to Dr. Hightower, but I don't think about it.

My eyes ache like hell. I've mostly been taking Valium lately, along with Darvon, other tranquilizers, and whatever else is available. For a few days Larry said he was never going to supply me with methadone again, and pills only once in a while. One afternoon he handed over two Valium and said, 'That's it.' When he got out of the car I took another from the glove compartment; luckily he ended up dispensing four more Valium anyway. My tolerance must be building up. I hardly get a buzz anymore, even though I smoke pot and drink vodka on top of the pills.

Well, one amazing thing. I just won, for the second year in a row, the non fiction category of the Canadian Author and Bookman magazine high school and university contest. The poetry and fiction winners were both university students. I won with an essay titled 'Streets'—it's surprising that my writing accomplishments are still happening while everything else is precarious. If nothing else, my relationship with Larry has produced two poems: 'Tambourine Man' (about the pills) and 'Hanging On' (about methadone and suicide).

I just wish my eyes would feel better. Larry and I are meeting this afternoon; he's taking the night off work and going to get the Valium.

May 29

Along with the other drugs, I've started popping Mandrax (a heavy narcotic sleeping pill, similar to Quaaludes). I'm terrified of what I'm turning into. Larry dominates my time; it's one in the afternoon now, and he's meeting me at two to give me some pills. The first time I took

Mandrax it was strange, I nearly fell asleep, and then when I closed my eyes this merry-go-round dizziness enveloped me, there were winking pieces of glitter in that darkness ... I'm trying very hard to cut down. I'm dancing as fast as I can—torn between the importance of my writing and the seduction of drugs. The colors of the pills are so pretty ...

High. I want to be a brilliant and successful writer, but the waters are sloshing over my head. I have more than straws to clutch, but it's still difficult, Dr. Hightower matters little, and that's wrong because he would help if I cooperated.

I could become one of the top writers in Canada, or I could be a drug addict, or I could die. Those are the choices.

May 31

This is Sunday afternoon. I have to write more often in these pages. I think writing even beats drugs; it's necessary for my survival.

Without Larry's knowledge, I worked Broadway Friday night. It was chilly and the rain was thundering down out of the blackness; I didn't see one other woman working. I had taken several Valium before going to work, so it was all right. No bad tricks.

Tomorrow Larry is buying methadone for me, from his friend Kyle. Since we've met, Larry has done juice about eight times and he vows not to do it anymore, or he'll be wired again. He had been on the methadone program for ten years and before meeting me, hadn't touched the stuff for almost a year. He also promised that he'd never take another Mandrax because they made him slur for days afterwards. My conscience bothers me. I shouldn't be drinking methadone, but it's a good feeling. I'm trying to take care of myself; I'd commit suicide without the drugs to keep me going from day to day, so I will just have to keep struggling. I've forgotten about death. Right now I hope to live long enough to make a name for myself from my writing; I'm even thinking as far ahead as moving to Toronto when I'm older.

June 5

This is Friday afternoon. On Wednesday Larry, his son Kirk and I met at a coffee shop.

Kirk was looking sick in the sunshine; he kept running his hands frantically through his thick dark curls. His skin was pale. I was doled out four Darvons. Kirk went to get his prescription filled and took eight Darvons, forgetting he'd popped four earlier. He had to get out of the car to throw up before climbing back inside, He sat in the back seat hidden behind opaque lenses that swam with color. We were going to rent a video and drive up to the apartment, but Larry said that he wanted to spend the night with me instead. Kirk and I both thought he meant he wanted to screw, and Kirk started crying. God, drugs can screw you up. Kirk cried for a long time behind his crystal hippie glasses. Then Larry started crying because he had just wanted to go for a walk with me. 'You only wanted to get your rocks off,' Kirk accused. I comforted them both. High. Tears and pills and me trying to hold them together.

We went to this house where Kirk vanished for a while and came back with two white blotters. He said the hippie who sold it had dropped one blotter and seen a flaming bowl in the sky, and added that he could go back and get me ten more double hits for thirty bucks. Larry accused me of caring about nothing except LSD.

June 9

Since taking some Darvons on Sunday afternoon, I've been straight, and it's now Tuesday. Wow! I'm really trying, though it's like being in a candy store with money, because I've got LSD, Valium, Darvon and Mandrax stashed away. Last night I had a nightmare about living at home and being ordered around—my parents had forced me to go down to the beach where a man who looked like Dr. Hightower stood. He would not acknowledge me; he didn't move. I was left staring at the waves. I must feel as though Dr. Hightower is giving up on me.

Went out with Larry last night for a few hours—he took a long break from work. He had a cold and was nauseated and feverish. I had a cold too, and realized in the restaurant that my cheeks were flushed, flaming to the touch.

He'd stolen Darvon from his mother, who needed them as

painkillers, and gave me three. I decided not to take them and put them in my bag. Larry had given me a black leather pouch that contained the key to his trailer; it also contained Melanie's key, two Rivotrils and some hash and pot. My fingers picked casually through the contents of my bag and then became panic-stricken—the pouch wasn't there! Luckily, there were no other drugs in there besides the marijuana.

We went back to the restaurant and checked and checked. I was frantic, terrified of Melanie's reaction to my losing her key, just when I was trying so fucking hard to prove I was responsible enough to handle Independent Living. We looked in the car, in Larry's bags, on the street; I dumped out the contents of my backpack five times. We spent an hour and a half looking for it.

I was wrecked. It must have fallen onto the street along the way and somebody had grabbed it. It was downtown after all, near Granville. Thank God I hadn't used the pouch for my other pills.

I was so upset on reaching home that I was screaming. Melanie was surprised, quiet. Then I realized that neither she nor Jennifer were going to take away my opportunity for Independent Living. It took me a while to calm down; at one point I dumped the contents of my backpack on the living room floor and started kicking my things around, yelling.

I took a Rivotril to go to sleep, which was around 12:30, and this morning I got up at 5:00. I'm really sick, have some form of the flu. Fuck, man, Larry should pay for giving me this. At least I've gone straight since Sunday afternoon. It's great to know that, although I'm so crazily ill!

Next time we do acid I want to go on the suspension bridge. Larry hadn't been there since he was little.

'What if we fall off?' he asked in all seriousness. We won't fall off, no, not that. How would that feel—dying? I'm sure I care whether I live or die; Jesus. But maybe Larry will tumble overboard. Do I want that?

I'm trying to stay straight largely because I ran into my former math teacher yesterday afternoon and we talked and talked. What are drugs and prostitution but a steady trip downhill? We know that. I'm trying hard—or so I always say.

I was half an hour late for my appointment with Dr. Hightower,

after taking one of my few precious Darvons. It took away the pain of
sitting in a smoke-clogged bedroom, playing depressing Dylan songs
at full volume and blaming myself for Larry's problems.

'Druggies are never on time,' Dr. Hightower commented.

Afterwards, I waited for Larry in front of the Dairy Queen. As
usual, he arrived twenty minutes late. His hands were shaking and
he'd given away the rest of his Mandrax, so I handed him a Rivotril.
His tolerance to tranquilizers was so high, though, that he wanted his
doctor to try another drug; he also said that if he continued speeding
the way he was, two weeks from now he would request to be put back
on methadone.

We went to Kyle's and his girlfriend Wendy's place. It took Wendy
five minutes to answer the door, wrapped in her bathrobe, slurring.
Kyle knows Wendy will never come off juice, but they help each other
through the ups and downs—like Larry and I do, I suppose ... sliding.

Kyle stumbled out, reeking of marijuana. Yuck. Their apartment
was a mess—lipsticks on the floor, dirty laundry, tables piled high
with old newspapers and measuring cups for juice. We had come so
Larry could buy me some methadone—he had confessed earlier in the
car that on Saturday night, when we'd both taken two Mandrax, he
had also juiced earlier in the day.

Kyle fell onto a couch that opened into a bed, and Larry slumped
on the floor. They discussed a heroin deal they've been working on
while I half-listened, watching the thin figure of Larry mouthing
ounces and grams and prices, watching Kyle answer with a drawn-out
voice, his face like sculpted marble. Larry asked about the juice and
Kyle said he didn't have any—we had been over an hour late and he
had thought Larry didn't want it anymore. He was getting some
tomorrow. Larry arched towards me, his lean face despairing, his eyes
like those of a frightened animal.

What could I do to calm him? Immediately I said I hadn't come to
see him so that he would buy me methadone, that I wasn't using him
for drugs. He stumbled up and fumbled in his bag, taking out four
Darvons, then raced into the kitchen and fetched me a glass of water.
I started swallowing the Darvons, shrugging at the scummy white
coating on the bottom of the glass. I decided to save the last one to get
me through tomorrow.

Larry crouched in front of me. He was shouting. 'Take the

goddamn thing! I'll stuff it in your fucking mouth if you don't take it.'
I tried to explain that I didn't have a prescription for Darvon like he
did. Valium is easy enough to come by—Larry can buy them off Kyle
in lots of a hundred—but I was dependent on painkillers as well. They
killed the pain not just in my body but also in my head.

Kyle watched. His eyes were large above his wide cheekbones and
hard jaw. 'What are you doing, Larry? Have you gone crazy? Why're
you trying to stuff drugs down this young girl's throat?'

'Just take the goddamn thing, before I get really mad!'

Finally I gave up and swallowed the capsule. Larry calmed down
and explained that he wanted me to get a buzz, that was all. I took the
last one only because he reassured me that there was more where it
came from.

Wendy wandered into the living room. Larry was mentioning how
I wanted to fix heroin once, just once, in order to experience the rush.
Kyle and Wendy looked at me with traces of despair and urgency on
their faces. Kyle pulled himself together and stared at Larry.

'You're insane. You don't know what you're doing. You're going to
give a young girl her first fix?'

I tried to explain through the weed and juice fogging Kyle's mind.
'I only want to do it once. I promise. I just want to feel the needle
going in.'

He couldn't understand. Wendy was telling me not to get into using
junk. Kyle tried to make me realize the seriousness of my desire. 'You'll
be back on the street, working twenty-four hours a day in order to fix.'

'I'm only going to do it once.'

'That's what they all say.' He looked away, back to Larry with a persistent look on his face and fleetingly it crossed my mind that Kyle
might be right. Larry gave in and didn't fix me. But I could never
become a heroin addict anyway. My writing comes first.

June 17

Larry is starting to use me more and more as a psychiatrist for his
emotional, sexual and drug-related problems. He thinks I'm to blame
for his being broke—he took a week off work when we first met, and
then every Saturday after that—and for not being home when he calls,

for his lack of sleep. If his ideas or accusations don't make sense and I simply look at him, he retaliates with, 'You don't understand, do you? How could you understand? I'm talking to a naive 15-year-old girl who is immature both emotionally and sexually and who hides in a corner whenever anyone around her gets angry!'

It looks like the relationship is coming to an end. There's more to life than Larry, Darvon and methadone. I'm often sick, but the last Darvon I took was two days ago. I arrived at Dr. Hightower's yesterday on time, perfectly coherent, and we rejoiced. I realized how wonderful it was to be able to work with him again, to think straight, to feel my body freeing itself of chemicals.

Last night I went to work. I swallowed four Valium before leaving the house, to make sure I wouldn't be afraid, even though the vision of a knife to the throat danced into my mind.

It went okay. Dr. Hightower peered into my face, as if he could somehow dissect me, and asked, 'What is it besides the money?' A lot of things, I guess—another example of self-destructive behavior, a replay of past abuse and helplessness. A kind of power and control over the johns themselves, that they would have to pay for sex, that they would find me attractive enough to pull bills out of their wallets before pulling down their zippers. The last appears to be the going theory among therapists about hookers, and I think it's closest to the truth.

I can dredge up a sob story to my advantage—a true sob story, because I am trying to save up for Independent Living and to go straight. But with prostitution, you begin to forget the motivations after a while.

June 18

When it was dark, Larry and I walked around the neighborhood where I lived till I was six years old. The memories came back, one by one, as we sat on the steps facing my former home and he held me like a father or a psychiatrist or somebody who could protect me from too much hurt. Memories like waking up in a sunlit room as a very young child and being alone in the house, crying because I thought my parents had abandoned me. I also remembered waking up past midnight in a cot with the sounds of my parents fighting in their bedroom; I used to be terrified that my mother with her shrill voice and her ability to inflict emotional wounds would kill my father, my father who was so close to me when I was small. He would come in when he heard me crying and extend a giant hand through the bars of the crib, let me clutch him. Then my mother would invade his comforting, the lamp light outside illuminating his ghostly face, and scream that if I didn't stop crying she would leave right that moment. What would I do then, she'd challenge, with nobody but a useless man who could not take care of me? I'd be out in the cold, gnawed by hunger. It would take a long time for my father to soothe me, though he couldn't ever take the fear away; he was never able to dispel the terror of his oversensitive daughter.

June 29

Larry called last night and we arranged to meet at 8:30. I told him hesitantly that Dr. Hightower had been right about our relationship and that it would be better for both of us to end it—especially for me, and in the long run for him. His heart lay in drugs; it was only temporarily in the hands of a fifteen-year-old girl whose love for him was indeed naive. I tried very hard to convince him that we should split up, after thinking about it all day. I wanted to leave Larry. Dr. Hightower, Dr. Graham, Jennifer and Melanie had pointed out that it could never work out between us, that we would begin using each other more and more. I love him now, but it would be better for him to return to his true love rather than to let the days and weeks drag onward—it would be harder for both of us later.

Larry wasn't about to see me to say, 'Goodbye, it's been nice knowing you.' Towards the end of the conversation the Dr. Hightower sitting behind me and helping me shape the final words began to evaporate, and I needed to see Larry; God I wanted to see him. Our relationship had been of such intensity that I could not break it off so simply, and in the end I gave in. Disappointed yet desperate, I headed off to see him. I tried to tell myself again to take it one day at a time, that everything was under control and why should my psychiatrist matter anyway, but I could not validate this way of looking at the situation anymore.

June 21

Larry and I talked for two hours in his car the other day. I explained why we should make a clean break, why it wouldn't work out after a few weeks or months. It would be easier now than later on. Later Larry would feel much more bitterness towards me, the fifteen-year-old slut who had devoured a man who felt he cared too much for her.

I was very dizzy and didn't want this to be happening. I wanted Larry to leap out of the driver's seat and pin me down, hold me there, stop Dr. Hightower's words from sprouting from my mouth, stop this struggle for life. But Larry didn't do that. He had his dope; he had everything he needed to blot out the pain of the next few days without me. But without Larry, I would have to go straight. The unfamiliar dizziness overwhelmed me till I was weaving in and out of consciousness.

Then Larry did leap out of his seat. He raced to my side of the car and flung the door open. 'Okay, if you think you're being so mature. I have to go to work now. So your shrink has the world by the nuts, eh? You think he understands people? Do I get paid a hundred dollars an hour for seeing you?!' He was shouting, back behind the wheel before I could move. My legs and feet were leaden. The wheels of the car began to spin, and then he was gone.

I got up early yesterday morning, around 5:00 to put a cold cloth over my eyes, which hurt from the methadone I had bought from Wendy and Kyle, then fell back into a deep sleep until 8:00. I reached Larry at 10:00, not feeling quite on top of the world anymore—every drug has an aftermath, and methadone is no exception. I was slurring and sick.

But everything was cool. I apologized for my stupidity during our prolonged farewell. He forgave me instantly. We spent Saturday together—I managed to trade three Darvon from him for five Valium, then a Mandrax for two Rivotrils. I was pretty sick from the methadone and needed to relax; I was also very tired. We went to bed not much past midnight, and my exhaustion was overwhelming—the battle between Dr. Hightower and Larry had utterly confused and drained me.

June 25

I ask myself if there is any purpose in continuing this journal. The drugs make it too difficult to write, and if I do OD and jump off a bridge anyway, these pages are going to be drenched with a lot of water. Is it all a lot of work for nothing?

On Tuesday, Melanie and I went to my parents' house to collect my belongings. It was right after my appointment with Dr. Hightower, during which he sat like a lump in his chair and wasn't helpful. Larry has convinced me that Dr. Hightower can't do anything, that he doesn't care. Is believing Larry's words self-fulfilling? Dr. Hightower observed that I appeared frightened about going back home after well over a year, but honestly I wasn't. I thought it would be fun to prance obnoxiously back into my parents' lives and make them pay for the fourteen years in which they'd created this messed-up human being. I remember being very tired during the session, having adopted Larry's sleeping patterns and thus hoping to make it better for him. Too many drugs, too much stress, broken and difficult sleep.

My hands started shaking when I was in my old bedroom. Dr. Hightower had not prepared me for this. I had no problem dealing with my family, but being in that house again overwhelmed me. I was no longer the same person and felt like an intruder, a stranger. I had to take several Valium to mellow out, though I'd wanted to deal with the situation straight.

Afterwards we thought it had been a success; bags and boxes of possessions weighed down Melanie's car, and a grin of accomplishment spread across my face. It wasn't till later, when those possessions were in my bedroom, that I began going crazy. It was too much to deal with. There were hundreds of pieces of mail, including rejection letters, acceptance slips, magazines I'd been published in at twelve or thirteen. The awards that had lined my walls. There were armfuls of books, and I sat there arranging them over and over: smallest to largest, paperbacks and hardcovers, fiction and nonfiction. There were schoolbooks and magazines. I sat there amidst the books, the newspaper clippings about me mocking me from the floor. I was nothing now but a drug addict, a failure. A failure. It struck me then. I hadn't grown enough as a writer over the past year—where had the dedication gone?

A former success. It was one of the worst nights to get through in my life. A Rivotril, warm milk, half a Mandrax, a Darvon—sleep would not come. My room was littered with a talented young stranger's trophies.

The next day I began to piece myself together. It was Wednesday. Larry arrived with some methadone that wasn't that strong, but it was a gorgeous day and we were down at the park. Just when I had sunk into depression, the crescent of the juice lifted me up and I was high, happy. I bought four Darvon off him, then remembered Wendy and Kyle's advice—'Be totally honest with Larry, that's all'—and decided to tell him that I had worked the streets while seeing him.

We talked about it. Larry appeared to take it well and said he still loved me, was still able to accept me. I was warm, relaxed, loving.

That night I had been invited to do a poetry reading after a twenty-minute play. I was greeted by a woman who had read my poetry in Prism International; she said it was the best she'd seen in that magazine for a long time. She must have been crazier than I was.

The reading went superbly. Usually I'm nervous and bothered by the fixed stares of the people in the audience, feeling as if I'm speaking in a foreign language. But when I looked up from my crumpled poems, I saw understanding and mesmerization in their faces. They cheered at the end, and the woman gave me a rose. People came up to me and said they had identified with the images and the issues, that I had inspired them to begin writing again. I felt so happy there.

When Larry came to pick me up, he looked grim. Apparently he hadn't accepted that I'd been working the streets after all, and had gone bawling once again to Kyle and Wendy. Suddenly I was reduced from the budding West Coast writer to a fifteen-year-old slut, whore, bitch ... It was a heavy down. I suddenly felt exhausted. I had been exuberant, and then that other side of my life took over.

Larry's stiffness upset and enraged me. He didn't understand; it was as if I'd enjoyed sucking strangers' cocks! How would you like to feel that much of a slut? I started crying uncontrollably.

Dr. Hightower had said that Mandrax brings on episodes of psychosis, and that's what seems to be happening to me. Yesterday morning when I was upset about my two lives—the one before I left home being good, the one now being bad—I slammed the bathroom door so hard into the wall that the handle went through it. Often in the mornings the rage wells up and I scream as if I'm in a padded room.

June 27

I know I must keep writing here, whether I am drugged or straight. This journal may never be read by anybody else, but at least it deals with some of my confusion. Right now drugs and writing are on the opposite ends of a teeter-totter; it's never gotten to this point before.

It's hard for me to write. The past few days have been filled with drugs and bewilderment. This is Saturday night. I can't go for a day without dope anymore.

A lot of people were working last night. It was the craziest night; everybody was drunk, and because school was out there were carloads of guys ripping past yelling obscenities. A couple of women shared my corner; cops were watching us. An orifice for abuse, I was not interested in turning tricks or making money, only in the degradation and possibly in someone cleanly blowing my brains out. I went out to prove that yes, I was nothing but a whore. All the women wore masks: bleached blond hair and crudely painted faces. I turned just one trick and became teary when he drove me home as he reminisced about the sixties, as I read my poetry to him. He was a decent guy who felt bad afterwards, but he wasn't any different really.

Larry called at noon, and we arranged to meet at eight. I needed something—why? what? I took half a hit of LSD and drank vodka. There was a lot of pain. Unfortunately, Melanie realizes I'm still seeing Larry.

So what is this pain, that it needs to be obliterated? I stumbled into Larry's cab, and everything was all right between us, but the acid and the vodka hurt. I didn't think I could live. Too much confusion; I'm scared that I've burnt out as a writer. Drugs have become too important to me. I can't even figure out why anymore, except that the idea of being straight for even an instant is intolerable.

June 29

This is Monday evening, and I've managed to stay clean since Saturday night. The poisons must be draining from my body, because aside from bouts of weariness and depression, everything is fine. I think I'll survive this with few problems—this being not an attempt at complete detoxification but rather a rest. I need sunshine and a vacation from the pills that have broken open and flowed through my body for the past two months.

The sky is an ocean of blue and the heat is beginning to dwindle, though the past few days have been marvelously like summer. I need to be strong, and have decided not to worry so much about my writing for the next few days at least—it's time to catch some sun and do some long-neglected reading. Fuel for every writer. Many years ago someone told me that to be a writer, one has to be tough-skinned, but I hadn't taken that seriously till now. Before, it had seemed a smooth road to travel.

The math teacher who pulled me through my worst subject in school has been terrific support. I ran into him on the bus again and we spent several hours together today. He's coming over next Monday for a work session in which I'll write and he'll study material from his summer course. I'm amazed that people are helping me pull through, that when I'm most likely to fail or give up they appear and offer strength. My tutor has been a source of discipline and inspiration for me; Melanie was so impressed by his influence that she was willing to hire him to continue with the tutoring over the summer, but he doesn't want that conflicting with his school board contract. We will keep in touch, though.

July 1

Days of being unable to touch my writing, of almost deciding to give up and resort to the full-time occupation of drug addict and whore. I stayed clean till last night, but then my eyes burned holes into my head and the pain was profound—I took a Darvon, a few Rivotrils and a Mandrax. But I am returning to this land of waiting white pages, after a Valium to calm down.

Okay, so you want to lead a full, satisfying life. But talent is something that has to be nourished, and drugs won't do it. Don't think of failure. Evelyn, you're going to be sixteen tomorrow, and that might sound young, but it isn't right now. You may not reach adulthood.

But that's bullshit. I will make it as a writer. The other life isn't at all glamorous, as it may appear to some people and as it once did to me.

It isn't a movie where the young actress is full of potential but in the end loses herself to drugs. How then would you be able to face the mirror, face yourself. You were born to write—don't waste it.

July 7

Dr. Hightower's face wrinkles as he watches me standing there before leaving the office. His eyes survey my body with concern. 'Your bum's disappeared! I don't know how much weight you've lost, but you're starting to look ... funny. Maybe ... I don't know. Don't worry about it yet.'

Me, becoming too thin? Yet over the past few months, starting with the Darvon, I've lost twenty-five pounds. Bones are popping out of my flesh and striking me. Most of my clothes don't fit anymore, sagging like deflated balloons around me. Dr. Hightower said that with my body type I can't lose this much weight without beginning to look like I've walked out of a cartoon.

I want to be healthy and to be able to write if there is hope and inspiration. There is both. Perhaps work will lead to something better than this. However thrilling, drugs are a superficial aspect of this diary, merely a coating. I don't want it to be all about drugs—ups and downs. But I think I'm too afraid of having an 'ordinary' life. The blankness of such a life would easily become a pit for depression—what creativity could spring up from that kind of well?

July 10

I want to run to Toronto, that cold city people tell me I will hate. If I end up staying here, it would seem like too much of a failure. What will I do then—let Larry move in with me, Larry with his scrawny body, Larry and his bottles of pills? Who wants to help whom now?

I want to put my right fist through a window so I could hold it up bleeding, stuck with chunks of glass, and say, 'Well, now I can't write until this gets better.' That would give me all the time in the world to play with drugs, wouldn't it?

So it finally comes to light that Evelyn is lazy. Evelyn is no longer the child prodigy who churns out the naive poems about a president who won't stop to smell the flowers or look at the mountains because he's too busy building nuclear weapons. It's no longer, 'Look at Evelyn Lau, she's had so many successes and is blessed with so much talent, and she's only _____ years old.' There's an adult world out there where there are thousands, maybe millions, of struggling writers, and take a good look at the competition. Who's going to be fascinated by the writing of a kid who has ability but chooses time and again to run away, take drugs or prostitute herself? A bored psychiatrist, maybe: 'Oh, this looks like an interesting case.'

Who said writing would make you rich? It's easier to go on welfare. But all I want to do is get my writing published.

July 13

Funny how in the process of writing I've straightened myself out. This typewriter beckons and beckons, needs to be tapping forever into the silence. It won't allow rest; it refuses the sunshine; it throws up at the sight of pills.

What madness. Now I find drugs to be too costly in recovery time and in the dulling of my creativity. At night I dream about getting published—short dreams in which an interested publisher phones me, long dreams in which I race from one publishing house to another with a manuscript, receiving rejections and no encouragement.

I seldom leave the house, glued to the typewriter or submitting poetry and short fiction. Larry's profile, colored with the dying sunshine, is thoughtful. 'I'm just worried about what will happen to you if your writing doesn't work out.' That's a thought I don't even consider. Can you imagine Evelyn simply shrugging, finding a cheap apartment and returning to a Grade 10 classroom? I can't swallow failure, even if it wouldn't be that in other people's eyes.

July 20

I've been racing around for a week like a chicken with its head cut off, planning to move into my apartment and working on my writing.

Something is driving me here, won't let me rest until an allotted number of pages have been revised.

But I've fucked up. I would very much like a small cup of methadone to stop the world for a moment, to stop all this shit, to stop me from running to the Outreach office to find one very angry kid without a place to stay and the office closing down two hours early because there's no staff. To find Jennifer gone so that now I'll have to wake up early tomorrow to pick up the damage deposit, then dart over to the apartment to give it to the landlord. I was supposed to get the check today.

I hate it when I go in to get a massage, and the therapist probes my muscles and asks if I take Valium. 'Your muscles are very, very relaxed. But it feels unnatural.' Is it that obvious? I may as well walk around with a shirt reading, 'I Take Drugs—My Body Is Screwed for Life.' I'm fighting the fucking drugs, working like a madwoman on my writing (dealing with the past at the same time), preparing emotionally to live on my own, fighting the streets, realizing I'll be returning to high school, knowing I may never be able to 'make it' as a writer ... Yes. That's all. I'll throw in an extra whimper and add that I'm only sixteen.

Because of my impatience (justified, considering the lethargy of editors) and lack of prolificness (unjustified), I received a sarcastic and very humiliating letter from the editor of *West Coast Review,* who had read the last copy of *Prism International* and realized that 'The Quiet Room' (which he'd accepted along with 'There Once Was a Commune in My Back Yard') had already been published. But if I hadn't made simultaneous submissions, it would have taken ten times as long to get to where I am today, which admittedly is not very far. I don't write enough poetry or short stories to wait six months for a batch of them to be accepted or rejected. I've always made simultaneous submissions and should have expected that one day two magazines would simultaneously accept and I'd be up against a wall. Now *West Coast Review* won't publish the other poem either and is unlikely to consider my work again, sparing me only because I might not have known about the policy—being my age and all, you understand.

Why not go and work tonight? The money wouldn't go unappreciated. Larry isn't calling anymore, and his promise of 'Once you go out on Independent Living, I'll hit you with at least an extra two hundred dollars a month' has obviously vanished. Along with him, the asshole, and I paid for most of my drugs too; he got all the free blow jobs and triple orgasms! Jesus I hate this crap, want to just collapse but can't now.

July 30

Today I was at Dr. Graham's for nearly an hour, skirting around him, dancing with words, trying to get a week's prescription for Valium. He was adamant about not giving me one, though my argument was reasonable—I'd get it anyway. And if I got it off the street, I'd have to pay for it, which would mean working the streets, and the hassle of buying the pills, and I had only two left! Unimaginable. He kept saying no. It blew my mind. I wasn't going to go in the next week and ask for Darvon, the next for Mandrax, the next for methadone. What did he think? I told him that if he gave me twenty-five, a week's supply, I'd make it last for a month. How else am I supposed to cope with strenuous situations, especially things like seeing my parents?

'I'll do anything, Dr. Graham.' (Blow job blow job blow job please)

'I said no. You know, on the appointment book, I mixed your name up with another girl's. She was native Indian; I saw her over a six-year period and watched her go downhill on Darvon, speed, Valium, everything. She overdosed.'

When I stepped out of the office, his face was turned away from me. Reluctantly but impulsively I went over and hugged him. 'Thank you … I guess.'

What desperation is this, as I constantly interrupt this entry, restless as hell, putting pleading calls through to Larry? His phone's been busy for over an hour; he must have taken the receiver off the hook in anticipation of my call. No Mandrax? How could that be even remotely possible? Got in touch with Kyle and will be able to see him late afternoon or early evening. Methadone. That's not really what I want, but it'll do; it has to. It has to work. Yes. It will.

I spun into Dr. Hightower's office late—had to hitchhike to make it back home in time. A man in a white Mercedes picked me up, and even dishevelled as I was in shorts and a T-shirt, rubbing involuntarily at lumpy mosquito bites, he wanted a blow job.

I talked speedily about the deepest, darkest things with Dr.

Hightower, but like he said, echoing disappointment through me, 'You're just relating them. You're recording these experiences, not feeling them, not reliving them. The drugs are a protective barrier. You can't start real work until you stop doing them.' And God, more than ever I need to resolve what's happened in my childhood or else I can't go on. I just need to reach Larry, that's all!

August 11
'You've become what all the workers who ever cared about you or worked with you have feared. Their deepest fear. A junkie whore.'
Dr. Graham, trying to dispel my lethargy, digging for anger.
'The truth hurts, doesn't it?'
He was listening to me saying that I didn't care about my writing anymore, that for the first time in my life it didn't matter. All that mattered was drugs, and even those weren't as good as they used to be—my body was becoming more tolerant of the chemicals. And I had thought I was immune! Simply a reporter standing by with her journal, perched on the very fringe of the drugs and the streets, tampering with them a little, just experimenting—I'd never thought I had a normal body, a normal mind, that could be sucked in as easily as any other human being's. Never thought that.
'But those workers didn't care. If they did, it was just because they were paid to care. They wouldn't have listened to me if they'd been bank tellers. They were social workers, and so they were paid to listen and to pretend to be concerned. Most of them probably don't remember me now.' It was true.
After the session I asked for my usual two-week supply of sleeping pills. With anger freezing his face into stone, Dr. Graham refused. No more Rivotrils.
Oh God no. Didn't he see? It was all falling apart. Those visits with my parents, me in their bathroom watching a reflection in the mirror gulping pills, the writing meaning nothing, not wanting to ever write again, the drugs that were my world and my death.
I thought I would faint. My heart was going too fast, I was sweating, but there were enough pills to kill me. I counted out twenty-five Rivotrils, five Mandrax, five Darvons and poured them into one

bottle. There was enough. I threw my writing into a Smithrite bin and headed towards my apartment. A bottle of vodka on the dresser, cigarettes and an ashtray. Everything was ready.

The pills emptied out onto the dresser were enough to kill me, I knew that. I began taking them, one by one by one. There seemed a lot more than there were at first, so many in a sickening heap. I swallowed the Darvon, then the Mandrax, then the Rivotrils until they were all gone. Misconceptions: I did not fall flat on my face onto the floor. Lights flashed across my eyes and something buzzed around my head, but I had enough strength to crawl into bed. I was elevated, as if my soul were leaving my body, except my soul was black and going nowhere. The pills fought and screamed and banged inside me. They hurt so much; I was so sick. Oh God. I can't tell you what it was like. It wasn't easy; I thought death by overdose was painless! It was the worst thing in the world. Most of all I saw Jennifer's face, her blue eyes, her pale skin, the blue of her goddamn eyes that had enabled me to have this apartment, that had stopped the running, that had listened and understood. I couldn't disappoint her. She had done so much for me! I thought of Larry whom I loved, and then after that through the lightning in my eyes and the levitation and the insane sickness I said Dr. Hightower's name out loud.

As the blackness started to leak from above, I got scared. Terrified. Don't you know, Evelyn, that death is forever, not like methadone, where it's for a few hours? I struggled up from the bed, forced myself to vomit, and went into the other tenant's apartment to use his phone (he wasn't in). I dialled 911. I didn't know whether the pills had reached my bloodstream yet. Four policemen arrived, and an ambulance waited outside.

After that I blacked out. When I came to, I found myself on a bed in the hospital in the acute care section. A doctor was forcing a tube, with charcoal in it, down my throat for me to swallow into my stomach. I kept gagging and pulling, but he restrained me. It was awful; you should never change your mind and chicken out if you're going to commit suicide. They pumped my stomach and plastered heart monitors over me and stuck IV tubes into my arms. I never thought this would happen. It happened through a darkness, a hell. When I woke up there was blood and charcoal all over the sheets and tubes snaking in and out of me. I was groggy.

They took me to the Psychiatric Assessment Unit, where women were screaming and men were talking incessantly. One woman was crying in a Quiet Room; another woman claimed that she had been there for forty years and only someone on top of a mountain flicking a switch could let her out for a while. There was the same doll-like nurse who instantly asked if I'd found religion yet, and the same stone-faced psychiatrist, who talked to me with two female students. Then Melanie arrived and they talked to her. I remember thrashing around last night before falling asleep, pleading for Dr. Hightower, but they wouldn't bring him. It was all out of some dumb movie I wanted to end! Why hadn't I gone to sleep under the covers and let the pills dissolve? Why was it so painful, why was everything so fucking painful? When am I going to die? I can't take it much longer; I can't take any of this. I'm so sick.

No more sleeping pills, no way to die except off the bridge. Oh God. Jennifer came today and Melanie told her I wasn't ready for Independent Living after what happened; the people at the hospital told her that too and now she doesn't know if the Ministry will approve it for September 1. The possibility that they will is very slim unless I go drug-free and follow certain rules. More games to play. I wish I could die easily. Oh God it hurt so much, swallowing that tube with the charcoal splattering everywhere, the blood. I want to die.

And Jennifer's blue eyes were crying there on the couch and I went to her and wondered how, how can you care about anybody, please don't, DON'T, you'll only get hurt. I couldn't disappoint her, but I'm hurting too. I want her to be happy. I want people like her who care too much and hurt too much to just be happy. She deserves so much better than this. It hurts and there are tears and blood and I really doubt if I can make it this time.

PART VI

august 14 to october 1 1987

August 14

Now having to play different games and tell lies, even to my psychiatrist. How did it ever get so out of hand? The fear is engulfing, the anxiety, and yes—now the depression; it sinks in, weary and nauseating. Each nightmare is like a card from a deck, flopping one over the other, rapidly—Melanie saying I'm not ready for the apartment, the supervisor postponing Independent Living, Dr. Hightower not helping, Larry with his drugs—alone, no pills, wanting to die. It's too late now, Evelyn, you chickened out at the crucial moment.

My anxiety about being able to move into my apartment on September 1 is overwhelming, coupled with my general weakness after the overdose. The place seems so beautiful now. I couldn't love it more. It was seeing the apartment and Jennifer's face hovering around it—Jennifer, who had made it possible for me—that made me vomit and call the police. If they delay the plan under the delusion that I won't be safe living on my own—as if Melanie is any support, as if I couldn't as easily kill myself there—then I'm scared about what will happen. School starts in September; if I can't move into my apartment then, I basically can't go to school, because I signed up at a school in the East End.

Dr. Hightower admitted that it was the politics, that if I killed myself in my apartment social services would look bad. That's very sad. It's hard being this angry and unable to take any of it out, because if I did, then the whole mental health care system would open its jaws wide and swallow me up; there would be the torment and the depression and most of all the feeling of being trapped, and then I don't think I would be able to come out again.

Now I'm left with the fear of coming home to Melanie's each night, the fear that is no different from when I was living with my parents and it engulfed my every tremulous step towards 'home.' I am terrified of this place and of Melanie, knowing that no matter how I act she will still be against me. The anger feeds on itself inside me and grows and grows. It's ready to swallow the world—this immense hatred, resentment, hostility.

Still it is the drugs that can take me away, temporarily, from something that could be developing into a nervous breakdown, this intensity and suppression. The methadone helps for a while, but it isn't enough anymore. I woke up last night at 3:30 a.m. itching everywhere from the drug, the nightmares tumbling in assorted realities around me, sleepless and frightened.

I need to be in my apartment where I move around like a neurotic housewife, touching this and that, making sure everything is in its rightful place, beaming with desperate pride. I am really so alone in this. If I hadn't chickened out that night, none of this would be happening right now. The apartment would not be wafting in the air of the future. I would not still be so careless with drugs and so lonely, upset without them.

August 16

The only friend I have is Larry. I don't have any more sleeping pills except when he gives me Mandrax. Last night we did methadone together and it wasn't enough, but with not working I can scarcely afford what we're doing as it is. We also went to buy Valium from Kyle and Wendy. A day without drugs drags on forever, is hardly endurable—isn't it funny how a year ago I had wanted to go into Detox for the experience, and Dr. Graham had looked at me with amazement. Then I was dropping LSD and smoking pot. And on Monday Dr. Graham looked at me and said, 'Why don't you go into Detox?' I wouldn't now unless somebody physically forced me; I couldn't bear going straight. But when lines of poetry wriggle into my head, I can't write a poem. I don't feel attracted to my writing at all, and once again it's all right. It's not a major crime. A major crime is going for a day without drugs. Larry and what he can give me to feel normal and even—yes—happy is the only support I have, the only thing I can count on, the only thing I feel good about. Living at Melanie's is like a prison term, and it's no longer a matter of am I going to be a writer or am I going to be a drug addict? That doesn't matter; that's ridiculously irrelevant compared with the everyday struggle, the delicious pleasure and reprieve of methadone or Mandrax or something to keep me alive (which I want to be) yet satisfied with both myself and my world.

August 18

On my way home from Larry's last night the bus stop was excruciatingly cold, so I stuck out my thumb. A man in a long dark blue car pulled up. C. was in his twenties, with heavily sprayed blond hair that feathered over his forehead, a hooked nose. There was a computerized message area on the dashboard, and doors that could be locked by the driver. He was wearing a long-sleeved, pale yellow shirt. I slumped in the passenger seat and asked him to take me to Kitsilano.

C. cruised around the West End for a while, apparently looking for his coke connection. We decided to park somewhere for a blow job. A quick trick, I thought, knowing only that the money was necessary for methadone. C. had been in group homes and foster homes before, and he now owned three cars and hired girls from escort services. That was all he told me. In the parking lot he wanted me to take my top off, or no thirty dollars. Cheap bastard. I said I could make a lot more dressed up and told him to fuck off. He really wanted it by then, though, so he agreed—thirty dollars for head, nothing else.

C. got violent in the middle of it. He tore my bra off. When I started to protest he said over and over, 'Be a good girl, or I'll give you a spanking.' He would have beaten me up afterwards anyway. He shoved my head up and down, then climbed on top of me. I was struggling by then. It was dark and the parking lot was empty except for us. I writhed and tried to push him off, but he was much stronger than me. He wanted to fuck, and I was afraid he would take out a knife. He tore my shirt off and then came all over me, squirting over my breasts and my stomach and my thighs. I want to disown this body now, cast it forever into the winds. It is too gross to be mine, it will always be scrawled with oozing white semen.

I stopped struggling and relaxed, stroked his hair fondly, caressed his arms and his back. I mumbled that I was too cramped; would he get back into his seat for a moment?

I grabbed my bag and scrambled for the door handle. When I couldn't find it, I almost wept.

'You're locked in.'

Click. But I found the door handle a split second before he reached to lock the doors and the door swung wide. God. The night. I tumbled out with my top half off and my bra dangling. God. God.

I didn't know what to do, but Emergency Services was three blocks away. I went there to wash off. A social worker told me to write up a description of the guy, and then he drove me home.

August 25

Fifth day of staying clean. It feels like it's been a month, but I know I can't stay on drugs forever. Walking in the too-brilliant sunshine, I am envisioning Larry in his car opening the glove box and waving a bottle of methadone back and forth, back and forth, hypnotically before my eyes. The third day was probably roughest—depression and exhaustion combined with severe nausea and a suffocating sensation. I couldn't seem to get any oxygen.

There are so many people I want to impress on paper—to impress period. The writing is coming back, and that's what's keeping me going: hours at the typewriter. Through the stifling heat I walk and breathe the need and want of my writing.

My session with Dr. Hightower today was very productive; we did more work in that one hour than in the past several months, probably since I've been on dope. I was so ready to work and so proud of being clean. Dr. Hightower wrote down what emerged after thirty-five minutes of talking about prostitution:

'... I was fulfilling someone, which I couldn't do as a child with my parents.'

I said that! He didn't. It came out of my mouth. It's just a sentence, some words, really very simple in fact, but after the initial euphoria and pride, the fear set in. The anxiety. The feeling of having the stuffing bled out of me, of being lost, of being stripped.

'Do you realize the importance of what you just said?'

It's too heavy. It's probably been evident to everybody else for a long time, and evident to Dr. Hightower. By giving blow jobs that resulted in orgasms, I had fulfilled somebody, which I couldn't do as a child with my parents. It hadn't mattered that it had only been a trick, a customer, a john. It was somebody. The worst part of this realization is knowing that I hadn't ever been able to satisfy my parents, and I certainly can't now. That it's hopeless. That I have to give up trying. That Dr. Hightower was right in saying there's no use in hoping they'll change—yet unconsciously I had nourished that hope. I didn't know there was all this inside me!

I want some Valium. But I won't touch it, I swear I won't, except Larry called this evening and I could have gotten methadone, I could have hooked him again so easily, but instead everything wavered and I tried so goddamn hard to push him away with a calm voice, though that shook too. The familiarity of Larry's voice. The gift of drugs it could bring. We were both cool towards each other, but I did ask him to call back tomorrow morning. I just couldn't resist! I can't do it! The allure of drugs. I felt a sense of betrayal, as though I'd been cheated, on hearing Kirk had signed himself into Detox. I want him to fail, need him to come back out and rejoin us, need that whole community I have tried these past few days to give up.

Yet I also want to be myself, turning to my journal like this when I have a problem, writing it out instead of muffling it further into my subconsciousness with dope. I want to feel whole, healthy and happy, and be able to deal with things straight. I want to eliminate my compulsive attitude towards drugs so that it won't deter me from progressing as a human being with potential. I want the very best for myself. Please keep me strong. Yet, oh God, I want Larry to be there tomorrow with methadone. I want it badly and the feelings that come along with it—all's right with the world and with me. Those feelings! Who said that things get easier? I hope you, my writing, can help. Don't weaken now, when you need to be stronger than ever, when you need to be attractive and absolutely irresistible.

August 30

Groping through the Valium mist, I was spectacular at the meeting about Independent Living today. Melanie appeared nervous, and I wanted to reach across the table with sympathy in my eyes and press a tranquilizer into her palm. Jennifer sketched my activities during the five months at Melanie's and left it at that; I answered questions, posed suggestions, explained, elaborated. It was all like some brightly lit dream in that fluorescent room and I was fine; everything was just fine. Nobody had to say anything; I could have carried on the meeting by myself. I even suggested that for the first month I spend weekends at Melanie's, to adjust. They approved the Independent Living, of course, on the following conditions: weekends to be spent at Melanie's in September, weekly contact with Jennifer, school, an end to prostitution, continued therapy with Dr. Hightower, continued progress with my writing, a self-defence course. Jennifer and Melanie were astonished at my behavior, anticipating outbursts, tears, running from the room. They didn't know that now I always had the magic of Valium within reach and could cope with anything.

It occurred to me later that maybe I didn't want to live alone after all, didn't want to ever be alone. My apartment in the basement no longer shone with an unattainable beauty—there were the stains on the carpet, the baby spiders hatching in the cupboards, the silence. I wondered why I'd struggled so hard for it, seen it as a salvation. Larry isn't around much anymore, and perhaps I had begun to see the apartment as an oasis not for growth and a return to education but for sex and drug-taking and ultimately death. But I'd spoiled my chance at death. Ironic that I should have floated convincingly through the conference only because the pills Larry had given me were holding me up. Without them I'd have drowned; it would have been the disaster it perhaps should have been.

August 31

Larry has become an inconvenience attached to the blessing of drugs, ugly wrapping that has to be patiently peeled away before the gift can be snatched. Something in me hates him so much for what he's done that it wants him to die, wants to kill him in fact, and sometimes it looks like he's not that far from death—he's sick all the time. But he mustn't die; where would the prescriptions come from then, and the methadone?

I don't want to appear desperate or hooked, if that's what I sound like, because I want to believe that's not the truth. Tomorrow is the first of September, time to move, and I shouldn't have denied that I still hope it will be a big change from this existence, a leap into some paradise or other, a whole new life in fact.

September 1

Well, I feel I should have something to show for today, this first day of my independence. Hence the obligatory journal entry. No, it's not really that, it's just that I'm upset because there were the makings of a story lurking in me and I wrote copiously before tearing it up. It was too daring. I'm not ready yet, or is that a cop-out? I haven't written a short story for over a year, only the odd vignette. The latest idea came from a dream. Dr. Hightower had said that it had all the makings of a story. But it scares me too much, this idea of creating something that is actually a miniature book. I try to tell myself it doesn't matter but it does; that's the problem.

I don't think I'll ever prostitute myself again, not after working through the reasons with Dr. Hightower. The idea is barely conceivable now—Evelyn, a prostitute? No, the two don't go together, so why try and make them?

I don't feel like writing. Sorry, another time. Just checking in to say that things are fine and that maybe they'll turn out, no promises, just maybe. I'll work hard.

September 3

Again, I couldn't make it past the sixth day of staying clean. Dr. Graham had revealed that the third day isn't the hardest, not with methadone—it's the sixth, seventh and eight days that are most difficult. And here I'd been thinking that I could treat myself once a week and thus cleverly never be addicted! He said that so long as I juiced even just once a week, my body would continue to be wired.

It wasn't particularly difficult for me yesterday; it was the availability of the methadone that finally overtook me in the evening. I'm doing really well in this apartment otherwise, grateful for the space, feeling much more motivated to continue with my writing. I feel whole and complete, and pleased at being able to manage. I feel safe, as if I belong to the house, not cut off, not jailed in any way.

But except for a few hours, I haven't slept for four nights. No Rivotrils. I'm anxious, too, and have headaches and incessant nausea. I'm worried about not having enough money; this apartment would vanish if I were caught working the streets, which has become too genuinely horrible and frightening to consider now anyway.

Larry spent the night and I got four hours' sleep. The methadone gave me a sense of well-being, relaxation and wholeness, but my pupils didn't get as pinned as they used to. He also gave me four Mandrax, two tranquilizers and two Darvon. Larry professed to feel guilty and immoral about providing me with methadone, but wasn't that only because I didn't pay? He sounds like he's not going back on the methadone program, though: 'Going back on methadone would be like being in a snowstorm wrapped in an electric blanket, but with no place to go.'

Anxiety sometimes takes control of me. Perhaps I can't really cope with this idea of adulthood. My parents stole my childhood and most of my adolescence; now I'm not really a teenager and never have been. That's tough. I hope that I'll start doing some serious writing in my English class at school and that gradually the negative shit will be gone; I want to be like a snake wriggling out of its old skin. Above all, with Dr. Hightower's help, I hope to be able to integrate my childhood experiences into the present—no denial, no blocking out—and go on to develop the self-esteem I've been lacking.

September 6

If it weren't for the sadness it wouldn't be so bad. I've been seeing a lot of my parents, partly to be with my sister Karen, partly to pick up my old belongings from them, partly for self-punishment. If it were just the rage at my mother's unchanged personality and my father's unchanged silence, then it would be manageable. But my mother persists in making small, desperate, pathetic gestures of love; my father persists in attempting an understanding silence. It tears me apart. It makes me want to kill somebody or destroy something while simultaneously committing suicide. The sadness is unbearable, watching my parents try to contain themselves, try not to do anything wrong or alienate me again. Yet their attempts are so obvious, clumsy, revealing all the more starkly what they are trying to hide. Their efforts fall short but are efforts nonetheless, and it makes me feel immensely sad, a sorrow that burns and washes in the biggest fires and oceans. I want to protect them, throw my arms around them and demonstrate total, self-sacrificing love. And I know I can't because it isn't there. Hope is etched plainly in their faces; perhaps their hearts are in their throats waiting for some gesture of acceptance from me. I sometimes put my arms around them, casually, but that's when I'm stoned. Which is most of the time.

I've lost the battle with drugs for a while. Sometimes I'm so out of it on downers, early in the morning, that I lurch and weave and have to hang on to Karen for support, but my parents never notice. Their ignorance protects them, their tremendous resistance against the truth—I have no hope of breaking through that wall because it shields them so well.

I've told Larry I hate him and want to kill him, but we spend more and more of our time together. It's compulsive. I can't seem to exist without him, my body, a space in me craves him—he too is perhaps a space—but when he's there and I'm straight he's intolerable. So it's Larry's drugs that melt me towards him and away from lucidity. I've been taking methadone too often again; yesterday it didn't even pin my pupils. We're going to have to double the dosage. I slept three hours last night, scratching at myself, leaving trails. I don't know what to do, am at too much of a loss, am frantic with stress or weak from lack of sleep.

Larry is coming over tonight, in an hour or so, after work. The light is on above the desk and I'm typing here, groping for words, shaping them out of the nothing porridge of my brain. I spent the weekend dutifully at Melanie's, or part of it anyway, enough to make the obligatory gesture we perhaps all know is nothing but a gesture. I hated it.

It was an inconvenience, with my typewriter and books and personal belongings left here in the apartment. It made things worse, brought me to the brink of depression.

One of my old regulars phoned at Melanie's on Saturday morning, and after much hedging, after telling him plainly, 'I don't do it anymore,' I agreed: a hundred dollars for head at his place. The money didn't matter; it was only paper money. I had been able to resist until I asked why he wanted me so much and he said, 'Because you're different.' Still snatching at something that might define my individuality in this mess, I went for it, and we drove to R.'s home, drinking rum and Coke and smoking his surprise, which he proffered with irresistible childish delight: a joint of hash. 'Saved for my sweetheart.'

I couldn't refuse, and as usual popped Gravol in the bathroom to prevent the flags of nausea from swamping me, twirling and choking and dragging. R. was fat and disproportioned, and he got a kick out of me because I was 'down to earth,' refused to sip my drink and bat my eyelids—what's the use anymore? Dr. Hightower would be curious as to why I went for it, since I'm no longer a prostitute and no longer have any need for that identity. But familiar things are still safe. Even if that safety is on narrow, treacherous ground—like R., a ball of white fat lolling on his waterbed on top of me, ready to fuck me. I had to roll him off like a beach ball—can't, I'll get pregnant, don't you know? One day someone will not be afraid of that word. But then there won't be another day; it was what we call an Isolated Incident; it probably won't happen again.

At our next session I'll be too drugged to be able to do any therapy with Dr. Hightower, anything of significance; I feel no urge or curiosity. With the drugs, I slip too far back in progress to make it seem worthwhile, this psychotherapy.

I wonder, you know, if I shouldn't just give up. It's becoming tiresome; I have nothing to fight. The people who still bother to interest themselves in appearances are satisfied: Hey, it looks like Evelyn's healing; she's got her own place; she's seeing her parents; she's going back to school. And indeed all these things are happening, but boy if you knew the rage and the despair, the sickness, the unspeakable and inexpressible sadness, most frightening yet most desirable of all the pure blank space that sometimes flops listlessly between my ears. That is all. I exist and go from day to day, waiting for something internal or external to explode or come painfully together, standing there on the pavement while everything, the dreamscape, moves gradually past ... Wanting to surprise Larry with a knife spurted right through him, the end and then the slow, happy construction of the beginning.

September 8

'Who wants to be down when they could be up?' as 'Alice' had written in her journal, Go Ask Alice. I think I do. Deadened. It's what I've been searching for my whole life; now I realize with surprise why downers are so attractive.

Yesterday morning at school went all right, nerve-wracking at first, but I approached it with the right attitude after preparation by Dr. Hightower. Not like last year, when I went there aloof, hating the authority figures of the teachers, holding my worldliness in front of me like a shield. The community inside a school isn't so horrendous after all. Ran into Lana and we talked a bit; I connected with a few people, behaving like myself, not defensive. A teenager. Semblances and stretches of normalcy.

September 9

We take ten minutes each day in English to write a journal entry, so from now on I'll incorporate some of what I write in it:

'The teacher sounds like my psychiatrist. 'Don't censor your thoughts. This could be therapy for some of you. You can record dreams if you want.' He steps back and spreads his arms. Laughter.

'Perhaps I could write out my desperation, the piercing thought that school is no more tolerable than it was before, that I need out! Valium. I could call Larry before lunch and he could arrive, no questions asked, no unnecessary meaningless gestures of love, with his spice bottle of methadone. I could float happy and untouchable through Science and French. Little else matters. Drugs and school weren't meant to have a plus sign between them (besides, what would they equal?), but I want it now, with a wild passion—who can stop me? The paper swirls. No mind-blowing new thoughts; I told you that drugs would be a boring topic in the end. They permeate my thoughts mercilessly. I dream consciously of an ocean of bitter, horrible-tasting yellow liquid, child of Kyle and Wendy, flowing over this pale marked desk, over these virgin pages, over my blue fingernails ... Over me. Over me! I want to smother in it.

'Drugs are no inspiration whatsoever, after the first few joints, the first two or three acid trips, maybe the first experiment with methadone. There is nothing left to write about that anybody might be interested in. What conceit, to think that someone would want to read a journal in which the promising young author rattles incoherently about dope. They would be angry. I, however, am not angry, only desperate. I want something so bad! Would drop a hit of acid if it would make everything disappear, but we know from experience that it wouldn't do any good.

'I have Valium, Mandrax and LSD in my backpack, along with the school duo-tangs, the peanut butter sandwich for lunch. I want to be seen through by teenage X-ray eyes as somebody trashed. Where am I going to make it if not here? I've run out of ideas, tactics, inspirations. The thought of suicide flops like wide canvas cloth over me, suffocating, convincing in its finality.'

Today was rough, although it doesn't seem so bad now that it is 1 a.m. and I'm still riding the methadone, each typewriter key hitting the page a shock to my system. A lot is happening and it's frightening.

Here at school, faced once again with the problem of fitting in, the only kids I have anything in common with are the rockers. People have called me 'brazen'—have they thought that brazenness hides awkwardness, loneliness? I still want to fit in and have begun to hang around with the kids in black leather jackets, who love heavy metal, hate homosexuals and nerds, who put people down, who literally can't say three words without 'fuck' hurled in for good measure. They are probably more conformist than any other group, but one of them has attached himself to me.

I barely got through today, bursting into tears several times when no one was around or looking; I was dying for methadone! It was really bad and finally I took a Valium.

The classes are long and difficult. I've totally forgotten my Science and French; you must remember the time that has lapsed between Grade 10 at my former high school and the present, which would be enough for a lifetime for some people. I spent my free block, lunch hour and after school with my new friend, listening to the ravings of him and his friends about heavy metal, drugs, their laughter over suicides. I knew I would be immediately dismissed if I showed even a glimmer of intelligence, insight or creativity, if I said 'I don't have any' instead of 'I don't got none.' So Evelyn said, 'I don't got none,' and was accepted. For me, that's torture. This whole business turns my stomach so much that I'm about to puke over these mocking typewriter keys. Oh Christ. Yet with my experiences there's no one else to fit in with, to talk to, to have anything in common with. But it can't continue, I realize that now. For me to speak in monosyllables, to bite back my individuality, is nauseating, is chewing through me.

I'm actually feeling ill. I don't know what to do. School is hell and the irony is (if I can smile at it at all) that I'm going to be taking something every day in order to get through. Tomorrow at lunch Larry is picking me up to buy Valium. Oh God, help me please.

September 10

'The people in this classroom rustle back and forth. It doesn't matter what I write because the teacher looks for quantity, not quality. I am starved for education, but at the same time school is a waste of time. I don't know how to act anymore, the appearances have been stripped by methadone.

'Once at my former high school, during Science class, the students scrambled to the windows to watch a kid being arrested outside for dealing weed. He was kicking in his cage of blue arms. It meant nothing to me then.

'The silent buzzes, hum of fluorescent lights, as if in sympathy. The teacher has left the room and some of the kids have turned around, chattering loudly. I'm getting fed up with all this, though a part of me is attracted to the textbooks, opens them eagerly like a dog seizing a bone. Yet most of me hates this, needs more dope to fight it—Larry gave me four Mandrax and three tranquilizers yesterday.

'Giggles. Whispers. The juice has left its scars—scarlet welts (burst vessels?), lumps, thin lines where I scratched too hard in sleep. The poison oozed through my pores, the excess.

'The bell rings. The students have been poised for the past several minutes and now rush like a tidal wave out the door. Alone in an English classroom, finishing off—what?'

If the apartment didn't bolster my spirits, I would consider committing suicide, but instead I sit here with a throbbing headache, slightly drunk. I found my own locker today, though my new friend and I are causing trouble in Math Modified; I had an argument on sexism today with the teacher simply because he was conducting a girls vs. boys competition on the blackboard. Embarrassed afterwards, I couldn't remember what I had said. I'll be lucky if I pass any of my subjects, except English. Jennifer isn't available; I could be working the street for all anyone cares. No one really does; I want to kill someone but know that if anyone dies because of Evelyn it'll be Evelyn herself.

September 15

It has been five months out of my life. Five months of Valium, Darvon, Mandrax and methadone dependency. Methadone was at first a three-day high, but now it's no more than a change of mood, a relaxation. I take it to keep myself going, to maintain what has become 'normal,' to prevent pain or discomfort or panic—or work on my writing. Five months have been taken out of my life, and I am angry. I am not going to continue this way, not when a one-minute oral report in English leads to a notation in my datebook: 'Valium!' I refuse to be hard on my body and most of all on the strength, the life-force, the healthy part of me that includes my writing. There are too many side effects—forgotten conversations, lapses of time, unbidden hostilities, nausea, desperation, incredible anxiety, insomnia. There are bottles around my apartment with Mandrax, Valium and the odd Darvon in them and I shall keep them, they aren't going down the toilet, but it's not a huge supply and I won't be using them recklessly. Larry is going. I will be strong, healthy; I will fill the hundreds of hours he has stolen, the hours of mock suicide through pills and liquids, with learning and writing and sleeping and friends.

I am going to stop taking methadone. I am going to stop seeing Larry. I am going to cut down on the pills, which will free my drug-preoccupied mind for more interesting escapades. These are not deprivations—these are the destruction of roadblocks, these are the paths towards growth and what has always been my destiny: success as a writer.

Dr. Hightower made it clear for me today. I'm growing up. I'm back in school, which occupies most of the day, and I've stopped working the streets. I have my own cozy apartment. He said that I was not seeing Larry to get drugs; I was doing the drugs to see Larry. This enraged me before I understood what he meant. Larry has been an anchor for the past five months; he has become safe, familiar and reliable. I have become hooked on him as much as the drugs themselves, because I could swing him around my little finger. A power I have unwittingly craved. He was handy as a companion, lover, therapist and supplier of some form of happiness.

Recently I wanted to refuse methadone more and more, but I kept taking it because I was afraid of losing Larry without it, since I couldn't tolerate being with him straight. And if I lost him the methadone wouldn't be there if and when I really did need it, in times of panic. We were supposed to juice tonight, though I felt no need.

I am secure. I have turned down the ringer on the phone. I'm going out tonight to meditate with the Zen Buddhists. Dr. Graham gave me a few Rivotrils to help with the anxiety, so they will cut out the necessity for Valium, pot, and the crazy blue Mandrax that I succumb to at 4:30 a.m., preventing me from making it to any of my morning classes.

I am not going to take methadone tonight, I do not need five Valium to get through one minute of standing in front of an English class, I do not need to be dragged down by Larry, who has become less of a person and more of a symbol, I do not need to take a path that culminates in a dead end. Evelyn remains a writer and a whole human being, not someone broken and chipped into fragments. I don't even need to be vindictive to Larry.

Five months is almost half a year of my life, and it's been enough numbness for a while. I'm not going to pretend that it's going to be easy, but I am going to continue, free of methadone and free of Larry.

September 16

'It was a symbolic suicide, each pill, each cup of methadone. So many times, lying sleepless at night, I have longed to direct a gun at my head and thus spiral dizzy sparkling colored into the original pattern of things. The pattern before the separation of birth.

'After the first elation, there is the emotional and physical coping. Larry is gone, for good, for GOOD, do you hear that, you little dark side that aches here in this English classroom, suffocating. Knowing you would be content and talkative if you had received the present of methadone delivered into your hands? Seeping through future and destiny, coloring mine black. There is no other way to do it. As Dr. Graham had said, it's now or later; a few months later it would just be harder.

'I will be good to myself, forgive myself, for at that first point of contact—pills into hand—I did not know. I really couldn't have known. In fact Larry deserved worse than the short mild good-bye he received; he deserved far worse. I hope he goes to fucking hell! Well, all right, he is living his hell here on earth, as are most of us. I hope he dies painfully, knowing that he was and always has been a coward, a failure, that he was never able to rise above the excuse of narcotics.

'I won't look for other Larrys; I refuse to relive the nightmare only with a different man, a different drug. The small black voice claims that it wasn't all a nightmare, there were the pleasures, the ability to cope, the successes. His gentlest touches, his being there. The voice says that I would not have been showered with applause and praise at my poetry reading had I not been on methadone and therefore calm enough to perform.

'I don't want this entry to end this way. I am free now. There will be space (not emptiness), the space he once occupied, to be filled with creativity. Larry ceased to be a person and became only a name—one of hundreds of sugar daddies and drug suppliers who directed hundreds of bad, trite movies that killed the actresses.'

September 21

'Suddenly everything invades. The fluorescent lights wiggle over my forehead and lip in sweat. Glowing worms of light, heat in bars, writhe—they want to come off the blackboard and squirm between the posters on the wall. It shouldn't be me. What are you still being punished for? The lights come between your eyes and the paper in fluorescent eyelashes. Once you latch onto a savior you never let go! These teenagers are unfamiliar creatures; you shouldn't have come here like this. How can you exist not wanting to be stoned? I can't let this happen; there have been too many experiences to integrate, hot tears sparkling in my eyes, the blow job and titfuck you remember too vividly and him with his stiff blond hair. Suddenly all this snow. I am shaking too much inside. Brilliant snow. The acid should have been in the teacher's coffee, not mine. You weren't going to punish yourself again. You were petrified, like the snowed-in spider in its agony of poison spray, too huge for imagining. I am writing on a beam of fluorescent light, I am like that lone bomb out in the ocean. How can I go home after what is happening now, all this incredible white light in slivers and fur around each of us, barriers or openings?

'This is the teenage world and I've seen so little of it for so long that this must not happen. I cannot understand teenage humor, or is it cruelty, the looks, I cannot stand the looks, the eyes must be cut out. Who can relax when teenage creatures surround me?

'My whole life exists in one basement. If something happens to the basement I am dead. I depend wholly on the basement being there. I am terrified that they will take my home away from me! I would rather be raped a million times than have that happen; in fact if something goes wrong that will have to be the case. Out there again on the street corner.

'Where do these ice-cream rainbows come from? This is not real life in this room. How can these people allow themselves to be dissected and examined as though they were something minuscule under a microscope, trying to curl up into themselves, defending and sparring, each of them looking for safety. What you, Evelyn, don't realize is that you're the only one receiving the snow and the quivering rainbows in your eyes. Everything is so totally different, yet no one notices. I hate you who stand for one minute in front of an English classroom and think that you can be judged. The layers of multi-colored writing underneath this paper are more real to me than that one minute in front of a fucking English class. I am getting really freaked out because why am I here in this too brightly lit room; why are there spun silences I can put fingers through? How has it become that the basement has become more than a life? But shit, it takes up more space in the universe than I ever may, space that can be filled with rainbows and worms. The light is in patches and it radiates in jagged prisms. All of you are too contained within your bodies. An English II classroom. Girls, have you ever been out there, sucking off an old man's prick, seeing the ugliness behind the concealing blackness, legs tottering tattering on heels? It frightens you too much, doesn't it, the men stopping and the women bending over, needing money to pay for the fleeting happiness that all of us snatch at: that one thread in the neon darkness. When the cars stopped you always hoped it would be different, that somebody would step out and hold you and stop the shaking. Too much is exploding, the suicide with the pills on the dresser. These people weren't there. I have to go back to my apartment; I'd rather be out on the street fucking fucking fucking old men to keep that space. Oh God, help me, I'M AFRAID I'LL GO BACK TO THE STREET TO KEEP AN ILLUSION ...

'People are joking about rape. You try it. You fucking try being in a car fighting for whatever's left of your life through a swamp of Mandrax suddenly realizing: You could be dead ...

'Fuck, I would rather be out on the street than in this classroom to keep my apartment. That familiarity is easier ... None of you know ... My two worlds are too far apart. I'm in the hallway now, hard on the ground, I don't want to die with my life still full of shit. You weren't going to have to come back to school. You were going to be able to take it to the street, to the real world, and be able to survive and pay the rent and be different, BECOME A WRITER. You were going to be given the time, space and resources to do that, because they all knew that otherwise you'd die and there was something they saw that they could not let die. But it can in school hallways; it's going to get trampled here.

'They cannot invade. They are all seeing too much of me. I can take any invasion of body, but not this. It is worse than anything.

'Sometimes I think I'd rather be out there sleazing so long as no one ever saw me. They can see too much of me here. She goes out to seek the blind spots, where no one can see her, where she can hide and perhaps be her true self: a girl in the sun.

'This writing is so much better than sex: the union of paper and pen. Bodies are all around me and moving.'

September 24

Yesterday I freed myself from all sorts of mental and emotional anguish by deciding to quit school. Dr. Hightower had warned me against it, saying that after so many times of attempting to return to school, dropping out again would bring my self-esteem crashing down and I would get screwed up enough to lose my apartment, end up in a group home, run away, try committing suicide (and perhaps succeed), be hospitalized. No! I listened to what he said, and though I left his office and went into the sunshine with a determination to stay in class, it just became too much. I had difficulty fitting in, and without masking myself, I couldn't fit in at all. That was the main thing. Then there were the long hours, the work. My acid trip this week revealed a few things: I often think about killing myself simply because I can't fit in anywhere. I allow a lot of people into my life and open up to them, but after this initial intimacy I withdraw. They can't see how insecure I am inside. They never really know who I am.

On Tuesday, with Dr. Hightower's approval, I called the police, and a cop came by to take notes about what had happened with Larry. Larry could, at this very moment, be doing the same thing to a susceptible kid or woman that he did to me. Dr. Hightower had also pointed out that Larry's doctor was being watched closely by the police—he overprescribes to his druggie patients, who are, as I know from experience, selling parts of their prescriptions. But it wasn't solely for these reasons that I allowed Larry's full name, his reality as a living, weak person, to slip past my lips. I do have a need for revenge—on behalf of my writing, my dreams, the essence of who I am. Violation has taken place. The police likely won't be able to do anything, but maybe something will come of it.

Last night I went out to Larry's apartment. It was too big to trash. Besides, I never go out of my way to hurt people. Being there brought out sadness and desire; I remembered vaguely the many nights on the couch and in the bedroom, doing the junkie nod. It had seemed like a piece of paradise then. I went over the apartment methodically, curiously, opening drawers, looking under couches. There were pictures of Larry and his old girlfriend, cards of love; I tried to peer inside this woman who had come before me and had also torn herself away. She too had sought safety and gentleness in Larry, away from her life as a dancer and a hooker.

In the apartment were two televisions, a VCR, lots of tapes and books—stuff I could have impersonally destroyed, but I didn't. It would have been a childish thing to do.

After deciding to quit school, I felt tranquil, happy. Suddenly there was creative independent time again, in which I could enjoy my apartment, write, read. School had prompted me into drinking (yes, early in the morning). It's kind of hard to pay attention or write tests when your head is fogged up, your eyes are sleepy-shut and you wobble to and from classes. I figured my health and clarity were more important than education. Yet I have trepidations about losing my friends and relatives as a result of this decision, which they might perceive as a failure.

Jennifer returned from her vacation yesterday but has been too busy to call back, so I'm waiting to talk to her. There may still be other options—i.e., correspondence school—but my main concern is whether or not social services will leave me alone if I don't go to school and refuse to budge from my apartment. I could work the street a couple of nights a month and pay for rent and food; I also have money in the bank, saved from prostitution. I had vowed not to touch the money until I received Independent Living and needed it. If worst came to worst, that would give me two months to think things over and come up with something, although I'd probably be back on the street before long.

But I am calm. Why worry too much about things until you know what the alternatives are?

October 1

I am sick and tired of swallowing the guilt and pain of everything. Alcohol does not make me prolific or brilliant. I can find no normalcy in being a writer; I am not even on the same plane as other crazed authors. I am sick of blank waiting paper, but it is the only thing I have. I want to get out, take a few Mandrax and see if they'll do the trick, slice something sharp and radiant across something soft and malleable—a throat. I want to plunge a knife into someone who is not myself, but I lack courage. Who is it you're afraid to injure? Why is he more important than you? I am consumed with rage. I hate men. I could never turn a trick again because it would fuck up everything, as if there were anything here in the first place to fuck up, what a lie, what a delusion, fuck you, Evelyn, you bitch, you cunt, you fucking cocksucker. I can't stand this earth with these men and want to get out. I want to get off and spiral who fucking cares where, this is all shit, there's so much shit being flung in my face from every direction, you think you see safety and let down your barrier for an instant and wham you get it right in the face. It happens every time. I'm not so drugged anymore that I can't see it. Reality is ugly.

I don't know whether to cry (as if that were possible anymore) or cut myself open a little or scream or burn the house down. A man picked me up hitchhiking a few weeks ago. J. looked and sounded like my psychiatrist, intelligent and insightful, so comforting, a friend, someone to trust. He called tonight and said we had a 'friend' in common, I couldn't guess who. It turned out that he knew a girl from New Beginnings who had remembered me, though we hadn't lived together. I'd met her once when I'd gone back to say hello to the housemother—a thin blond girl, addicted to Talwin and Ritalin, who worked the street. J. had known her for eight months—they'd met in the same way we had—and they'd slept together twice. Apparently she considers him a friend, though she is too drugged up to really care or notice, the little fifteen-year-old girl. Tonight, drunk, J. was all over me, me biting into myself, hating it, him misreading and thinking that he could love me, that shit again. It won't work this time, that shit about needing me, God who needs that, I don't, do you want to look for another Larry? Is that it? Do you want to feel smart and beautiful on a street corner? Fuck you, Evelyn, go dig a hole and crawl in. I really let down some big barriers for this guy J. because he appeared trustworthy, a friend, oh yeah sure, he was too insightful, hey look at Larry—ALL MEN ARE THE SAME. I'll go run off and abandon them all to find a rich publisher who'd love me, God, anyone, anyone, anyone who for once wouldn't lie, but how could I tell now? How could I tell? After almost two years of being out in the world this bitch still

trusts, still can't figure out who's an asshole and who's half-decent—
but maybe that's because there's no one decent. Take anyone, thrust
him in front of me, and automatically he'll take advantage. Try it! God
I hate men. I hate life.

PART VII

october 9 to december 20 1987

October 9

I crawled into my basement neighbor Ed's bed last night and slept there. Someday he will be a character in a book or story of mine if I ever get dialogue right. I'm fascinated by him—he admits to being vulnerable and insecure, yet he's honest about his emotions. Despite that honesty, Ed is impenetrable. When he hides behind his sunglasses, he seems walled off; I don't know where the secrets lie.

He thinks of me as a friend and shows no interest in having sex with me. I feel frustrated and inadequate (especially after crawling into his bed—is that an invitation or what?), though I know that if our relationship became sexual it would be difficult living here, and he would lose his unattainability, which I find so riveting.

He watched me sleep, not used to another body in his double bed. I woke up at 5 a.m. and lay quite still, the bed shaking as he tossed and turned. At times he pressed himself against me, and ran his fingers down my body. In sleepy triumph I thought, hey, he is seduceable, subconsciously at least—but when Ed realized I was awake and we started talking, he said that he'd just been trying to nudge me farther over and was sorry. Jesus fucking Christ, this is exasperating.

When I woke again at 8:30 he was holding my hand, but that was probably because it had fallen over him or something.

So why not settle for friendship, like when Tommy sleeps over? I must admit that it has to do with ego, as if I am not good enough for him, not attractive enough. Must I stand on Broadway to prove that I am not totally ugly?

I went to King Edward Campus yesterday to pick up the results of my assessment and was pleased that I'd passed Basic Math and had only a few mistakes in Writing and Reading. I took the results to the head of the Basic Training and Skills Development (BTSD) program, to find out when I could sign up, and he was flabbergasted at the scores. 'You could go to university tomorrow. You did better here in English than 90 percent of the university graduates.'

Compliments are always welcome, but they don't publish books and they don't pay for rent and food. I was excited but in a doomed way.

He called up Jennifer and told her I shouldn't have to enroll, but that didn't change the situation: Evelyn is sixteen, Evelyn is living independently with the agreement that she will go back to school, Evelyn wants to go to college or university but is crippled in Math and Science. He sent me down to talk to a counsellor, and this is what we've agreed on:

I will go to King Edward full-time from October 26 to the beginning of December, to cram one year of Math and one year of Science into—get this—one month. I will write a résumé stating where I've been published, my writing contacts, etc., and we will approach the Dean at Langara College to ask for a Special Admissions. We hope she will allow me to start first-year courses at Langara in January.

It's a lot. It's like growing up all at once; I didn't seriously think I could make it to college. And maybe I won't, maybe I'll stop myself. Prostitution is simpler and it pays the rent too. Dr. Hightower keeps saying that I feel as if I don't deserve an education. What if it's just laziness that's holding me back? Nobody's impressed that I might go to Langara with a Grade 9 education anyway, not Jennifer, who is sick of writing letters to different supervisors justifying my Independent Living contract. She's bringing over a one-to-one worker soon who is going to spend ten hours a week with me. I'm tempted to give him a hard time, whoever he is.

October 10

Melanie had predicted that I would have a hard life. Both she and Dr. Hightower had given me a practical rule to follow for when I moved into my apartment: Never have sex with anyone who lives in the same house.

The reprieve from anxiety couldn't last forever. Yesterday afternoon I dropped a double hit of acid. The reasons weren't good: Jennifer was bringing the one-to-one worker over, and I was angry that this previously unstipulated condition was being added to the contract; I was furious about the night in bed with Ed—my ego was badly shattered and I felt ugly and rejected; what I'd described as a 'vacation' from my writing was turning into a writing block; I was terrified of the Math-and-Science-in-one-month plan, and even more terrified of going to Langara with a Grade 9 education.

I decided to go for a long walk. Two hours later, I headed back, irritated that there was more head stuff than hallucinations going on. The acid exploded the anger and fear; I was not yet feeling suicidal, but enraged—a little at Ed, more at myself, at my age, at social services' protectiveness, at Jennifer's relative powerlessness, at the BTSD/Langara plan.

I slumped in a chair in Ed's apartment and told him about the acid. He'd been sleeping and appeared annoyed that I was hobbling and weaving my way towards him for help again. Wasn't it enough that he'd saved my life, though inadvertently, once already? (Without his phone at the time of the overdose, I couldn't have called the police.) I wasn't going to budge, though. Then the landlord arrived and we went back to my place.

The colors in my apartment swam. I still couldn't focus my eyes. At least the apartment was tidy—'I must admit, you've fixed it up nicer than any tenant who's been here,' the landlord conceded—or I might have been kicked out then and there. I was obviously stoned or crazy; things were getting out of hand. I sprawled on my bed and kept my mouth shut.

After the landlord left I maneuvered myself onto Ed's bed. He was highly uneasy, positioning himself safely across the room, shaving and cleaning things up. Everything was wavering, spinning, flowing deep through and around me. My body screamed for pain. I hated my apartment, hated writing and the prospect of school.

'If I get through tonight, I can get through anything,' I said. I knew that acid made things worse than they really are, but that knowledge was not enough to pull me through and help me trust that things would be better the next day. My life seemed silly, useless and absolutely, absolutely horrible. Never had I been so sure that things would be the same in the morning, that sleep wouldn't make them go away.

Ed eventually sat on the edge of the bed and I held onto him. We lay on the bed and I murmured some of my confused images; he watched television aimlessly and held me back. His arms around me. We talked, and finally we fucked. I was only the third woman Ed had slept with. With the first woman he'd been drunk at a party, didn't know her name and never saw her again; with the second he was straight, but they didn't have any contact after that night. This time was clumsy, embarrassing and hilarious. Ed was different from any of the multitude of men I'd tricked; he was a boy in comparison. It was just a relief to my ego.

Afterwards we talked. I'm not used to naked bodies very much, you know, only parts of bodies—forearms or faces or hands or penises. The whole thing is overwhelming. It was okay, even if Ed had lost his unattainability by sleeping with me. He had been afraid of rejection, jealous of friends like Tommy whom I hug and kiss, and had even thought of marrying me if I lost the apartment. (SEE, EVELYN DOES KNOW HOW TO SURVIVE IN THIS WORLD. SHE DOES, IF NOT WITH HER WRITING, THEN WITH HER BODY.)

Of course, this latest development presented problems. Our friends, interests and lifestyles are so different—he's shy, introverted, without ambition. We lived in such close proximity that we couldn't avoid each other.

'This isn't unusual for you, is it?' Ed asked, meaning sleeping with someone I hardly knew.

Well, in a way it is unusual, because Ed in his inexperience and shyness is different from the tricks and the other men. He wants to carry this relationship further; I guess you can't hop in and out of bed and pretend it never happened when you share a bathroom and the same entrance.

I am apprehensive and would be regretful if I didn't know that I would have trashed myself even more and felt even uglier if we hadn't slept together. Life is confusing. The anxiety level is almost back to where it used to be except I'm trying to Block Out. What worries me is that this could be a pattern—I struggled and worked to move out, to be independent, and now Ed and I are almost living together. I will just have to be mature; after all this is my life.

October 11

Some people have to be uncovered slowly. Sometimes I'd rather people kept their clothes on, or only unzipped the necessary portion; clothes protect. The worst thing is when somebody is before you naked and you hardly know what they look like—he's suddenly a stranger, an intruder; you curl up inside.

Where is Larry? How many pink Darvon and sun-warmed nauseating cups of methadone are dissolving in that diseased frame? Being with him was a demeaning experience, one no longer necessary because my apartment is a package that includes better people, a better life. Now that I am re-acquainted with health, he is too sickening for consideration. (How many illnesses are not self-inflicted? Kirk and I have both been hypochondriacs, slumping in front of Larry to be showered by a rainbow of pills and juice.)

Where is the woman in the pictures who Larry also poisoned with his caresses? We never met and she remained a mystery, the woman who escaped from Larry's wildly needy clutches after eight years, whole. Even as I write I find myself missing him—missing the gentle death he represented.

'Do not go gentle into that good night
Rage, rage against the dying of the light ...'

It was unnecessary poison. We have to measure the amount of health against the amount of sickness and then realize it wasn't worth it, not for anything. It was an experience, that much can be said, but experiences don't seem to be lacking, don't appear to be rare exactly.

Why am I even thinking of Larry, the skin hanging in folds on his face, his kidneys discharging many white bumps on his upper arms, the subtle exchange: countless blow jobs for the spice bottle of urine-colored liquid that could leave me relaxed/debilitated for days? Could he have hoped it would be a lifetime? How strange men are, and even stranger the women who do not go through these things, who live in a deceptive cocoon of safety. Perhaps he was wrong, you know, perhaps Bob Dylan's 'Mr. Tambourine Man' never was a heroin dealer. Larry read drugs into anything and everything. I don't want any more rejections from prestigious magazines complimenting my poems but asking for ones that don't describe drug experiences. Flipping through my files first in boredom and then in alarm, I realize that there are no unpublished poems that don't deal with drugs.

Have I ever been able to look at a man I am sleeping with and accept him? Certainly not an old dried-up junkie, not a faceless trick with a bulge in his pants. I am a virgin when it comes to a true relationship.

Sometimes, looking back, it is hard to believe I was not on drugs the whole time I was a child, popping cute blue Valium to get through any crisis, to make me acceptable to others when I never could accept myself.

Let's get married, typewriter; stay with me through what Melanie perceives will be the hard years.

'Do not go gently in that good night ...'

My words and my emotions will be brilliant, and they will never go gently into the night.

October 20

Dr. Hightower felt that I'd said something clear and accurate that I should record in this journal: 'I needed to know that a man would want to have sex with me.'

We had been discussing the unpleasantness of intercourse for me, how sex and love do not seem to equate. For the first time in his office I broke down, with the seemingly insignificant confession that my mother used to go to the bathroom without closing the door, and she often chose that opportunity to want to talk to me so that I would have to stand in the doorway and watch her urinate. As a child I had been both aroused and repulsed; I learned to associate genitals, especially female genitals, with something dirty. I still don't want to know that my vagina exists, casting it away as something horrible and ugly.

Usually whenever I've had sex I've popped Darvon beforehand because I'm not turned on and it hurts. It hurts with Ed too, but I need to be held by someone and it's only a fair exchange. No. I know but don't want to admit the truths. I have this great difficulty with sex and intimacy together; I lie there counting and wondering when it's going to be over, hoping it'll be soon. Probably the worst thing in the world for me would be to have to look into the other person's eyes while having sex with him, to see the vulnerability, the nakedness, his trust, and have him see me exposed, or living a lie.

My body is broken up, my vagina 'somewhere down the block' as Dr. Hightower described it. Becoming even half-whole sexually is going to be very difficult. Can it be accomplished in one lifetime?

October 23

I feel mute. My fingers must write or be paralyzed. I am praying, not for help but for something else. Maybe I'm simply trying to block everything out with the sheer frenzy of prayer.

The last few times Ed and I had sex were horrible. I had to throw myself miles away, irretrievable, in order to give him head. With all the nameless penises that have been shoved into my mouth, how could it happen again? It felt exactly like prostitution and it didn't make sense that there wasn't any money involved, that Ed could look at me the next day with what appeared to be tenderness in his eyes when that had happened. But how could I have expected him to understand the enormity of what happened to me when we had sex— the rage, the repulsion, the incredible endurance?

Yesterday I was depressed and upset, hating Ed for the part of him that was normal male desire but still liking and caring about the rest. Not knowing what to do about it. I called Larry twice and begged for methadone with an outrageous abandonment of pride. He didn't care, though I broke all my rules and told him that when he'd needed me back in April I had tried to respond, and now he wouldn't do anything for me. But Larry didn't give a shit about what happened to me, though I told him that it was either methadone or I'd go out and work the street immediately. It didn't touch him. It was no more than an idle threat, and I'd lied to him before. He probably couldn't even remember my face, I was that unimportant. Afterwards I sobbed at the silent phone that I still needed him and had always needed him— the night in the apartment, the drugs, his gentle touches, the only things that could work for me.

I made myself dress up and go out. I decided to punish myself, and working straight was the best way. It was unfamiliar, though. I'd forgotten how to act like a prostitute—I didn't look anything like what I'd remembered or what people fantasized about. But I made myself go out anyway, without a knife or a bus pass, so that I would have to hitchhike and be at a man's mercy.

The guy who picked me up en route to Commercial and Broadway was twenty-seven years old, with wavy dark brown hair and a short nose. He drove a Corvette. I had forgotten how to smile, what to say, and opened myself up to him as though he were an intimate friend. I made the mistake of telling him I was scared and lonely; I made the mistake of deciding to trust a john completely so (supposedly) he would be unable to betray that trust; I made the mistake of going out on the streets to look for a friend.

D. took a long time to come during the blow job and kept grabbing me with his hands. It didn't matter except it was like a bad acid trip where you wish you hadn't done the drug, except worse because it was reality. I had turned one trick and that was all that mattered; I'd degraded and dirtied myself enough. I asked D. to drive me home, but he seemed so friendly and considerate that I didn't say anything when he bought a bottle of wine and started driving to his place.

D. lived in an apartment in Richmond. He seemed to need someone to talk to as badly as I did. We sat on the couch and D. said he'd found a friend in me—yes, so naively and so trustingly, incredible after this long on the streets, I decided to believe and did not protest when his arm went around me.

D. tore my clothes off and raped me. I knew how not to get hurt, by not screaming or kicking. I pushed against him, but it wasn't any use; I kept my voice insistent, but it wasn't any use: 'Maybe we shouldn't do this now, D. No. Not now. Let me go. Please. I can't do this—no—' And I'd already told him about my sexual problems; maybe secretly he was a necrophiliac, who knows?

If the bastard got me pregnant, I'd never be able to live with it. Ever.

Afterwards my voice was hollow, but I managed to persuade D. that I liked him and would go out with him Saturday, but no, I mustn't stay tonight; I wouldn't give him head as he drove. Thus he drove me home. Thank God for small mercies. It was terrifying. I have learned so well with my parents that by complying I won't get hurt, by looking blank and docile I will come away without too many visible scars—the bleeding's internal.

It was midnight. I knocked on Ed's door, unable to cope with being alone, and climbed into his bed. I was in shock, numb. I expected him to hit me, throw me out, yell, but he held me, and although I knew he didn't understand and could never understand, at least he wasn't going to immediately give me hell. We went to sleep after a long time.

Early this morning when his alarm clock rang for work, Ed touched me and then he was above me saying, 'Hold your breasts together' in a quiet voice, not like the voice of the blond man, that titfuck in the car in the parking lot when he demanded and threatened and rubbed his penis angrily up and down my breasts and came all over me. Ed did not know and could not have known, but he was making me relive another assault. Oh God, I thought in a daze, each part of me detaching itself and disappearing forever: Oh God.

It was for some reason not a surprise that Ed should guide my hand to his penis and touch me after I'd been raped. Last night in his bed I wished that I'd killed myself two months ago with the pills. I don't know now what to do with my body except go compliantly through the motions of cleaning up, doing laundry, washing dishes. I am scared. I'll call Dr. Hightower, avoid Ed—no one from social services can know about this, which means I'll have to be strong, I'll have to be really strong, I'll have to go through the motions. I am here now at the typewriter. I am here and I must on the surface stay glued together for the time being.

October 29

I talked to Ed about many of the things Dr. Hightower and I discussed in our last session. I tried to explain how our relationship frightened me because familiarity is safety and I'm familiar with men on the street; how prostitution kept me from becoming too involved with him; how hooking is a form of gaining control. It is frightening to be in a relationship, to share experiences, to divulge vulnerabilities, to do things together. I never developed any social skills before leaving home because my parents refused to let me go out, and then I found myself in situations where the social skills I acquired were how to take drugs, how to manipulate johns. How can I do anything ordinary, like going to a movie, without tranquilizers to get me through the evening?

But Ed doesn't understand these exposures. I can't blame him because he doesn't see things the way Dr. Hightower does. He thinks I'm self-destructive, end of discussion. Yet I need him to understand because it would help us so much, help me! I wish he would. I wish I didn't have to drink and do drugs in order to smile, make conversation, pretend.

Yesterday Steve, my one-to-one worker, and I went to Langara to see the head of the English Department. He was impressed by my portfolio and felt strongly that I should enter first-year English at the college, but then the registrar said that I was not old enough and would have to complete Grade 12 before entering. Steve said afterwards that he had to bite his tongue to keep from lashing back at her. Dulled from Valium, I did not even cry. The registrar seemed to feel that life was hard and in order to make it you had to follow all the rules, no matter how inapplicable.

However, she will talk to the Dean and they will come to a decision. I thought that I should finish my journal and retreat into drugs and prostitution as a way of life. Then after everything was over somebody could write an epilogue like in *Go Ask Alice* to the effect that I had died—accidentally, or was it premeditated?—and somebody else could publish it and it would become a big sensationalist hit.

I went to work last night at eleven. The world was washed and drenched; the roads slick black. I was not afraid, not after another Valium.

November 11

At least my period will keep me off the streets for a while. Dr. Hightower wants to know why this is going on, says I am becoming psychologically lazy—I'm using the techniques I've learned to cope with everyday problems but refusing to progress to the core of the problem. But he is unwilling to push me, happy at least that he doesn't have to worry from week to week whether or not I'm still alive. I don't feel suicidal anymore, since my life has become quite ordinary and quiet—except for the other side, except when the night begins and the city lights dance. Prostitution has become my outlet, and the Valium my reward for making it through another day.

It is ironic that some of the people we have been taught to respect, the teachers and the businessmen and the 'authority figures,' are the same men who cruise the streets looking for young girls to affirm their manhood, their desirability. Refusing to believe that it is an act, and that somewhere inside they know it.

Life is going okay. I wonder what the Dean at Langara will say tomorrow, since they have decided what to do with me. Are they going to place hoops at the exact height where I cannot jump? Then what? Although I am integrating prostitution into my life, making it something normal, I don't think I could do it out of necessity. That would not be good. That would make me old in no time.

November 14

I realize now that a large part of why I am still working the street is that that is where I am recognized as a somebody. That's the last thing I would have expected, since I used to feel that the johns treated me like a piece of meat, but as it turns out the street is the only place where I am actually appreciated. Otherwise, I'm a nobody. A young, struggling writer—and a prostitute. A prostitute who can make money, satisfy customers and be praised. Finally, people are giving me total approval. That is the response I would like with my writing, but it hasn't happened yet, maybe never will happen. I am becoming more frustrated; salvation right now is when I can say to myself that hey, you're not just a probably-won't-amount-to anything writer, you're an active prostitute! It's something you're successful at right now!

November 18

Although Dr. Hightower thinks I need to start considering other people's feelings—'You've been immersed in your own, which is fine, you're still trying to discover your identity'—he doesn't think I'm selfish. I've been so busy trying to understand myself that I haven't taken the time or effort to know anybody else well. He thinks I'm doing '300 percent better' because I don't run away from situations anymore, but I still react to everyone I meet as if they are my parents.

I talked at length about Ed. 'A couple of years from now he'll probably tell his girlfriend or wife, 'I once went out with this crazy bitch.' No. He won't do that.'

'That's right. He'll probably say, "A few years ago I was with a girl whom I couldn't understand, but she was a really nice person."'

That's worse, somehow, sadder.

Ed has stepped back visibly. I don't blame him. In some respects I'm doing really well. When I bumped into Art today at King Edward Campus, he said I looked like a college student. That's good. School is turning into something positive, providing a dramatically different lifestyle from my life on the streets at night, holding me together in its stability. I'm even beginning to do my homework, and not just strictly on the bus either.

I had been planning to work tonight and was jumpy when F. phoned and offered to take me to work and keep an eye out for me. Playing pimp. I wasn't sure what I was getting into but decided to take him at face value, as the friend who had been giving me driving lessons and taking me out. Unfortunately, when I was dressed up and he was knocking on the door, Ed was in the hallway doing his laundry. If he doesn't want to be with me, it's up to him—I do work the street and that's a part of my life that's there right now. I won't give that up for Ed, because then I'd only resent him, feel trapped by him. He's pleaded with me to ask him for money instead of going out on the street, but out there at least I have my individuality and independence, a remarkable feeling of specialness and power that wasn't there when I first started. I used to feel like trash. Now it's the other way around—out there the men appreciate me and I am strong. Dr. Hightower says I am choosing a very, very lonely life, but I'm keeping it together okay right now.

F. parked his car where I brought most of my tricks, off Broadway, and the night went well. It didn't take long to break the hundred-dollar mark, and the first two men drove Mercedes. The second had picked me up before, months ago when I was with Larry. It seems like a long time ago, because when I did place him I also remembered that the money had gone immediately onto the kitchen table in return for a cup of methadone. I am so much healthier now. I chatted for a while with another hooker who went off with a guy who'd approached me earlier for sex. She was older, she'd been addicted to Talwin and Ritalin but was now relatively straight. The women on Broadway were bundled up, raincoats over their working clothes, which meant that I too could get away with not freezing my ass off, could wear a jacket and pull it back to flash the breasts. Tonight the men were good and fast and it was only early evening.

F. bought me a pair of fishnet stockings, so I obligingly put them on for him back at my apartment. He started kissing me and touching my breasts, leaving me in the same old predicament—I didn't want to reject him by saying no outright, hurting his feelings, so I sat there stupidly passive while he took my underpants off and buried his face between my legs. I'll have to learn soon. It's just that I'm so reluctant to hurt anybody, hoping that they'll stop before actually putting their penis inside. So they are justified in getting angry, accusing me of being a cockteaser, leading them on. I like warmth and body contact that is nonsexual, and by now I have come to view my body as such a nonsexual, nonprivate thing that even somebody feeling my breasts and vagina is normal.

November 23

Tommy slept over last night, so I went over to Ed's and slept with him. We began kissing and touching, and then Ed's fingers moved in me too deeply, too many of them. It was painful at first, and then it got worse, beyond endurance. He couldn't see my tears. 'Is that better?' he asked in his innocence, and I managed to choke, 'Yes.' It was an agony, but I was experiencing what had happened with Joe on the coast, and ultimately what had happened at home: always being unable to talk back, always silently screaming. Those screams weltering up and up from inside and drowning me, but I couldn't say anything when Dad was hitting me after I had gone to a court appeal instead of Social Studies class, when Mother quizzed me about my homework, as she had ever since I was little, for hours on end, hours and hours without pause so that I would know everything inside out. She had a ruler, or her hand, and always her mouth, but I never was allowed a mouth. It was like standing on a street corner and screaming inside while telling a trick he had a nice big cock, biggest I'd ever seen.

I went to the bathroom abruptly and he was half-asleep when I came back. There were colors to the mass of pain: My chest was orange and green; my feet and hands were red and blue. I felt like I'd been sliced open, but it was better to say nothing because speaking out would have been more painful—something I had learned in my childhood. The swords up my stomach made me forget how to breathe, and as I hovered over the rim of sleep my body began to spasm, waking Ed. He had his arm carefully over me, thinking it was the methadone. A switch finally flipped somewhere and for five minutes I shrieked with laughter, beyond reason, hysterical, and then I fell asleep.

December 1

Ed told me he loved me. We were lying in bed, and he looked down at me and said, 'I love you.'

I made the usual romantic Evelyn comeback; I laughed and said matter-of-factly, 'Oh, yeah? Wow, what a shock. Why? How could you?'

'I just do.' He didn't flinch outwardly, although he must have inside. I shy away from anything that suggests a softening, a merging into another being. Because there is another person inside me, the hard one, the one that cannot be melted. The other is just the surface. The real one is ugly and unloveable.

Ed had taken a leap into that core being, into me. In my mind I retreated, facing him in terror, then turning and beginning to run. I didn't need to hear anymore to feel threatened.

The wind blew, lifting the passersby off their feet, making their bodies twist and jut. A woman walking past me said to the man she was with, 'She should have been killed.' I snatched that phrase, wrested it from the air into my being. Yes, she should have been killed a long time ago. They should have killed me a long, long time ago.

I was going crazy. I wanted to hitchhike far away, somewhere warm, to get away from the Christmas season, when most of my friends would leave and I could not be with the remaining people because I would be too exposed. Once again it would be the bleak time of year that would be warmly and glitteringly lit up, and I would be alone. I wanted to be on a beach somewhere, baking in the sun, thin and brittle and drugged. I wanted to bleach my hair blond and starve my body wiry, and have vacant eyes. I wanted to be another kid prostitute and then one day be found lifeless and buried by a stranger, without ceremony. I wanted to make up a different name for myself—an initial would do. Then it would be all right; the rest would be erased.

I came home in the late afternoon and took two hits of LSD. I was frightened by Ed's saying he loved me. I very much needed my own life separate from anyone else's; I wanted to touch intensely but only occasionally. I wanted to go somewhere warm but didn't know what I would do upon getting there, being alone. I wanted to know who Ed really was. I wanted him to destroy me. I wanted to destroy him by making him destroy himself. I wanted to get back at the intruder who had dared to say that he loved me.

I stirred one hit of LSD into a cup of herbal tea and took it to Ed.

He had never dropped acid before. He had smoked hash and eaten mushrooms once, but that was the extent of his drug experience. While I was letting the blotter melt and swirl into the tea, I was quite high, but that was not the reason why I did it.

Ed was, as Dr. Hightower said, my laboratory animal.

He drank the tea trustingly. I was between giggles, the rush of acid, and an apprehension and vague sorrow. He even picked up what remained of the blotter and chewed it, thinking it was a tea leaf. Half of me believed that the acid wouldn't have any effect on him, couldn't.

After a while Ed looked at me with the slightest suspicion. 'My stomach feels queasy. Are you sure that was nothing but tea?'

'Yep. Of course. How's your headache?'

'It's gone now, but I'm feeling queasy and my head feels sort of numb. I have this really funny feeling. My body's tingling all over. Are you sure you didn't give me something in it?'

'No, you know I wouldn't.' I grinned. He was actually feeling it! We were in for one long evening.

A few minutes went by, then: 'Look, Evelyn, I won't be mad if you tell me the truth. I definitely feel different. It's like a rush from hash; I feel light and weak all over. I will be mad at you if you keep denying it and then I find out you slipped me something, so tell me now.'

'Okay.' I looked at him and couldn't suppress the giggles, half from nervousness and half from excitement. 'I put acid into the tea.'

At first Ed was exasperated, but then he said, 'Well, okay, we can't do anything about it now.' I was flying, and he was the weaker one. I was curious about what would arise, what aspects of his personality he had hidden that would be revealed, what truths would come clear. He was in my control, and though it was not consciously as cruel as it may sound, I was aware of it. I already knew that I would be kind and helpful, but in power.

Ed was overcome by giggles. He was actually glad that he had been coerced into accepting the gift of LSD. That, of course, was acceptable only to a point—it could not be a purely good trip because then it would erase my purpose. I could have given him the tea and then left the house if I had been vindictive, but that wouldn't have accomplished anything either.

While Ed was helplessly giggling, I was peaking and becoming reflective. We were on his bed and Ed touched me with something like awe—apparently my body felt warmer and softer. In contrast, his fingers felt cold on my skin and I was withdrawn. He said he felt much more sexually aroused, something I did not expect. I've heard conflicting reports from men who've had sex while high on LSD—that it was nightmarish, the woman's skin crawled and so forth; that it was absolutely beautiful, an amazing experience. As the person who had dropped the acid into Ed's tea, I didn't know how to respond to his arousal—I was afraid he would see crawling skin and be repulsed, and of course thus see my true self, the ugliness that was hidden just below the surface and could rise so easily. I responded by shaking my head no when he asked me to take off my sweater, and suggesting that now was not a good time.

Ed persisted, however, and had soon removed my clothing. His kisses and touches were cold. Despite my protests, he loomed over me and wanted to rape me—later he confessed in bewilderment that he had enjoyed the feeling of taking control of a woman, of being the aggressor. He tried but couldn't. I told him over and over that I didn't want to have sex, but he persisted, sliding himself in and out of me. I turned my face away and cried. He said that maybe I should just jerk him off instead of him trying to fuck me—his precise words—which was too much like what a man on the street would demand. A jerk for twenty dollars.

I could have forcefully stopped him, instead of just pushing at his body. I could have bit and scratched and kicked and flung myself across the apartment, but then he might have become violent, and I didn't want him to have to live with that, or myself either. But aside from that fear—his loss of control was great enough that he could have been brutal—I wanted to see what he would do, how powerful his sensitivities and values really were, how much he respected me.

And so I conducted the ultimate test. Ed, who had morals and the ability to care, did not and could not stop. He was out of control, pleasure overtaking guilt. He continued to fuck me while I continued to cry, push at him and tell him to stop.

Afterwards I saw Jennifer in my mind, her pale wedge of face, her blue-shadowed eyes, and wanted her to know the truth and therefore help me. I found myself missing Melanie and the little responsibility that was required of me in her home, Melanie who listened and knew me, standing there powerful in her bright kitchen. Above all, the acid and the experience with Ed integrated me completely for a moment with the little girl I had been before leaving home. I saw the twelve or thirteen-year-old Evelyn sitting lonely on the piano bench by the balcony, hiding behind the drapes when people walked by outside. I was that little girl. I was the hidden-away Chinese girl whom the other kids in school had ridiculed and put down mercilessly, who had been beaten by her parents in hopes of giving her a better life. I was sitting on the piano bench convinced that no man would ever be able to bear touching me, much less in a caring manner. Ed had violated that. I had proved on the street that men would love me and love me and love me if I dressed and made myself up a certain way, and even that was a small violation, though it was also an act of defiance; I threw it back to mock the little girl, to try and kill her, oh to so desperately try and kill her forever. Without realizing her beauty, without realizing that she in her loneliness, ugliness and despair had given birth to my writing. With the drugs and the prostitution I had quickly covered her up, but the veneer was so thin that many times her face showed through it and other people did see her. I had tried to lead a violently different life to prove that she was not real, did not exist and never had existed, but she was always there, she was myself. I realized that my life was a lie.

The recent session with Dr. Hightower has made things much clearer and I'm able to accept what happened both during the week and last night. I was able to become one with the little girl for a long period and feel her pain flowing powerful and bottomless. I know that trying to kill her will always be unsuccessful. Now all there is to do is remember Dr. Hightower's final words:

'You can explore and try to figure out your own psyche, but you can't go and destroy somebody else's. Once is morally acceptable, but don't do it twice. This is beyond psychology and psychiatry—I don't talk like this often, but now I'm speaking in the world of right and wrong. Don't do it again.'

December 7

I would choose prostitution over high school. I would choose prostitution over living with my parents. Dr. Hightower said that the pain of what I have gone through since leaving home is far less than the pain I experienced at home—and yes, there is no comparison. I often wonder how that little girl that was myself managed those long hours by the window, at her desk, shrinking. No wonder she became withdrawn and, at a young age, eccentric. Some people think I am peculiar. I don't know how to take that, except that it must be something that sets me apart, makes me different. Being different means it isn't easy to belong, isn't easy to be accepted, but it is also a measure of safety.

There are only slices of hell in my life now, where at home life was one swallowing endless hell shut in a bedroom looking out the window. I recognized a slice of it last night, sitting in a restaurant eating frogs' legs, wearing fishnet stockings. Sitting beside a lump of a human being that could easily be tucked into one big beach ball and rolled wherever convenient. I winced when he ordered yet another drink. To perceive that it was a slice of hell was like lightning, sudden yet clear. I was with R., one of my regulars, trying to focus my aching eyes and clear my head. The two acts were not hell: a blow job in his waterbed, and then later, another one in front of the rented porno movies gasping from the TV screen. They were easy. God, it's one thing you don't have to have any brains for, one thing where intelligence is not expected (though I can boast that I would have been hurt many times if I hadn't been able to talk and feel out the man's psychology). No, that was not hell; the acts were comparable to housework, like washing the dishes or vacuuming the floor. Even simpler than that.

The hell was the time, the energy and the small affections. Affectations. I spent seven hours with R. yesterday. Hell was hugging him, stroking his arms, kissing him with practised passion, calling him 'darling.' Hell was exposing myself in that restaurant—for why else would a young Oriental girl be with a grossly overweight, wheezing middle-aged Caucasian man? God, it's so obvious, so funny really, after the hangover has passed, after the clothes reeking of his cologne are in the laundry basket. It seems hilarious now, in a slightly sad and whimsical way. The rain, the greyness of winter always makes me feel like that—lost, lonely, melancholy, wishing for something. Like a voice calling out in the wind. I thought smilingly in the restaurant how magical it would have been if it had been a publisher sitting next to me instead. I think.

It is also funny how the money that has accumulated from working means little and does little. It helps, of course. It helps make life more pleasant, and for that alone the actual blow job is worth it. It's the acting that's hard, sometimes the feeling of despair, trying to be light and life in a sordid blackness. Yes. And the truth is hard, the truth that money earned from prostitution is meaningless, fifteen dollars from a published poem could make me feel rich, could propel the days into a summer drenched in greenness and sunshine. That's the kind of money I earn with love, that's when I am whole and healed and beautiful.

December 8

I live in my own world of perceptions. It's a complex place, receiving a constant barrage of stimulation and swimming with thoughts. To think that every other person in the world is walking around surrounded by the same sort of enormous globe is boggling. To try and understand even one of these globes must be a lifetime devotion.

That is what Dr. Hightower does for a living.

I am like one of those Russian dolls. They are a womanly shape, wooden, with painted features. A line slices them in half. You take their two halves apart and inside is another doll, with the exact same features, only smaller. You peel them away, one by one, and there is always another one underneath—until you reach the core, the solid wooden woman, its features by now blurred. I am always surprised and disappointed that there are not more and yet more, multiplying, neverending, until the last one is so tiny it is microscopic.

Dr. Hightower believes that I have at least two personalities—myself and the little girl. I am her fantasy. I worked a long time to create myself, many long hours in bed and by the piano and over the desk by the bedroom window. Still I am not yet perfected. I am never quite another person, and this is a constant source of frustration. Wanting to be someone else, someone perfect, is what drives me. Yet I need to always be in touch with that little girl by experiencing her pain, and that pain of intrusion and oppression is best found on the street. Yes, there is something worse than giving a stranger a blow job, and I lived it for fourteen years at home. I must be in touch with that girl and her suffering because otherwise I might lose my writing, this writing that was nurtured and defended so fiercely by her, this writing that both her parents denied. This writing that her father would turn black and red over, rushing for the nearest ruler and smacking her arms while she sat meekly at the piano until her tears would blur the keys, the soft light of the lamp over the piano, her lessons propped in front of the water in lakes in her eyes ...

Dr. Hightower ventured to say that I am living out that little girl's fantasy, that being on the streets was her idea of freedom. That is the truth. I cannot help but live that fantasy, although it is dangerous. He cannot argue with a fantasy. I know I am ugly beneath the clothes and the makeup and cannot accept, though I try, what Dr. Hightower believes so wholly: that even then I was beautiful. No, how could he think that? He never saw me. I had to hide. I was powerless. I used to think that if only I could be beautiful or even acceptable enough to be a hooker, to be so far below and yet beyond my classmates, to have dared to do something none of them would dare to do, to be beyond reach—they would be sorry then. And that was how I would hurt them for what they had done. Not by being a writer—that was something else, that was something they could tease me about along with the clothes and my intelligence. Being a hooker, I would be shameless, and they would be afraid of my power. They would be envious of the money and the adoration. I would be somebody they could never dare talk back to.

One of my former classmates saw me out on the street a week ago.

She was unable to conceal her surprise and curiosity. 'Evelyn? Is that you?'

I was hitchhiking to work, my composure intact. 'Oh hi, Jackie. How's it going?'

'Are you going to school now?'

'Yeah, at King Ed. I'm taking some upgrading courses.'

'You're in the same grade as I am, aren't you?'

'No. It's a sort of catch-up program.' I didn't bother trying to explain. I was afraid that the inch-thick or so of me would fall away and she would see the real me underneath.

I want to be integrated now. I dare not believe that the little girl possessed something pretty. I have no idea what her body looked like then, though. Maybe it was the pain and the desperate need to belong, and the shameful thing her mother told her her body was, that made her ugly. The certainty that no one without greatly stifled repulsion could touch her.

I wonder.

Jackie looked at me. 'But I guess you're not getting the kinds of marks you used to.' Her eyes said, Remember? I know who you were. I went to school with the little girl.

'No.' I rejected her eyes. She went away. I felt triumphant that my mask had not cracked. If she was still as immature as she was two years ago—it isn't fair, but I still see my classmates as frozen where I left them—she would go back to school the next day and there would be gossip, there would be whisperings: 'Guess who I saw last night? Remember Evelyn? Yeah, EVELYN! Guess what she was wearing? Guess what she was doing?' And I felt triumph that she would do exactly that.

Out on the streets, it is both funny and sad.

I wonder now, trying to smooth my fear of going out and working tonight. I want to see. I want to feel this girl that I am becoming more aware of, that is growing inside me and, I think, shedding some of her ugliness as Dr. Hightower and I explore more of her. I do not fully understand her—and that means I cannot confine her in words, yet. But I feel her wholly. She is there, she is coming out, and I see with confusion and something like denial that she is not altogether ugly.

December 9

Five a.m. I've been up all night. The black rain falls outside with plopping noises, as if the whole world is one black ocean. The window is open, to let in a slice of the morning. I am sitting here with cigarette smoke trailing heavenward. I am trying to integrate. What a lovely meaningless word. Again I see the Russian dolls, literally full of themselves.

Hours ago I went to work, unafraid. There is nothing left to be afraid of out there because it is my home; for some reason it is where I am most together. Everywhere else I am still unsure, worried that my mask is likely to crack, wondering how many people see through it each day, and I am ashamed. Out there, on the street, I don't have to be. You can act and talk any which way with strangers; they are the only people you can take that liberty with. Out there I am perfectly invisible.

There were a lot of cop cars sliding up and down Broadway. Dr. Hightower is certain that they know me, have a description. I argued that they most certainly did not; I am not ostentatious. Dr. Hightower says they're cleaning up the streets again.

I only stayed to turn two tricks. The second man was drug crazed and we did a little pile of cocaine together, the mound of whiteness spread and thinned into lines. Maybe that's why I can't sleep tonight, but it's all right; I knew even while coming down and inevitably wishing for more that there wouldn't be any. It gave me a high, but there was the paranoia and then the unpleasant though thankfully undramatic aftermath. The cocaine was bitter, flooding my nostrils and coming up my throat. The man lay on the floor on the back of his van and wanted me in control, loved relinquishing all of himself into my hands and mouth. If I had been cautious, I wouldn't have climbed into a pitch-black van with a frantic druggie. But I don't bother too much. I don't know what it is that protects me; maybe I don't care anymore.

Before I left Broadway several men wanted me, but I turned them down, and I saw a few of my old tricks cruise past. I see them in my mind as frozen around the corner of Broadway and Commercial, their cars gliding around and around as if it were a magnet and they had no control. I see people I don't want to see, out there. Trouble may be waiting, but surely I can stand a few bruises; I have been inordinately lucky.

I am fine. The human experiment with Ed is over. We don't love each other, but he has been security. He has been the 'boyfriend' I've confidently warned tricks away with; he has been the man next door, ready to defend me against potential danger with a nonexistent but unquestioned strength. It would be good to keep that, but otherwise it's not working out between us. I leave a lot of myself back on that corner, so there isn't much left over for him. We had sex hours ago. I did it clinically, so it was ridiculously unromantic. I wanted it that way, though; I wanted him to have an erection and then to put his penis inside me. A penis, not Ed's, not anybody's in particular. Penetration was all right. We confirmed without verbalizing it that we didn't feel anything for each other. I am in control of the relationship, but it is useless. It's been a learning experience for us both, that's all. Ed would rather masturbate than have sex with somebody who doesn't want it and doesn't respond—admirable, but that shows there's nothing there. We have so little in common. I guess we will continue to care about each other in our own minuscule ways and maybe even try not to hurt each other.

The unlikely hooker. I wept over my Grade 8 annual. Nearly all the kids who had written in mine either said I was too intelligent or thanked me—a slap in the face, a last sarcasm—for 'giving them the answers.' Some told me to keep smiling, that smile that was a tortured grimace. I looked at their faces, young and clean. I am not lashing back at them so much as at who I used to be, and still am underneath—that is the horrible truth. It was quite painful. I wanted them to see me wrecked on drugs, hooking. I wanted them to see me living on my own. For a long time I have wanted them and everyone else from my past to see me finally as a failure, stupid.

But what good is it? Instead I feel cheated by the frivolity they possessed, their cliques and so forth. I wanted that acceptance as desperately as anyone else. Now I'm too far beyond it, and it's painful to know that I never really had a childhood or an adolescence. I am asking why but cannot blame my parents, who didn't know or understand ... rather myself. The person they created.

I could go to sleep. But it is morning. I would like to know: What is going to happen now?

December 10

Ed is leaving in a few days to spend two weeks with his family. Often around Christmas I realize I haven't bothered to know my friends very well. Do I know anyone at all, have even a keyhole's vision into the globes they roll about in? Emotionally with Ed it has been a lopsided relationship; he knows more about me, my inner workings, my privacies, than I do about him. He doesn't volunteer information, emotional or otherwise.

Dr. Hightower had looked at me shrewdly, kindly, a few sessions ago and said, 'You shouldn't be so worried about appearing foolish.' Yes, I am afraid of that, as much as I am frightened of sex. When my sexual experiences began, with Joe, it was painful. I was terrified of intercourse for a long time, but when it did happen I was drugged. How ironic, that finally there was no pain; in fact at the time I didn't even know it was happening. I don't even remember who it was with.

I want to save that girl who was trapped in the relationship with Larry. I am angered at what a should-have-been-responsible adult did to me, not so much with drugs as with the head games.

The closest thing I can find now that is comparable to the pain at home is working the street. As integration takes place, as my faces mesh into one, things are coming up. Like today I realized with total clarity that ever since leaving home, even now, I have been afraid and certain that I will be forced back. There is no use arguing that nobody could make me go back there; there is no use arguing that even if by some bizarre choice I did go back, I would behave differently. For some reason that fear of re-oppression has hung over me and never really lifted. Prostitution is a reaction to that fear, although now it is much too cold to be out there and I am sticking to a few carefully chosen men. I still haven't brought anyone to my apartment. It is off limits, even if it means I don't turn another trick all winter.

It was inevitable that a part of my street money would go to drugs now, although without addiction. Without slavery. I understand the two by now and will not let the men of the street take all of me. They will never be able to make me work for them; I live by my own standards.

This is normal here in my world: sexual favors for money, and the availability of drugs. I am secure in what I do, more than ever; it is almost difficult not to become overconfident in my ability to read men and play it safe.

It is always a source of irony to me that I can deal with prostitution and drugs so efficiently, but I cannot do something like go out with a friend without a great deal of stress. How am I supposed to accept that hooking is ugly, when there are the overblown compliments, the men always calling? How, when that little girl wondered sometimes if a man would ever masturbate thinking of her? She didn't know what penises looked like then or how they would go about doing it, but that was irrelevant. She would never have believed that in a few years, hundreds of men would pay to touch her. She hates it now, but one cannot have pleasure without paying; one cannot triumph without losing at the same time.

I feel I am progressing rapidly. New emotions are coming up; there is a stirring inside me. I feel fairly secure and don't want that security tampered with, threatened in any way.

December 11

I no longer need Valium to work. I seem to be able to adopt the personality of the hooker in her heels clicking down dark frozen sidewalks without taking a pill; it's an automatic switchover to a different frame of mind. But anybody could look like a prostitute if they wore the right clothes and smeared on enough makeup, which disproves the compliments of men.

Is prostitution becoming too much of a way of life for me? My customers still remark sometimes that I am not hardbitten, that to find someone like me on the street is like finding a jewel. I don't know whether I take that as a compliment anymore or not, but that's irrelevant; at least it's a measure of safety.

But it's too cold, no longer possible to stand on a corner for very long. Today I started off by meeting a regular in the afternoon. I don't have many regulars because after a while they want more; they are not satisfied with a blow job and squeezing me, licking me, putting their fingers up me till it hurts. They want entrance to my apartment, to sleep with me. Although I could be considered careless, I am emotionally and psychologically careful with men—but that can't last;

some of them are intelligent, manipulative. Those are the ones to be afraid of, not the ones who seem strange or are physically overpowering.

I am happy. I work hard, but whenever my jaw aches or my arms fall asleep, whenever a man takes forever to come, I tell myself it is much better than vacuuming the house for my parents—which would be my 'day off;' in the evening I'd be confined to my bedroom studying again.

More of me is becoming detached. Kissing is all right but still a chore when it doesn't spark other emotions, lusts. Blow jobs are strictly business, an exchange of money for a somewhat ridiculous service. My breasts were amputated long ago—the men touch them so much, move them around, squeeze them. They are not a part of me. I am flat chested and asexual. The next thing that will go will be my vagina, because of their probing fingers. But maybe it has never been mine, maybe it has always been my mother's—Dr. Hightower and I wonder about that, if when I am on the street, I subconsciously wish it were my mother's body the customers are defiling.

And then there are the triumphs. Hitching back from Broadway, the guy who picked me up was young and very good-looking and drove this sleek little car. The good-looking ones scare me because they threaten the identity of the ugly little girl. They are so unexpected; I never expect to be propositioned by them. They aren't very safe for me emotionally; I knew that if he had gone to school with me he would have been one of the ones to ridicule me—this gave me a sense of power as well as fright. It shook my identity, violated my knowledge of who I was underneath.

December 14

The craving for cocaine is so immediate and intense. I could easily picture someone with a big bag of it never doing anything with their life except sitting around and snorting. It doesn't take intelligence; with the whiteness of it traveling up my nose I feel happily despairing, ethereal. I told Ed last night that if he caught me with it again, he was to take the stuff and flush it down the toilet—but he's leaving Wednesday morning.

I believe I've quit working the streets. It snowed last night. I took the first part of my Human Biology test at King Ed today and probably failed it.

December 15

I'm seeing Dr. Hightower in a few hours, and where has the integration gone? Is the fear of joining with the little girl prompting me to do coke? I can barely think straight; my nose is dripping constantly, hurts whenever I breathe. I went to my friend's last night, didn't have enough money, but he fronted me the rest, and we each pooled a white heap on the plate and snorted and smoked it up with one of his friends.

Ed is leaving tomorrow, but I didn't care. I believe I've triumphed over him by telling him to flush the stuff and thus placing him in an authoritative position.

Why do I keep trying to analyze myself? It's no good. What hell.

December 18

The rolled-up bill. The gray compact open, exposing two mirrors—one compressing her face into a square, the other broadening it into a circle. The square mirror is smudged with white powder and speckled with tiny chips of something white and crystalline. The razor blade lies alongside the compact, its edge the same blurred white. The paraphernalia is beside her bed.

The mirrors wait invitingly, one round, the other square. Neither is flattering, and she does not look at herself when she races a line up her nostril. She doesn't look at her bleary eyes. She doesn't look at her red chafed nose. She hopes only that her left nostril will continue to hold out.

The packet is almost empty. She will finish it before morning. It is 4 a.m.—another sleepless night. She doesn't worry. She does not know why she is not writing in the first person except that this is the way she often thinks. She likes to picture herself as a certain kind of person, a tragedy, a young intelligent girl who becomes a prostitute and a drug addict. It is suitable and dramatic. She realizes that there have always been people she has wanted to suffer, but in real life she hardly ever hurts anyone.

She wants to snap. She wants to knuckle under and stop fighting. She wonders mildly about her writing and why it meant so much. The entire irony of her life has hit her too suddenly and concretely. She has been a fantasy for many men, but for the one man she cares a little about, she cannot show pleasure or even interest. She cannot moan and beg as she does obediently now for the men over the phone, sometimes unable to conceal laughter, sometimes unable to conceal tears. Encouraging their fantasies of dominance, of inflicting brutality and pain. On the phone she goes down on hands and knees, doing what she would never do in real life. They believe her. They want to believe her so badly. She is Eve, the original sinner, the temptress, the woman with many faces. They do not know she is so young, nor would they care if they did know. She is better at phone sex than she would have thought possible. She pushes her guilt aside. She laughs secretly at them, and she cries too. Because she does want someone inside her. Someone who loves her, but not even that would be good enough. She wants to love herself enough to be able to want to be inside herself.

The magazines. The women he pretended to be making love to when he was inside her. The one beautiful centerfold at the bottom of the drawer—a woman with her legs wide apart, her hair black and upswept, her eyes green. The woman placed carefully and tenderly at the bottom of the drawer, smoothed out. The condoms in the same drawer. Him reaching into that drawer for a condom and me lying obediently on the bed without knowing. I concede that he has won this time. I cry over the white lines. I anguish for green eyes and become insane.

Her days have lost shape and form. The passing of time is marked by her body's desire for another line laid out. She wonders if she is becoming a good actress. She wonders what to do when he comes back. She knows she will get it together; that perhaps is the real tragedy. She is beyond running away and saddest of all beyond suicide.

It is, of course, when she can least bear her thoughts that she switches into this other mode of thinking, of being. She still does not like herself. She wonders when it will begin to hurt. She acknowledges that the pain has already been searing. She feels used. She knows she is not alone in that. She has violated her beliefs, is through her job promoting women as objects, encouraging men's violent sexual fantasies. All she can do about that is not think about it. It is a personal war, and though her person is political, there are other issues ahead of politics at present. She knows that he cares about her. She knows that because she fears no one could ever love her, she has made him to be too much. She knows she deserves more, and with this knowledge is a desire to do less.

She would love to disappear before he came back. It would appeal to her affection for trauma and melodrama to remove every trace of herself from the apartment in less than two weeks so that when he came back it would be empty. It would be like she had never existed. He would not know where to find her. He would be distraught. But it is not practical, not real.

She wants to be loved. She wants to love herself. She wants to give things to people, to spark off bursts of insight, to be dedicated to her writing. She wants to be healthy. She wants to be accepted.

She wants half of herself to die. She is no longer sure which half, or indeed if she is cut so neatly. She wants the man who made love to green eyes while she lay there with her legs open to hurt for a long, long time, but here she has lost some control. She wonders why she ever cared. She has all the control in all the wrong places. She wonders why she sometimes didn't care. She does not like or understand the rapid fusion taking place inside her. She wants another body, another face ... other eyes. She feels like she has lost something she never had in the first place, which is worse than simply losing something, because she also looks like a fool for assuming it was real.

She does not know which of her selves to be now, and therefore she will probably take the worst possible path by being all of them at the same time. She does not feel she could bear to have him touch her again, but that is a falsity, she could bear anyone touching her because her body is not truly hers. She has been there for him. Her breasts. Her vagina. She used to think that he had been there for her far more because he had seemed to save her life, but now she knows that she would have survived anyway. She has always survived, though by now it has made her old and worn and slightly crazy.

December 20

These sleepless nights and blurred days where the one definition is the lines on the mirror. My hands are shaking on the keys. Jesus, Diary, you mean so much to me—help me study, write, stay away from drugs.

This past week has been a sickness. I am so frightened of myself, my feelings, of being alone. The paranoia mounts. I am afraid of dying, of no longer knowing my emotions—the threads that tie me together as a person. The eternity. I understand at last again how I felt that night in August when I took those pills spilled out in front of me. I want to run back through these pages and yank that girl away, because I do love her, to see her suffering so much physically and emotionally is painful. I realize that I still need redemption, which can only be found by taking care of myself. I haven't been doing that lately, and am scared and small. It is part of the integration, of being a child living by herself, no more than twelve years old, and unable to cope. It's so powerful. It's like something inside me splitting apart.

I absolutely must stay together. I am like the little kid in the house where I was born, who woke up from an afternoon nap and found her parents gone, the terror of that, how convinced I was that I had been abandoned.

How could she have stood the terror of prostitution, the bad acid trips, the downers? I have to convince myself that I am still the person who did these things, who found myself smart in a previously unknown way in my handling of drugs and men. I know how to give a good blow job. No, don't think about that; you are too scared of men. Everything is all right. Calm down. It's just the coke. If you don't want to accept and acknowledge that little girl, you can tell Dr. Hightower to hey, slow down. He should have known. He should have anticipated this and not pushed me so hard. He must stop and take care of me for a little while now.

Oh Jesus. I'm so high I'm hallucinating. Don't make the fusion happen too fast.

PART VIII

january 4—january 20 1988

January 4

I am reaching the brink. My writing isn't moving, Langara classes are starting this Friday, and my King Ed upgrading courses are at a dead halt. I'm going crazy, and my appointment with Dr. Hightower isn't till Friday. I can't remember having gone through such a difficult time before, emotionally. I need help and don't care what form it takes.

Last night I broke things in the kitchen and there were shards of glass on the carpet, in the sink, on the counter, in fragments. I went out and hitchhiked aimlessly. A man named Spencer picked me up; he has an intelligence and an intuition of my needs that could be disastrous. He could manipulate me so easily if he wanted to. The view from his penthouse was tremendous, the city pooled underneath and the mountains a blue embrace around the balcony. We stayed there until 2 a.m., when I insisted on leaving. He relaxed me, his stomach a pillow I could be comforted by. Spencer wanted sex but wouldn't push it; he had no qualms about our age difference and was ready to marry me. I was at the point of not caring. Why not? Live in a penthouse and pretend that you got there with your writing, that you had fulfilled your dreams. I hate myself, no matter what guise I adopt.

Spencer said he had committed himself to love me because I needed love. I agreed to go out for dinner with him tonight and sleep over. I told you, my body is not mine. I know Spencer will let me down; I had seen him as a guardian angel in his sports car, unlocking the door and inviting me into his fairy tale. But in fairy tales men do not have penises. He was to be my father, my therapist. I am disillusioned, disillusioned. It is time to move out, but I don't want to give up this apartment; I would only move someplace absolutely sterile that no decorations could warm up, because it would most resemble me inside. Tonight I am going to sleep in this wonderful apartment and fantasize that I got here by working hours at my typewriter instead of waving my thumb out at passing cars. I had never thought that prostitution would become a substitute for writing.

January 5

When I stood on Broadway in the dimming light, men would often stop and say, 'I want you because you have a clean face, not like the other girls out here who are in such bad shape. I know you're clean just by looking at you.' I, too, had always thought myself immune from disease.

Dr. Hightower had said that I was living a dangerous fantasy. I am beginning to see that. I had carried with me a childlike belief of invulnerability. Yesterday at a clinic, I found out that R. had given me trichomonas.

It wasn't a big deal, but it was unexpected and defied my whole belief system of immunity—that because I was different, I would be protected. Also, R. had called me his little girl and above all his only girl, and told me often that he loved me. Another slip-up: once again a mistaken trust, when I should have known by now not to trust. I feel so hurt that I have to be hardened to protect myself not just emotionally but physically; trust had been my protection, but it's a flimsy one.

I went to the pharmacist to pick up my treatment and she was rattling on about her kid having been tormented in school, teased about her lunch box and her nose. In the cafeteria the entire football team would encircle her and make fun of her. At that point I broke down. Without any warning at all I started howling—the cruelty of people.

Spencer came to pick me up. By this time I was composed, hidden. He cheered me up, then looked at me and asked what I wanted from our relationship, saying I should be completely honest. I looked back at him in amazement. Spencer said he had friends who would pay over a hundred dollars for a blow job; I was sixteen years old and Oriental, big pluses. He said these men were clean. He said he could have me making ten thousand dollars a month if I wanted to, that I had been wrong in thinking that all there was was standing on a street corner blowing men for fifty bucks.

'Why limit yourself to that? You would be making twice as much, at least. I have already committed myself to loving and helping you, if this is the form of help you want. What do you want, Evelyn?'

I told him that between now and making it as a writer, I wanted to work for a magazine or a newspaper. Failing that, I would give blow jobs.

Spencer said that he knew the publishers of several newspapers, and if I would write four articles on a certain feature, he could see to it that I got in the door with them. I realized the truth then and blurted it out:

'Blow jobs are easier.'

It was the first time I had admitted that to anyone. I told Spencer that I wanted to meet his friends, I wanted him to care about me, I wanted him to pay for anything sexual we did together. He agreed.

With this established, we went out to dinner, went back to his apartment and then headed for bed. I stripped down and looked out at the mountains, the lights, the cars. Up there you could feel so superior to anything, and I tried to program my mind into the fantasy.

What followed was possibly the most difficult blow job I have ever been faced with, since he held back for half an hour; my mouth and tongue were quickly exhausted. Finally he came. I swallowed and gagged over the bathroom sink. I had certainly earned the money.

Now I am back home. Spencer wields a sexual power over me. He thinks I've got 'a wonderful mind and a marvelous body. You are intelligent, young and attractive. There's nothing you can't do.' Spencer has made me realize how many boundaries I have imposed on myself, when previously I thought I had broken down all the boundaries, transcended them. He frightens me.

January 13

I went over to Spencer's last night, in a cab in the rain. I thought I could sleep with him, drowsy from Valium. It wasn't until afterwards that I remembered the one other time I hadn't been able to turn a trick. That had been way back in the beginning when the trick with the joint of skunkweed had watched me toke. Then out there in the night, the pinpricks of headlights, the mud and grass, I had began to run. And stopped at the edge. Looked down. The man and the cliff. At least then I had an excuse, being more or less a beginner, still struggling with emotional hang ups about prostitution. It's been a long time since then. Like the billboards going up around the city beside bus stops: 'For some kids, getting streetsmart is just around the corner.' It is. I am.

I am alone with my frustration and inadequacy. There was absolutely no excuse. I am pieced back together now; in fact after the transition I was just fine, but in the bedroom the little girl had emerged and taken over.

It will be hard to describe. We got into bed and started kissing, cuddling. I was tired from the Valium and not enough sleep. After a space of blankness, during which I was emotionless about the situation, the little girl became me. She flooded my body and occupied my mind and emotions; I could not do it. I could hardly stand Spencer touching me, because he was touching her. And she was bathed in the most unendurable pain at what she had to participate in. She couldn't handle it—she was too young for intercourse, let alone prostitution! There was no way I could get back in control, although I tried. God knows I wanted the power that went along with it, but she wouldn't be convinced. She was so absorbed and overwhelmed by the pain that she was blind to me; she was swimming in an ocean of pain on the waterbed, embraced by Spencer.

She wouldn't let me do it. Back out in the living room, I was myself again, laughing while Spencer handcuffed me. But I didn't get paid for anything, and afterwards I was livid at myself. I should begin avoiding Spencer because he is close to falling in love with me. If I reciprocated caring, he would want me to move in with him, he said. In this business, once the men think they're in love with you, their fantasy is blown up to the point where they believe that you're in love with them too, and then the money is gone. Flown, out the window. Because then they believe you're enjoying it and that the relationship is based on caring, not money. Spencer is brilliant and intuitive; he has already grasped the dichotomy between the little girl and the streetwise teenager. If he were younger and if we hadn't met this way, I could fall in love with him. But with the present circumstances there is just agony for the little girl; perhaps her emergence is some sort of warning.

January 14

I don't even want to write about what happened last night. You know, there has been safety in prostitution for me. Now suddenly I can't work and am lost. The power and the fantasies had been so enjoyable. What happened? If this is what Dr. Hightower is trying to achieve, perhaps I shouldn't see him anymore. Perhaps I should live my life in what he would perceive as loneliness—a horrible choice, but at least I would be protected in it? Yes, at least with prostitution I was able to identify myself as belonging to some group for the first time in my life. I can seldom identify myself as a writer without being humored or laughed at, because I am sixteen. Like my friend said yesterday, 'I am the fringe of the fringe. I mean, when even the writers don't accept you, where can you go?'

The loneliness.

If the little girl could be slaughtered, then I could go back to it. I could preen in Spencer's waterbed overlooking the city. I could be bathed there in blackness, above swarming liquid lights. Above everything.

But even Spencer said I would have to give the little girl a chance to grow up and integrate with me, or else she would always be there: frightened, hurt, struggling to emerge.

I feel a great weariness when I think of last night, when I put my outfit on to go to work. I was straight, hitchhiking. A guy picked me up and promised to take me to my corner but stopped off at a friend's and left me in the truck. I waited and then got out, striding in the rain. The little girl was emerging bit by bit. Every step of the way I tried to stop her, but she wouldn't be subdued. She was not in pain this time so much as frightened and, above all, disgusted. I was afraid she would throw up if a penis got into her mouth. Stubbornly, though, I resumed hitch-hiking; a man picked me up and took me to my corner, but he asked if I wanted to smoke a joint with him. The little girl grabbed at this opportunity, and before I could stop her, she had said yes. It was a guarantee that she would not have to work.

She would rather be nauseated, vomiting and hallucinating from smoking too much marijuana than out there sucking skillfully on someone's cock.

But even then I persisted. I went out on the corner. I lasted two minutes in the rain and the cold. I did not prance or preen; I stood there feeling out of place, stoned and serious as hell. I couldn't act. And then I headed for the bus stop.

All the way home the little girl kept looking at her body and wondering why she was dressed up so comically. She felt horrendous. I felt horrendous. I do not want Dr. Hightower or anybody to strip away this occupation, which in a strange way makes life worthwhile for me, because it gives me immunity and a sense of belonging. I am tired of these struggles with the little girl who is transforming me.

January 20

A father figure. An unsuitable, emotionally frail father figure. Larry was just a few years younger than my father. Physically he was just as skeletal. But I had loved my father passionately as a child, with all my capacity. I had trusted him and depended on him and received great joy from him. That happened with Larry, at first, I was childlike in my ignorance of prescription drugs; I trusted that he was making me happy even while he was crippling my growth. And then, the turning around, when my father had become unemployed, withdrawn, impenetrable, dark and frowning. He decided that since I was female it was utterly up to my mother to take control. The bewilderment, like when Larry began to withdraw, to unconsciously play games. The trying so desperately to recapture the former joy and love so thick it was tangible. And then the end. My running away from home, like stabbing my father. All symbols: my wanting to retrieve that moment in Stanley Park with Larry so that he would have stabbed himself. Making my father see starkly what he had provided and what we had shared in my childhood and taking that away when he realized how he'd abandoned me. I hurt them both in the end. But I was not able to hurt Larry for very long or very deeply, because of his doped emotions. But then, with my father's unwillingness to change, refusal to accept my new life—it was no different. I could not go up to him and scream, 'Your daughter is a prostitute!' Everything in his mind would shut down, refuse to receive the incoming message, and he would be just as protected.

The comparisons, think of the comparisons. The similarities. And now here is Spencer, and why do I feel so strongly about him? It is not only that he has those material things that I have started to crave— why do I crave them, after all? It goes against anything that makes me happy, anything I truly value. It is more than waking up, being able to walk out onto the balcony and see the whole of Vancouver spread out before you, being pumped full of the feeling that you could conquer the city so easily, that you are on top of it all. It's more than that. Doesn't Spencer personify the preferred father, in his expensive clothing, his awareness of what is happening right now (not existing in a different decade, in a different culture), his humor, his playing with me as if I were little, his intelligence, his insight, his acceptance? But no, he is not accepting. And there's that battle again, wanting to be accepted by my father for who I am, the competition (wanting him all to myself, jealous of my mother and anyone else who might share or take my place in his attentions), wanting to play every role for him.

And Spencer! Spencer dangles bits of love before me, then takes them back. He promises to call, and doesn't. He promises to come over, and I wait up for him, and he doesn't. So when we do see each other I am grateful, because during the waiting and the expectations I have come to need him tremendously; it is like he was meant to save me from the struggles and the darknesses of my life. He has grown many times in importance. I have become grateful for the tidbits of love. I have become grateful for his strokes, kisses and pats as I rest my head firmly against his belly on the couch, needing to be suffused by the warmth and volume of his body as we watch television. I have hugged him desperately when he has finally shown up. I am jealous of his dispersed attentions, confused by his placing me in a central role in his life one moment and forgetting about me for days on end in the next. I don't know where I stand, and with this uncertainty comes a craving for reassurance. For equality. I am not dangling him along as I should, giving a little and taking a lot, handing out and withdrawing, the clever female games, until he has given me everything and is sprawled at my feet in blind and utter adoration. I am unable to do that because of my overwhelming emotional needs. Instead, he seems to be doing it to me!

Spencer is terribly intelligent; I found that out from the beginning. Is he deliberately doing this? If he is, he's succeeding, and I could end up giving him everything, just for the security of having him there, near me, the bulk of him, protection. How much would I sacrifice for the reward of feeling emotionally, psychologically safe? Isn't it true that I would sacrifice everything?

I am vying for Spencer's undivided attention. I need it as much as I needed that undivided attention from my father as a child, clutching at his pajamas and not letting him leave to go to my mother, basking in that viscous love at bedtime when he had exhausted his pile of stories. I was afraid of being alone. I was afraid of those feelings of emptiness and desolation that were like pain, that would cut through me as I lay there in the dark, not quite near sleep. They haven't yet gone away.

Larry and Spencer, the frail and powerful sides of my father. I am seeing Spencer through the eyes of myself as a very young child, and I am distorting his strengths. He is playing a dangerous game with me, consciously or not. I can feel once more what it was like to be lying in my bed; I can actually remember the bedside table, the lamp, the stacks of books, the scratches in the dark varnish of the table. I can see my father so much bigger than me in his baggy pajamas, colorful thin books in his big veined hands. I know what it is like to beg for the brightness to stay and suffuse you, and watch it walk out the door.

epilogue

It is painful for me now to look back upon this book. It represents a part of my life that I sometimes wish I could excise. In so many ways, after all, the girl in these diary entries—her rages, her self-absorption and grandiosity, her passionate and misguided beliefs—bears no resemblance to the person I am today. I think if she were to show up on my doorstep I would not let her into my house. Yet there are other things about her that I recognize even now in myself, and in my current work—her furious desire to write, and her quest for love.

The years following *Runaway* were turbulent in their own way. I had to remain a ward of the government until I was nineteen, and my agent and I encountered difficulties with lawyers and government workers in our efforts to publish the diaries. Meanwhile I was living on child welfare, and working periodically on a phone sex line to make ends meet. Editing the diaries was an arduous process, and many times I was tempted to tear up the publishing contract I had craved for so many years—I felt that once everyone knew I had been a prostitute, it would be impossible for me to ever secure love, or acceptance, from anyone.

Runaway was published in Canada when I was eighteen, to overwhelming attention. I had still not yet coped with much of what had happened to me, and while this attention was seductive and gratifying, it created its own stresses. Much of the interest from the media and the public was prurient, and some people saw me not as a young writer who had just published the first of many books, but as a one-shot wonder, a 'street kid' who had told her story and would now disappear.

Nonetheless, *Runaway* garnered many good reviews and became a bestseller. I kept writing, and over the next few years published my first book of poetry, *You Are Not Who You Claim,* and my second, *Oedipal Dreams,* to much literary acclaim. It was when *Oedipal Dreams* was nominated for the Governor General's award, Canada's highest literary honor, that I felt myself truly supported by other writers; this had an enormous impact on the way I felt about myself. The following year my first collection of stories, *Fresh Girls,* was released, and the year after that my third book of poems appeared, *In the House of Slaves.*

Looking back, I realize how difficult it was for others to take me seriously at first, given the sensational details of my background. Now, at twenty-three, with five books behind me and a sixth on the way, I am earning my living as a writer, and it is a constant source of happiness for me to at last have the validity I sought for so long.

If I had saved the story of my adolescence to write when I was older, it would have been a very different book. Likely it would have been less honest, less embarrassing, more judgemental as seen through the eyes of a relatively comfortable and established adult who perceives a fourteen-year-old on the streets to be a child, a victim. The fourteen-year-old I was in 1986 felt herself to be fully capable, even though she wasn't, and it was this conviction—shared, I believe, by most teenagers—that allowed her to write about her experiences with the frankness that is captured in *Runaway.*

Evelyn Lau
March, 1995
Vancouver, Canada

acknowledgements

I would like to thank the following people, each of whom helped propel *Runaway* into its final published form:

–The Explorations Program of The Canada Council, for its generous financial assistance,
–Denise Bukowski, my agent, for her perception and perseverance,
–Nancy Flight, my editor, for performing the difficult juggling act of pleasing both author and publisher,
–John Nicolls, Douglas Chalke, Robert Harlow and the innumerable others who gave their time and their advice while I was trying to settle the legal problems,
–Brian Burke, despite endings, for his intense support, and
–Sue Nevill, who became a friend in the present without needing to know the past.

I also wish to extend my gratitude to the many editors who continued to take interest in my other writings and to open up new opportunities for me while I was working on this book.